THE BETTER-WRITING CENTER

SHSAT
PRACTICE TESTS
NEW YORK CITY EDITION

By Won Suh, J.D.

This book is dedicated to the students who wish to pursue greater opportunities, academic and otherwise.

Dear Student,

In 2013, I published a practice test workbook for the TJHSST version of the SHSAT. The reception to the book was truly awesome. I was very proud of the work I had done, but I knew I could do more to help students preparing for the SHSAT, particularly for those students living in New York City. The first SHSAT workbook I wrote was modeled after the official practice test released for the TJHSST version of the SHSAT. What I realized, however, is that the official TJHSST practice test is actually easier than the official practice tests released by the New York Department of Education. Thus, I created this book to provide more challenging problems to help students be confident on the day of the test.

And because I intentionally made these questions more challenging than the questions you'll see on the SHSAT practice tests, don't fret if you find yourself struggling. I've provided very detailed answer explanations to guide you through the process of understanding how to solve the problems. If you should have any questions, you are more than welcome to email me at the address listed below.

Thank you again for purchasing this book, and I wish you the best of luck in your studies and in your pursuit of your future aspirations. God bless.

Yours truly,

Won Suh
President & Director
The Better Writing Center
Email: won.suh@betterwritingcenter.com

P.S. I am assuming you are already fairly knowledgeable about the SHSAT. If you are not, I strongly urge you to visit the New York City Department of Education website and download the SHSAT handbook, which contains two sample practice tests for the SHSAT. The handbook contains all the pertinent information you will need to know about the test format, question types asked, and more. The link to the webpage is http://schools.nyc.gov/Accountability/resources/testing/SHSAT.htm, so if you do not already have the handbook, please download it and do the practice tests.

Contents

FREE CONSULTATION

Thank you for your purchase. Your purchase entitles you to a complimentary hour of in-person private tutoring or academic consultation.* Just bring this book!

SCHEDULE YOUR CONSULTATION TODAY
won.suh@betterwritingcenter.com

*This offer is subject to scheduling and availability limitations and will be honored on a first come, first serve basis.

- -

TUTORING OFFERED

LEARN FROM THE BEST. LEARN FROM THE AUTHOR.

TESTING	MATHEMATICS	SCIENCE	WRITING
CogAT	Algebra 1 & 2	Biology	School Assignments
SSAT	Geometry	Chemistry	AP History DBQs
SHSAT	Trigonometry	Physics	Personal Statements
ACT	Pre-calculus	Computer Science	Application Essays
SAT	AP Calculus AB & BC		

- -

FIND THE BETTER WRITING CENTER

THE BETTER WRITING CENTER
7369 McWhorter Place
Suite 402
Annandale, Virginia 22003

the TESTS

SHSAT
NYC EDITION
TEST 1

PART 1 — VERBAL

Suggested Time — 75 Minutes
45 QUESTIONS

SCRAMBLED PARAGRAPHS
PARAGRAPHS 1-5

DIRECTIONS: The purpose of this section is to organize sentences into the best six-sentence paragraphs possible. For each paragraph, the first sentence is provided, but the remaining five are presented in random or no particular order. Re-order and organize these five sentences, if necessary, to create the **most** logical paragraph. Each paragraph is worth **two** points, whereas every other question type in this test is worth one. Partial credit will not be given.

Blanks have been provided to help you keep track of the position of each sentence in the paragraph. For instance, if you think a sentence follows the first, given sentence, write "2" in the blank next to it; write "3" next to the sentence that you believe follows "2"; and so on. When you believe you have arranged the sentences correctly, transfer your response to your answer sheet.

Paragraph 1

It may sound like a euphemism or kinder substitute for a profane word, but *fracking* is, contrary to how it may sound, not a fictitious slang word.

_____ **Q.** Traditional drilling only permitted access to the natural resources immediately within the reservoir accessed by the wellbore—a wellbore is the hole that is created by drilling.

_____ **R.** Whereas more traditional methods of drilling only permitted more limited amounts of oil and gas to be collected—oil and gas are frequently trapped between subterranean rock pores—hydraulic fracturing is a process that overcomes much of this limitation.

_____ **S.** After the wellbore is created, pipes are extended down into the wellbore that will reach out horizontally underground, allowing for the pressurized fluids to be pumped down to crack open surrounding rock pores and free up more oil and gas for extraction.

_____ **T.** Instead, it refers to the real-life oil and gas harvesting process known as hydraulic fracturing.

_____ **U.** Fracking, on the other hand, is able to access more of the natural resources that have become trapped in rock formations surrounding the reservoirs by using pressurized fluids mixed in with proppants, which are additives like sand and ceramic beads.

CONTINUE ▶

Paragraph 2

In 1859, a solar flare flashed so powerfully that it was visible to the naked eye and produced auroras, which are normally visible near the magnetic poles, over and near equatorial territories, such as Cuba and Hawaii.

_____ **Q.** Dubbed the Carrington Event, after Richard Carrington, an amateur astronomer who observed and recorded the flare, this solar flare remains the largest on record.

_____ **R.** What's even more amazing is that even though a solar flare is worth the energy output of billions, or more, of Little Boy nuclear bombs, a solar flare is worth only one-tenth of the energy released by the Sun every second.

_____ **S.** Putting that power into further perspective, a 100-megaton bomb, when detonated, releases 7,692.3 times the energy released by the "Little Boy" nuclear bomb that detonated over Hiroshima, Japan, in 1945.

_____ **T.** In fact, the energy released during a solar flare can exceed 10 million times the energy generated by a volcanic eruption and is the energy equivalent of millions of 100-megaton atomic bombs detonating simultaneously.

_____ **U.** And though the Carrington Event was atypical in magnitude, typical solar flares are still extremely powerful phenomena that result when the magnetic energy accumulating in the Sun's atmosphere is released suddenly, to produce the flare effect.

Paragraph 3

The goliath bird-eating spider, or *Theraphosa blondi*, as it is scientifically classified, is a massive spider, perhaps the most massive in existence.

_____ **Q.** Instead, after injecting their prey with paralyzing venom, tarantulas excrete digestive enzymes to liquefy its internal organs into a nourishing soup that they can consume.

_____ **R.** With legs spanning almost or just shy of a foot and a body mass of a couple ounces shy of half a pound, the bird-eater is the largest known tarantula alive.

_____ **S.** And like other tarantulas, the goliath bird-eater does not eat its prey in the traditional way we typically imagine; tarantulas don't chew and swallow their food or even swallow their prey whole, as snakes and some other animals do.

_____ **T.** With its massive size and inch-long fangs, the goliath feeds on a variety of prey, including smaller creatures, such as insects, to medium and larger (relative to its size) animals, such as lizards, small snakes, and even young birds on occasion.

_____ **U.** This entire feeding process is made possible by the goliath's stealth and strength; by sneaking up on its hapless prey, it is able to deliver the fatal, paralyzing bite that enables the massive arachnid to feed.

CONTINUE ▶

Paragraph 4

It is universally recognized today that the introduction of the iPhone in 2007 marked a turning point in consumer communications, paving the way for smartphones to become a staple in our daily lives.

_____   Q. While Blackberry was the smartphone market leader for a while, its total user base now only represents 3% of all smartphone users worldwide.

_____   R. Its rapid decline as a market leader can most certainly be attributed to the emergence of Apple's iPhone and a myriad of smartphones running on Google's Android platform, particularly the increasingly popular Samsung Galaxy S series, which have collectively sold over 130 million units since their inception in 2010.

_____   S. The iPhone wasn't the first smartphone—the first widely acknowledged manifestation of the smartphone was IBM's Simon, which was revealed at the 1992 Comdex computer show in Las Vegas—and it wasn't the first exceedingly popular one, either.

_____   T. How other brands hope to compete against these two smartphone behemoths remains to be seen, but one thing is certain: the line between smartphones and traditional computers has already been irreversibly blurred.

_____   U. That distinction belonged to Research In Motion's Blackberry line of smartphones, which led the smartphone market for several years with their QWERTY keyboards that facilitated the composing and sending of email and text messages.

Paragraph 5

Game theory is the study of strategic and interactive decision-making processes or how people make decisions when their decisions will affect the outcome of everyone else involved and vice versa.

_____   Q. They are taken to separate interrogation rooms and are encouraged to testify against each other for either a maximum sentence, if one accomplice sticks to his end of the bargain but the other does not, or a reduced sentence, if the accomplice agrees to cooperate.

_____   R. To best illustrate the basic tenets of game theory, we can turn to one of the most prominent scenarios presented by game theory experts: the prisoner's dilemma.

_____   S. What the police don't mention, however, for obvious reasons is that if neither complies with the interrogation efforts, then both will get off with the minimum sentence possible; ideally, for the criminals, they should stay quiet, under the circumstances, but in actuality suspects often fink on their partners.

_____   T. The prisoner's dilemma scenario is one in which two criminal suspects, who prior to the arrest had agreed never to rat on each other, are brought into custody for interrogation.

_____   U. And so game theory observes that the initial alliance between the suspects breaks down because the suspects do not trust each other enough and worries that if the other gives in and snitches, then he will receive a greater sentence than his accomplice will.

CONTINUE ▶

LOGICAL REASONING
QUESTIONS 11-20

DIRECTIONS: For each question, read the information provided and select the **best** answer choice, based **only on the information given.** In other words, even if you know more about a particular set of facts than is provided, do not use your knowledge of the facts to aid your decision-making process.

When dealing with logical reasoning questions, be on alert for certain placement or position and order words and phrases, such as **to the right of**, **above**, **before**, and **next to**. "The puppy is **between** the kitten and duckling," for instance, is not necessarily the same as "The puppy is **between and next to** the kitten and duckling"; one or more other objects may separate the puppy from the kitten or from the duckling.

11. Kevin has five differently colored dishes in his kitchen. He stacks them in either one or more vertical columns, according to the following conditions:

    1) The green dish is stacked immediately on top of the red dish.
    2) The yellow dish is placed between the blue and orange dishes.
    3) The orange dish is located at the very bottom of its column.
    4) The yellow dish is immediately beneath the blue dish.
    5) Each column has at least one dish.

    Based only on the information above, which of the following **cannot** be true?

    A. The green and red dishes make up one stack, and the blue, yellow, and orange dishes make up another.
    B. The dishes are stacked in one column, in the following color order, from top to bottom: green, red, blue, yellow, and orange.
    C. The dishes are stacked in one column, in the following color order, from top to bottom: blue, yellow, green, red, and orange.
    D. The dishes are stacked in one column, in the following color order, from top to bottom: blue, yellow, orange, green, and red.
    E. The red dish is at the very bottom of its column.

12. Martha exercises five times per week, no more than one time per day, from Monday to Saturday. For every exercise, she listens to a different genre of music, and she only listens to music when she exercises. Assume Monday is the first day of the week, with regard to Martha's exercise schedule.

    1) Martha runs earlier in the week than she lifts weights but later in the week than she rides her bicycle.
    2) Martha listens to jazz as she does yoga on Thursdays.
    3) Martha listens to rock music as she plays tennis, pop music as she rides her bicycle, and country music as she lifts weights.
    4) Martha listens to rock music on the day immediately after she listens to country music.

    Based only on the information above, which of the following **must** be true?

    F. Martha listens to pop music on Wednesday.
    G. Martha runs on Monday.
    H. Martha plays tennis on Saturday.
    J. Martha takes a break from exercise on Tuesday.
    K. Martha takes a break from exercise on Monday.

13. Bay Ridge School offers the football, track, and soccer, one sport per season during the school year. Thus, it is not possible for a student to participate in the same sport more than once per school year. Every Bay Ridge student participates in at least one, but not all three, of these sports per school year. Art, Lou, and Bob attend Bay Ridge, and each plays more than one sport; all three also participate in exactly one sport in common per school year.

Based only on the information above, which of the following **must** be true?

A. Art, Lou, and Bob all participate in football, soccer, and track.
B. Art, Lou, and Bob all play football, while Art and Lou both also participate in soccer and track.
C. Art, Lou, and Bob all run track only.
D. Between Art, Lou, and Bob, only two of the three will participate in two of the offered sports in common.
E. If Art participates in football and track, and Lou participates in football and soccer, then Bob participates in track and soccer.

14. A sleepover camp offers five sessions.

1) Stacy will attend the first two sessions, while Randy will attend the last two sessions.
2) Kim will attend three sessions, one of which coincides with one of Stacy's sessions and the other of which coincides with one of Randy's sessions.
3) Aaron will attend either one or two sessions and will never attend a session Kim will attend.

Based only on the information above, which of the following **must** be true?

F. Kim will attend the first session.
G. Kim will attend the second session.
H. Kim will not attend the third session.
J. Aaron will attend the fifth session.
K. Aaron will not attend the third session.

15. A zoologist visits seven animals at a local zoo, one animal per time slot. No time slots overlap with another.

1) The zoologist visits the gorilla after she visits crocodile but before she visits the iguana.
2) The zoologist visits the lion immediately after she visits the elephant.
3) The penguin is the fourth animal that the zoologist visits.

If the zoologist visits the tiger second, which animals can she visit in two or more time slots?

A. elephant, lion and iguana
B. crocodile, gorilla, and elephant
C. crocodile, gorilla, and lion
D. crocodile, gorilla, and iguana
E. gorilla, elephant, and lion

16. I can't go to my friend's house whenever my parents are home. I only go to my friend's house when it sunny out.

Based only on the information above, which of the following **must** be true?

F. If I don't go to my friend's house, it is either not sunny out or my parents are home.
G. If it is sunny outside and my parents aren't home and I don't go to my friend's house, then I am either too sick or busy to go.
H. Whenever it is sunny out and my parents aren't home, I go to my friend's house.
J. If I go to my friend's house, then my parents aren't home and it is sunny out.
K. If it is not sunny out, then my parents are home.

CONTINUE ▶

17. In the town of Edutopia, everyone is good at math. Some people in Edutopia are good at writing. Everyone who is good at writing becomes a journalist, novelist, or blogger, and nothing else. Henderson is an engineer.

Based only on the information above, which of the following **must** be true?

A. Henderson is not good at writing.
B. To be an engineer, one must be good at math.
C. If Henderson lives in Edutopia, he is not good at writing.
D. Henderson does not live in Edutopia.
E. If Henderson is good at writing, then he is not an engineer.

18. Six books are arranged along three shelves.

1) The history book is on the same shelf as the math and economics books.
2) The art book is on a shelf below the one holding the psychology book.
3) The geography book is on the middle shelf.
4) No shelf can hold more than three books.

Based only on the information above, which of the following **cannot** be true?

F. The psychology book is on the top shelf.
G. The art book is on the middle shelf.
H. The math book is on the bottom shelf.
J. The psychology book is on the middle shelf.
K. The economics book is on the middle shelf.

Questions 19 and 20 refer to the following information.

In the code below, (1) each letter always represents the same word, (2) each word is represented by only one letter, and (3) in any given sentence, the letters may or may not be presented in the same order as the words.

"Curt fixes cars and boats." means
U   T   O   N   P

"Meg flies boats and planes." means
L   S   U   V   P

"Lee drives bikes or cars." means
M   R   X   W   T

"Sue fixes bikes and planes." means
P   O   S   R   K

19. Which letter represents the word "Curt"?

A. N
B. O
C. P
D. T
E. Cannot be determined from the information given.

20. How many words can be represented by more than one letter?

F. 1
G. 2
H. 3
J. 4
K. 5

CONTINUE ▶

READING

QUESTIONS 21-50

DIRECTIONS: Each passage below has five questions associated with it. After reading a passage, answer the questions, based **only on the information provided** by the passage; even if you have a deeper knowledge of the contents of the passage, do not base your answers on any outside knowledge.

In the animal kingdom, only apex predators are relatively safe from predation; because they are at the top of their food chains, they are not often in danger of being hunted by other animals. This
5   is not, however, the case with creatures low on the food chain. So how do these "lesser" animals cope? Different animals depend on different methods of protection. A dizzying array of survival mechanisms, such as camouflage and pro-
10 tective armor, is available. Among these is the interesting evolutionary strategy of aposematic coloration, which warns would-be predators of the dangers or unpleasantness of preying on those animals employing this strategy.

15 The monarch butterfly's black and orange wings, speckled with white spots, are a common example of aposematic coloration. This unique coloration warns predators that it is not only repulsive in taste but also poisonous. It develops
20 the foul taste and toxicity from the milkweed plants, which are poisonous, it eats as a caterpillar. (Unfortunately for the monarch, a significant portion of its population is still eaten every year by animals that can tolerate significant doses of
25 its toxins.) Similarly, the viceroy butterfly also shares in the black, orange, and white colorations of the monarch and is bitter in taste, though its taste comes from its sequestering of salicylic acid; the physical similarities of the monarch
30 and viceroy and their unpleasantness as prey make them Müllerian mimics of one another.

Poison dart frogs, which describe the frogs belonging to the family *Dendrobatidae*, are another example of animals that use coloration to
35 deter potential predators. They are rather diminutive in size, ranging from less than an inch to 2.5 inches in length, but they flaunt big, vibrant colors that warn predators of their toxicity.

There are between 100 and 250 species of poi-
40 son dart frogs, but only a handful or fewer are toxic enough to be lethal to humans, with the golden poison arrow frog being the most toxic of them all—though it weighs less than an ounce, it packs enough poison to kill 20,000 mice.

45 Even completely harmless animals can benefit from aposematic coloration, even if they themselves do not employ this evolutionary strategy. Known as Batesian mimics, otherwise rather defenseless animals, such as milk snakes, increase
50 their chances for survival by copycatting venomous or foul-tasting animals. In the case of the milk snake, which is a species of king snake, the milk snake mimics the deadly coral snake; both species possess transverse bands of red, black,
55 and yellow, meaning these bands run orthogonal to the longitudinal axis of the snake's body, but the difference in the adjacency of the color bands of each species can be used to tell them apart; on the coral snake, the red and black
60 bands are separated by thinner yellow bands, but on the milk snake, the red and yellow bands are separated by thinner black bands.

21. What is the main idea of this passage?

   A. Top predators are safe from predation.
   B. Harmless animals benefit from aposematic coloration.
   C. Butterflies, snakes, and frogs benefit the most from aposematic coloration.
   D. Aposematic coloration is a significant evolutionary development.
   E. It can be difficult to tell mimics apart.

CONTINUE ▶

22. Which of the following statements is best supported by the passage?

    F. Müllerian mimicry is disadvantageous; resembling another animal increases the odds of being eaten by predators that can tolerate the other prey's toxins.
    G. Müllerian mimics look alike and are equally toxic to predators.
    H. Müllerian mimics always derive their toxicity or unpleasantness to predators from different sources, such as milk-weed and willow bark, in the cases of the monarch and viceroy, respectively.
    J. One Müllerian mimic is more unpleas-ant to predators than the others are.
    K. Müllerian mimics are at least somewhat noxious or unpleasant to predators.

23. Which of the following mnemonics can be used to distinguish coral snakes from milk snakes?

    A. "Jack doesn't like red next to black, but the dead fellow saw red next to yellow."
    B. "Red on yellow will kill a fellow, but red on black is a friend of Jack."
    C. "Red touches black, and surely the venom won't lack."
    D. "Yellow and red, you're not dead; black and white you're not alright."
    E. "Red on yellow won't kill a fellow, but red on black will kill Jack."

24. Which of the following can be inferred from the passage?

    F. Batesian mimicry is a form of apose-matic coloration.
    G. While aposematic coloration is a deter-rent, it doesn't always deter predators.
    H. The smaller the species of poison dart frog is, the more toxic it is.
    J. Apex predators are never themselves prey to other predators.
    K. The golden poison arrow frog's poison is able to kill an adult human within minutes.

25. Which of the following examples best exem-plifies Batesian mimicry, as described in the passage?

    A. a child hiding behind a larger child in order not to get bullied
    B. an owl butterfly's wings having large spots on them to make birds think they are looking into an owl's eyes and not at a butterfly's wings
    C. a child putting on a Halloween costume to receive more presents as she goes out to trick-or-treat
    D. a con artist dressing up as notorious out-law that every law enforcement officer is afraid of trying to capture
    E. a recruit shaving his head in order to conform to the haircut codes established by the military and to fit in with the other soldiers

26. In the context of lines 27-29, what does the author most likely mean by "sequestering of salicylic acid"?

    F. removing salicylic acid from the food source entirely, so that the food is no longer toxic
    G. adding salicylic acid to another more potent substance
    H. concentrating salicylic acid so much that the salicylic acid will kill predatory birds within seconds
    J. isolating salicylic acid by itself inter-nally in order to make the butterfly taste more bitter
    K. diluting and weakening the concentra-tion of salicylic acid internally so that the acid does not cause internal damage

CONTINUE ▶

In the field of biology, few have achieved the prominence that scientists Watson and Crick have, for their contribution in the discovery of the molecular structure of DNA and the implica-
5 tions of this discovery. What many people don't realize, however, is that others contributed heavily to the discovery of the double helical structure of DNA, including Maurice Wilkins, who shared in the 1962 Nobel Prize in Physiology or
10 Medicine with James Watson and Francis Crick, and especially Rosalind Franklin, who was unfortunately unable to share in the Nobel Prize because the Nobel Prize is not awarded posthumously—she passed away from ovarian cancer
15 four years before she could receive the award.

Rosalind Franklin, born into a wealthy family in 1920, was admitted to the Newnham College of Cambridge University in 1938, where she studied chemistry, and went on to earn her doctorate
20 in physical chemistry, also at Cambridge. After working as an assistant research officer at the British Coal Utilisation Research Association, where she studied the porosity of coal, and at the Laboratoire Central des Services Chimiques de
25 l'Etat in Paris, where she learned x-ray diffraction under crystallographer Jacques Mering— her tutelage under Mering would play a significant role in her pioneering work with the structure of DNA—in 1950, Rosalind joined a team
30 of scientists at King's College in London that had been studying living cells. The team leader assigned her to study DNA, but tensions quickly arose between her and graduate student Maurice Wilkins because he had initially assumed that
35 she was there as a technical assistant—it was uncommon for women to take leading research roles in universities at the time—and the differences in their personalities didn't help, either.

Despite the tensions between herself and Wil-
40 kins, Rosalind made tremendous strides in her research and study of DNA. By using x-ray diffraction techniques and by photographing the results, she and her student Raymond Gosling discovered that DNA had two forms: a dry 'A'
45 form and a wet 'B' form. Photograph 51, which was of the 'B' form, became one of the keys to solving the mystery of the structure of DNA. But unbeknownst to her, possibly fueled by the

strain in his professional relationship with
50 Rosalind, Wilkins shared her research (Photograph 51, in particular) with James Watkins and Francis Crick, both of whom had also been studying the structure of DNA at Cambridge University. The missing pieces of the DNA structure
55 puzzle became immediately apparent to them, and they raced to publish the first paper on DNA's structure.

Rosalind had come very close to solving DNA's structure, but Watson and Crick were the ones to
60 prevail in the race to publish the first paper, titled *A Structure for Deoxyribose Nucleic Acid*, on the complete structure of DNA in the April 25, 1953, issue of *Nature*, one of the world's most prominent scientific journals. It is impossi-
65 ble to say what would have happened in the history of biology if Watson and Crick had not been exposed to Rosalind's research, but her contribution to science cannot be understated.

27. Which of the following best states the purpose of this passage?

    A. to suggest that Rosalind Franklin was a better scientist than either James Watson or Francis Crick was
    B. to promote the idea that Watson and Crick could not have figured out the structure of DNA on their own
    C. to bring to celebrate the life and accomplishments of an often underappreciated figure in scientific history
    D. to show the significance of x-ray diffraction and the role it played in the discovery of the structure of DNA
    E. to detail the negativity that existed between Rosalind Franklin and Maurice Wilkins, which led to the unfortunate theft of her Photograph 51

CONTINUE ▶

28. Which of the following statements about the tension between Rosalind Franklin and Maurice Wilkins would the author most likely agree with?

   F. Wilkins did not believe Rosalind had the educational background necessary to take on a leading research role.

   G. Rosalind boasted to Wilkins excessively about her having been able to obtain a leading research role, despite her being a woman.

   H. Wilkins was confused about Rosalind's role in the laboratory and thus treated her accordingly.

   J. Wilkins and Rosalind clashed because their personalities led them to disagree about every little detail of their work.

   K. Rosalind tried to boss Wilkins around because she thought he was a technical assistant in the laboratory.

29. Which of the following was NOT true of the timeline of Rosalind Franklin's life?

   A. Franklin obtained her doctorate in physical chemistry.

   B. Franklin was hired by King's College in London in 1950.

   C. Franklin worked for the Coal Utilisation Research Association as a lead research manager and officer before working for the Laboratoire Central des Services Chimiques de l'Etat in Paris.

   D. Franklin studied x-ray diffraction under crystallographer Jacques Mering while she was working for the Laboratoire Central des Services Chimiques de l'Etat in Paris.

   E. Franklin was admitted to the Newnham College of Cambridge University at the age of 17 or 18.

30. Why wasn't Rosalind Franklin included as a recipient of the 1962 Nobel Prize in Physiology or Medicine?

   F. She had passed away in 1957, five years before the Nobel Prize would be awarded.

   G. Maurice Wilkins, out of spite, prevented her from being a recipient.

   H. Only three people are permitted to receive any given Nobel Prize, and since she had passed away, she was not included.

   J. The Nobel Prize was not awarded posthumously.

   K. It was later proven that Photograph 51 had no influence or bearing on the determination of the structure of DNA, so she did not qualify for the Nobel Prize.

31. Which of the following can be inferred from the passage?

   A. Photograph 50 was of the dry 'A' form of DNA.

   B. Rosalind Franklin's family's wealth allowed her to get a lead research position.

   C. Photograph 51 was of the wet DNA form.

   D. Cambridge University was the greatest institution to pioneer breakthroughs in the understanding of DNA at the time.

   E. Watson and Crick are the most revered names in biology today.

32. In which year was the complete structure of DNA revealed to the public?

   F. 1920
   G. 1938
   H. 1950
   J. 1953
   K. 1962

CONTINUE ▶

By writing and publishing *On the Origin of Species by Natural Selection*, Charles Darwin would forever alter the scope of biological theory by giving birth to the core of modern evolutionary theory. First published on November 24, 1859, *On the Origin of Species* laid out the framework for future theories of evolution by theorizing that species evolve over time by the process now familiarly known as natural selection, which, in stark contrast to artificial selection, was in effect nature's way of weeding out the weakest and otherwise least fit characteristics or traits for survival. So if survival and the promulgation of one's genetic material is the engine driving evolution, how do we explain altruistic tendencies scientists have observed in animals?

Altruism in animals species can be defined as the practice of increasing the fitness—we will say that fitness, in this context, is the ability of an organism to survive—of another, distantly related member of the same species while concurrently reducing one's individual fitness. That is, altruism is the phenomenon of an animal increasing the likelihood of another's survival, and therefore the likelihood that the other animal will be able to reproduce and pass down its genes, while reducing its own fitness.

Vervet monkeys, for instance, sound out warning calls to their fellow monkeys when danger approaches, to their own detriment; audibly warning others of danger allows the others in its group a better chance of survival but naturally draws more predatory attention to the individual issuing the alarm. Vampire bats, which have extremely fast metabolisms—so fast that if they don't feed within 36 hours, they will die—display altruism, too, albeit in a different way. Given how important obtaining food is for these bats, it would seem strange, then, that they have been observed to share food with those that returned unsuccessful from a hunt, even fellow bats that are not of immediate kin.

At first glance, then, altruism is at odds with natural selection. Upon further analysis, however, the logic behind altruism becomes more apparent when altruism is applied at the group level, in what is referred to as "reciprocal altruism."

With reciprocal altruism, the individual's chances of survival also increase, since it is likely that the individual will also benefit from the altruism that the other group members demonstrate.

For example, if only one Vervet monkey per group signaled imminent danger, then it is quite likely that that altruistic trait would have been naturally selected out over time, as any Vervet monkey that was prone to signaling danger would expose itself to greater risk of harm. But if every member of the group was given to signal danger, then the entire group would be afforded increased protection and likelihood of survival. In that light, it makes sense why altruism has not been eradicated through the process of natural selection. And in the case of vampire bats, by sharing food with an unlucky hunter, they increase the odds that those they helped will reciprocate if they return from a hunt empty-stomached.

33. What was the author's main purpose for writing this passage?

    A. to explain how altruism works in Vervet monkeys and vampire bats
    B. to examine a curious evolutionary phenomenon using two specific examples
    C. to discuss Charles Darwin's revolutionary theory of evolution
    D. to summarize a critical chapter of *On the Origin of Species by Natural Selection.*
    E. to illustrate how sounding warning calls or sharing food can be advantageous to an individual's survival

CONTINUE ▶

34. Which of the following best exemplifies altruism, as it is described in the passage?

    F. A philanthropist leaves his fortune to a charity in his will.

    G. A father runs into his burning home to save his infant children.

    H. A lion allows a gazelle to live after chasing and trapping the gazelle.

    J. A mercenary signs a contract to fight for and protect his employer, even though the job is a very high risk one.

    K. A volunteer neighborhood watch patrolman rushes in to tackle someone he believes to be an armed robber.

35. Which of the following statements would the author agree with?

    A. Altruism works because generosity increases societal happiness and gratitude.

    B. Altruism works because members of a group don't let the others starve.

    C. Altruism works because every species requires charity to function properly.

    D. Altruism works because enough members of a group are prone to reciprocating altruistic behaviors.

    E. Altruism would work in a group setting even if every other member of the group only displayed selfish behaviors.

36. Why might it be counterintuitive that vampire bats share food with others?

    F. Vampire bats have been known to share food with those who are not immediate kin, a counterintuitive behaviorism.

    G. Vampire bats only drink blood, so it's impossible for them to share solid foods.

    H. Vampire bats have such fast metabolisms that they risk endangering their own lives by sharing food.

    J. Vampire bats are successful hunters, so they have no reason to share food.

    K. Flight demands that vampire bats expend more energy than do other mammals.

37. Which of the following would the author agree is NOT an example of behavior showcasing the "engine driving evolution," as the phrase is used in lines 14-15?

    A. a tiger at a zoo caring for piglets that the zookeepers had disguised and scented as tiger cubs

    B. a soldier cowering behind foliage in the middle of a battle and then fleeing for his life at the first chance he gets

    C. two male lions fighting for control of a pride of lions and then the victor promptly driving out or killing all the male cubs

    D. an untrained driver speeding excessively around a snowy, narrow mountain pass for fun, while there is no one watching

    E. a grizzly bear charging a camper because it believes that the camper is posing a threat to its cubs

38. Which of the following can be inferred from the passage about "artificial selection," mentioned in line 10?

    F. Artificial selection is most likely not about nature's way of weeding out the weakest survival traits.

    G. Artificial selection is the process by which people breed animals selectively for the traits that they find desirable.

    H. Artificial selection is the process by which people actively eliminate animals selectively to get rid of the traits that they find undesirable.

    J. Artificial selection is the process by which two sexually incompatible animal species are bred to create animals that suit humanity's needs, such as is the case with mules.

    K. Artificial selection is the process by which animals help each other to prevent the weakest traits from being eliminated from the gene pool.

CONTINUE ▶

Scientists are hailing graphene as the "miracle material" of the 21st century. Its structure is simple to conceptualize—just think of a lattice of hexagons, similar to the patterning of honey-
5 combs, comprised of carbon atoms—but precisely because of its structure, graphene seems to have the potential to be used universally, from the construction of super-efficient and safe vehicles to the production of computers that can han-
10 dle unfathomable speeds.

Not only is graphene 200 times stronger than structural steel, making it the strongest substance ever measured—James Hone, a professor of engineering at Columbia University, offered the
15 possibility that it would take an elephant balanced on a pencil to break through a sheet of graphene with the thinness of Saran Wrap or an equivalent plastic wrap used to wrap up leftovers—but it has also been shown to be the most
20 conductive material in existence, surpassing even silicon, which is currently used as the basis for virtually every transistor included in modern computer processing units (CPUs), and there are quite a few transistors included in every CPU—
25 current generation processors each consist of anywhere from 900 million to 1.4 billion transistors.

In addition to its strength and conductivity, graphene has much potential as a building material.
30 For one, it is extremely elastic for its crystalline lattice structure; a sheet of graphene can be stretched up to 20 percent of its length, though it is also the stiffest known material—even stiffer than diamond. It is also the most impermeable
35 material ever discovered. Graphene is so impermeable, says Dr. Leonid Ponomarenko of Manchester University, that not even helium atoms can squeeze through. (For reference, helium is the second smallest element after hydrogen.)
40 The impermeability of graphene could thus be used to construct ultrasensitive gas sensors, for instance, because it may be possible to use graphene to detect even the smallest quantity of the majority of gases.

45 Once graphene's properties became increasingly apparent, this uncanny material has become the focus of much academic and research interest:

almost 3,000 research papers were written on graphene in 2010. Moreover, because graphene
50 could have extreme economic potential, more than 200 companies have begun investing in graphene research, as well. Samsung, the Korean electronics behemoth responsible for the international smartphone sensation, the Samsung Gal-
55 axy S series, has demonstrated a 25-inch touchscreen using graphene, and IBM has created a 150 gigahertz (GHz) transistor from graphene (silicon transistors, by comparison, top out at 40 GHz). Unfortunately for consumers,
60 the practical integration of graphene into current electronics is still a ways off because of its limits, such as the inability to properly control graphene's conduction properties.

While the commercialization of graphene is not
65 upon us yet, it is inevitable; it's just a matter of time before the major, necessary breakthroughs happen. Companies like Samsung and IBM may be the ones that bring graphene down into the realm of practicality, but credit must be given to
70 Professors Andre Geim and Konstantin Novoselov of the University of Manchester for discovering this fascinating material in 2004; the duo was awarded the 2010 Nobel Prize for Physics.

39. Which of the following is the author's purpose in writing this passage?

   A. to discuss the properties of a substance that may play a large industrial role in the future
   B. to suggest that graphene should be used immediately to replace many other substances that are currently used
   C. to give credit to the professors who discovered graphene in 2004
   D. to publicly reveal a breakthrough made by the scientific community that had previously been relatively unknown
   E. to illustrate the various ways in which graphene is currently being used and researched around the world

CONTINUE ▶

40. Which of the following is NOT a property of graphene discussed by the passage?

    F. impermeability
    G. elasticity
    H. conductivity
    J. structural strength
    K. reactivity to gases

41. Which of the following would be reasonable to conclude from lines 30-44?

    A. Graphene is so impermeable that it can be used in gas sensors to detect all gases, including hydrogen and helium.
    B. Graphene's lattice structure may permit the passage of hydrogen atoms.
    C. Graphene is among the most unique and quite possibly universally applicable substances to be created.
    D. Because graphene is so relatively elastic for its stiffness, it has many wide-ranging uses as a building material.
    E. Graphene will inevitably be used in all gas sensors in the future.

42. Which of the following statements can be inferred from the portions of the passage discussing the structure of graphene?

    F. Because it would take the weight of an elephant balanced on a pencil point to penetrate a sheet of graphene as thin as Saran Wrap, no substance will ever supplant graphene as the world's strongest material.
    G. The hexagon lattice is the most perfect shape ever to be created.
    H. Honeycombs have at least somewhat of a crystalline lattice structure made up of hexagons.
    J. If titanium molecules were arranged in a crystalline lattice, the resulting product would be even stronger than graphene because titanium is denser than carbon.
    K. Graphene's crystalline lattice structure makes it impervious to all known gases.

43. Why isn't graphene yet commercially viable as an alternative for silicon in the manufacture of transistors?

    A. No one in the world needs transistors that can support clockspeeds up to 150 GHz, as even 40 GHz is unheard of.
    B. The cost of replacing silicon with graphene would be astronomically high.
    C. Graphene hasn't yet been mass produced in large enough quantities to be used as the primary component in commercially available transistors.
    D. Graphene's conductive properties are either not yet fully understood or unable to be controlled.
    E. It is currently impossible to fit 900 million to 1.4 billion graphene transistors onto a CPU as small as the ones that are used in computers these days.

44. Which of the following assumptions does the author make in writing the passage?

    F. 2010 was a record setting year for interest in graphene.
    G. 3,000 research papers and the interest of about 200 commercial entities indicate the highest ever interest given to a subject matter.
    H. If the interest in graphene hadn't been so high in 2010, then Professors Andre Geim and Konstantin Novoselov may not have won the Nobel Prize in 2010, considering that they discovered the substance in 2004.
    J. Graphene will be used in a significant number of commercial products within 10 years, at the latest, considering how quickly technology advances.
    K. 3,000 research papers about a given subject matter are more than the average number of research papers written about other subject matters.

CONTINUE ▶

The history of navigators and explorers is rife with prominent names who have etched their names into the annals of antiquity by discovering new territories and lands, so it is difficult in
5 modern times to be recognized for an exceptional feat in exploration—not many feats remain to be accomplished, unless they involve some scientific marvel or phenomenon. Yet, as recently as 1988, one Australian woman by the
10 name of Kay Cottee did what no other woman had done: she circumnavigated the world in a single-handed, non-stop journey.

Kay Cottee, born Kay McLaren, was born into a family of yachters—her father, Jim McLaren,
15 had built his own yacht, the *Joy Too*—so it seems that it was inevitable Kay would spend considerable time at sea; in fact, she had her first seafaring excursion when she was but a few weeks old. Even when she was in class at
20 school, she often gazed out to sea and daydreamed of setting off across the ocean. Before too long, although to someone so enamored of sailing it probably seemed an eternity, she would get her chance to make a mark on the world of
25 sailing. Her first real opportunity came when she received a sponsorship from Blackmores Laboratories to compete in two races in 1986: the Two-Handed Trans-Tasman race to New Zealand and the Solo Trans-Tasman race back to
30 Australia, the first of which she sailed with her friend Linda Wayman, winning their division in the yacht she had built and originally christened *Jimmy Mac*, in honor of her father, but had to rename *Cinnamon Scrub* to get the sponsorship.

35 With a solo race under her belt, Kay hungered for more: to become the first woman to sail the world solo and non-stop, which means she would have to fight the urge to make landfall, on a trip that would, as global circumnavigation is
40 currently defined, span a distance of at least 21,600 nautical miles, crosses the equator and every longitude, and finishes in the same port as it starts. After lengthy preparation, Kay set out from Sydney, Australia, on November 26, 1987,
45 to realize her dream. And after overcoming significant obstacles, such as capsizing off the coast of southern Africa in 100-knot winds and 70-

foot waves—she was only able to survive because she was harnessed to her boat by two
50 safety lines—she returned home on June 5, 1988, thus completing a journey that saw her traverse 22,100 miles in 189 days, 0 hours, and 32 minutes. At least, that was the officially recorded time. In actuality, Cottee had arrived at
55 the coasts of Sydney after 187 days at sea but had to wait off Sydney Heads, which is the entrance to Sydney Harbor, in miserable weather, no less, to appease her sponsor and arrive home on a Sunday. Why her sponsor wanted her to ar-
60 rive on a Sunday is anyone's guess, but, regardless of her sponsor's idiosyncrasies, there's no question that Kay Cottee's circumnavigation of the globe was an incredible feat.

45. What was the author's purpose for writing this passage?

A. to chronicle the details of Kay Cottee's life, both personal and professional, from childhood to adulthood
B. to explain how and why Kay Cottee became a sailor
C. to briefly introduce a pioneer and celebrate her accomplishments
D. to encourage readers to become more ambitious and set loftier aspirations
E. to emphasize that there are still many feats that have not yet been accomplished, so this is a prime opportunity to make one's mark in this world

46. Approximately how much disparity was there between Kay Cottee's official time for her global circumnavigation and the actual time she took to complete it?

F. 1 day
G. 2 days
H. 3 days
J. 4 days
K. There was no disparity between the times.

CONTINUE ▶

47. What can be inferred from lines 48-50 of the passage?

    A. 70-foot waves can only be generated by 100-knot or faster winds.
    B. Kay Cottee would not have survived if she had been harnessed to her boat by only one safety line.
    C. If an expert like Kay Cottee capsized in 100-knot winds and 70-foot waves, the average casual sailor would have drowned in that situation
    D. Capsizing off the coast of southern Africa was by far the worst obstacle Kay Cottee faced as she sailed around the world.
    E. If Kay Cottee had not been properly harnessed to her boat, she would most likely have died.

48. According to the passage, what does it mean to circumnavigate the globe?

    F. Global circumnavigation is defined as the traveling around of the world, starting and ending at the same port.
    G. Global circumnavigation is defined as the traveling around of the world by crossing every latitude and longitude and starting and ending at the same port.
    H. Global circumnavigation is defined as the traveling around of the world by crossing every latitude and longitude, starting and ending at the same port, and traveling at least 21,600 nautical miles in doing so.
    J. Global circumnavigation is defined as the traveling around of the world by crossing the equator and every longitude, starting and ending at the same port, and traveling at least 21,600 nautical miles in doing so.
    K. Global circumnavigation is defined as the traveling around the world by crossing every latitude and longitude, and traveling at least 21,600 nautical miles in doing so.

49. Based on the passage, which of the following statements would the author most likely agree with?

    A. If Blackmores Laboratories had not sponsored Kay, she would never have gotten her chance to race competitively.
    B. Kay would not have gotten into sailing if her father had not been a yachter.
    C. Linda Wayman was Kay Cottee's partner for both of the 1986 Trans-Tasman races Kay participated in.
    D. Kay would have not changed the name of her yacht to *Cinnamon Scrub*, if she didn't need to get a sponsorship.
    E. No other woman after Kay Cottee has successfully completed a global circumnavigation.

50. Which of the following best describes the author's tone in the passage?

    F. admiration for Kay Cottee and bewilderment towards her sponsor who made her wait two days before setting her official global circumnavigation time.
    G. applause for Kay Cottee and disgust for her sponsor who made her wait two days before setting her official global circumnavigation time.
    H. amazement at Kay Cottee's achievement and skepticism about the reports that Kay could have survived 100-knot winds and 70-foot waves
    J. disdain for Kay Cottee because she did not beat the men's global circumnavigation record.
    K. complete objectivity

CONTINUE ▶

PART 2 — MATHEMATICS

Suggested Time — 75 Minutes
QUESTIONS 51-100

GENERAL INSTRUCTIONS

Answer or solve each question or problem. Once you have arrived at the correct answer or come up with a satisfactory answer choice, mark your answer sheet accordingly. **DO NOT MARK ON YOUR ANSWER SHEET OTHER THAN TO FILL IN YOUR ANSWER CHOICES.**

IMPORTANT NOTES:
   (1) Formulas and definitions of terms and symbols are **not** provided.
   (2) Diagrams may not have been drawn to scale. Do not make any assumptions about any relationship in a diagram unless it can be figured out or derived from the given information.
   (3) Assume that all diagrams are drawn in one plane, unless the problem specifies otherwise.
   (4) Graphs have been drawn to scale. Unless the problem states otherwise, you can assume relationships based on how they appear. For instance, if lines look perpendicular on a graph, you may assume they are perpendicular; the same goes for concurrent lines, straight lines, collinear points, right angles, etc.
   (5) Reduce all fractions to simplest terms.

---

51. If $p = 9$ and $n = 16$ in the equation $\dfrac{m}{45} = \dfrac{n}{p}$,

what is the value of m?

   A. 3.2
   B. 27
   C. 36
   D. 72
   E. 80

---

52. Find the value of z that satisfies the equation $5z + 3(4z + 5) = 4(z - 6)$.

   F. -26
   G. -3
   H. 1
   J. 4.5
   K. 52

53. If x is an even integer, which of the following **cannot** be true?

   A. $2x + 1$ is prime.
   B. $x(x - 1) = 0$.
   C. $0.5(x + 1)$ is even.
   D. $(x - 1)(x + 1)$ is odd.
   E. $x^2 + 6x + 9$ is odd.

---

54. What are the distinct prime factors of 798?

   F. 1, 2, 3, 7
   G. 1, 2, 3, 133
   H. 2, 3, 133
   J. 2, 3, 7, 19
   K. 2, 21, 19

CONTINUE ▶

55. $\left(\dfrac{4}{9} - \dfrac{7}{15}\right) \div \dfrac{13}{10} =$

A. $-\dfrac{5}{13}$

B. $-\dfrac{2}{117}$

C. $\dfrac{82}{117}$

D. $\dfrac{13}{585}$

E. $\dfrac{533}{450}$

---

56. $\dfrac{3|5-2-7|}{\left|(1-2)-\frac{1}{2}(10)\right|} =$

F. -2
G. -1
H. 0
J. 1
K. 2

---

57. Ahmed has a box of 23 crayons. 7 are blue, 6 green, and the rest gray. If, after removing 7 crayons from the box, the probability of Ahmed picking a gray crayon is now 0.25, what is the probability that he removed at least 1 blue crayon from the box?

A. $\dfrac{1}{7}$

B. $\dfrac{6}{13}$

C. $\dfrac{1}{2}$

D. $\dfrac{7}{13}$

E. $\dfrac{6}{7}$

---

58. If N = $3.46\overline{2462}$, what is N as an improper fraction?

F. $\dfrac{1153}{333}$

G. $\dfrac{3462}{999}$

H. $\dfrac{3462}{1000}$

J. $\dfrac{1730}{499}$

K. $\dfrac{3462462462}{1000000000}$

---

59. Set V = {930, 931, 932, ..., 1044, 1045}
Set W = {967, 968, 969, ..., 1112, 1113}

How many distinct integers are contained in the union of Sets V and W?

A. 183
B. 184
C. 216
D. 232
E. 263

---

60. $\left(-\dfrac{161^3}{23^4}\right)^{-1} =$

F. $\dfrac{21}{345}$

G. $\dfrac{343}{23}$

H. $\dfrac{49}{23}$

J. $-\dfrac{23}{343}$

K. $-11\dfrac{21}{23}$

CONTINUE ▶

61.

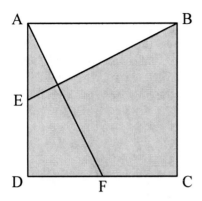

Square ABCD above is drawn in the rectangular coordinate plane, with the following coordinates: A(0, 8), B(8, 8), C(8, 0), and D(0, 0). If E is the midpoint of $\overline{AD}$, and F is the midpoint of $\overline{CD}$, what are the coordinates for the point of intersection of $\overline{BE}$ and $\overline{AF}$?

A. (1.6, 4.8)
B. (1.6, 3.2)
C. (2.67, 5.33)
D. (2, 5)
E. (2, 6)

---

62. What is the least common multiple of 510 and 1,122?

F. 2,805
G. 5,610
H. 11,220
J. 33,660
K. 572,220

---

63. How many unique ice cream cones can be made if each ice cream cone consists of one scoop of ice cream, of which there are three flavors, and a choice of either no toppings or one topping, from a list of two toppings?

A. 3
B. 6
C. 9
D. 12
E. 15

---

64. On a blueprint, 1 centimeter represents 7 feet in actuality. If the base of a building takes up 70 square centimeters on the blueprint, how much area does the base of the actual building take up?

F. 49 ft²
G. 196 ft²
H. 392 ft²
J. 3430 ft²
K. 4900 ft²

---

65. Audrey scored a mean of 4 goals in her last five field hockey matches and a mean of 3 goals in three of those five matches. What is the least she could have scored in any one of the remaining two matches, if she never scored more than 8 in any of her matches?

A. 0
B. 1
C. 2
D. 3
E. 4

---

66.   5.39 jings = 15.4 hings
4.9 hings = 2.8 gings

According to the conversion rates above, how many jings equal 1 ging?

F. $\dfrac{7}{20}$

G. $\dfrac{7}{40}$

H. $\dfrac{5}{8}$

J. $\dfrac{49}{80}$

K. $\dfrac{20}{7}$

CONTINUE ▶

31

67. Lisanne is $2n + 3$ years older than Alexis is and n times as old as Sandra is. If Sandra is 14 years old, and Lisanne is 42 years old, how old is Alexis?

    A. 42
    B. 33
    C. 29
    D. 17
    E. 14

68. Octane and ethanol are mixed in a ratio of 9 to 1, respectively, by volume, to create gasoline. The mixture's volume, however, was only 80% of the sum of the individual volumes of octane and ethanol. If the gasoline will ship out in 1,000-gallon tanks, how much octane is needed to make a mixture that completely fills up one tank?

    F. 720 gallons
    G. 900 gallons
    H. 1072 gallons
    J. 1125 gallons
    K. 1250 gallons

69.

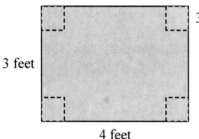

3 feet

3x inches

4 feet

Kon has a rectangular piece of cardboard with side lengths of 3 feet and 4 feet. He will cut out a square with side length $3x$ **inches** from each corner, whereupon he will fold the resulting flaps up to make an open box. What is the resulting box's volume?

    A. $3x$ ft.^{3}
    B. $3x(3 - 6x)(4 - 6x)$ ft.^{3}
    C. $x(3 - 0.25x)(4 - 0.25x)$ ft.^{3}
    D. $0.25x(3 - 6x)(4 - 6x)$ ft.^{3}
    E. $0.25x(3 - 0.5x)(4 - 0.5x)$ ft.^{3}

70. A horse breeder is packing sugar cubes into a box that measures 2 feet by 3 feet by 18 **inches**. If each sugar cube has a side length of 1.5 inches, and a bag of 5,000 sugar cubes costs $25, what is the total value of sugar that the breeder is packing into the box?

    F. $3.60
    G. $11.52
    H. $23.04
    J. $29.27
    K. $34.56

71.

Super Ant Colony Demographic

Ant Role	Number in Colony	Percent of Colony
Queens	9	
Soldiers	x	y%
Workers	36,000	
Drones		2%

Total Super Ant Colony Population: 45,000

Researchers found a super ant colony comprised of exactly 45,000 ants, 9 of which are queens and 36,000 of which are workers. What percent, to the nearest hundredth, of the number of soldiers is the number of drones?

    A. 5.61%
    B. 7.97%
    C. 9.14%
    D. 11.12%
    E. 12.20%

72. Car A, with tires of diameter 20 inches, travels $16,000\pi$ feet. Car B's tires, whose radii is x times Car A's tires' radius, each spins 3,840 times to travel $16,000\pi$ feet. Find x.

    F. 1.25
    G. 2.5
    H. 4
    J. 5
    K. 7.5

CONTINUE ▶

73. On Wednesday, an aquarium at a pet store contained 230 pink fish, 310 blue fish, and 110 yellow fish. On Thursday, 37 yellow fish and 48 pink fish were sold. How many blue fish must be sold on Friday so that the combined population of pink fish and yellow fish will be five-sevenths the total fish population by the close of business on Friday, if no pink and yellow fish will be sold on Friday?

A. 102
B. 167
C. 208
D. 357
E. 510

74. The point A in the x,y-coordinate plane has the coordinates (2, 3) and undergoes the following transformations and translations:

1. a reflection over the y-axis, and then
2. a horizontal shift to the left by 3 units.

Which of the following transformations and translations would NOT bring the point back to the coordinates (2, 3)?

F. a reflection over the line $y = x$, followed by a vertical shift up by 8 units and a horizontal shift to the left by 1 unit
G. a reflection over the y-axis, followed by a horizontal shift to the right by 3 units
H. a reflection over the x-axis, followed by a horizontal shift to the right by 7 units and then another reflection over the x-axis
J. a horizontal shift to the right by 7 units
K. a reflection over the y-axis, followed by a horizontal shift to the left by 3 units

75. A battalion of 520 soldiers goes through 16,380 pounds of rations in 3 weeks. If 780 more soldiers join the battalion, how many tons (1 ton = 2,000 pounds) of rations would the battalion now need to sustain its soldiers for 5 weeks?

A. $13\frac{17}{20}$
B. $20\frac{19}{40}$
C. $34\frac{1}{8}$
D. $40\frac{3}{20}$
E. $68\frac{1}{4}$

76. $\{1, 2, 3, 4, 5, 6, 7\}$

a and b are numbers whose digits are taken from the set of numbers above. a is a 2-digit number and b is a 3-digit number such that $a \div b = 0.5$ and a and b do not share any digits. In other words, no number from the set above can appear as a digit in both a and b. Which of the following statements could be true?

F. 5 is one of the digits of a.
G. 6 is one of the digits of a.
H. 3 is the last digit of b.
J. 2 is one of the digits of a.
K. There are exactly two possible combinations for the values of a and b that satisfy the conditions set forth above.

77. The ratio of girls to boys in the robotics club is 3 to 4. If there are 27 girls in the club, how many members does the club have in total?

A. 9
B. 36
C. 50
D. 56
E. 63

CONTINUE ▶

78. Yoshi can mow a lawn in 45 minutes; Luigi takes 60 minutes to mow the same lawn. With their rates of mowing, how long would it take them to mow a lawn 14 times the area of the aforementioned lawn, if they started mowing the lawn together at the same time?

  F. 6 hours
  G. 6.25 hours
  H. 6.33 hours
  J. 6.5 hours
  K. 7 hours

79. Juanita has x pens, and Connor has y, and Ramone has z. Juanita gives Connor one-fourth of hers. Connor, in turn, gives Ramone two-fifths of his new pen total. Ramone now has 30 more pens than before. How many pens did Ramone receive, in terms of x, y, and z?

  A. $0.1x + 0.4y + z = 30 + z$
  B. $0.4(0.25x + y) = 30$
  C. $0.4x + 0.25(x + y) + z = 30$
  D. $0.4(0.75x + y) = 30$
  E. $0.4x + 0.75y = 30 - 0.67z$

80. There are 10,000 square meters in 1 hectare and 1,000 millimeters in one meter. How many hectares are in 10 square millimeters?

  F. 1.0×10^{-9}
  G. 1.0×10^{-7}
  H. 1.0×10^{-3}
  J. 1.0×10^{3}
  K. 1.0×10^{9}

81. Find the value of $\dfrac{(x-6)(x+8)}{2(\frac{1}{2}x-3)(x+2)}$ if $x = 4$.

  A. 1
  B. 2
  C. 4
  D. 6
  E. No solution exists because it is not possible to divide by 0.

82. Which of the following expressions does NOT have a rational number equivalent?

  F. $-(\sqrt{7} - \sqrt{13})^{2}(\sqrt{7} + \sqrt{13})^{3}(\sqrt{7} - \sqrt{13})$

  G. $(1 + \sqrt{2})(1 - \sqrt{2})$

  H. $\dfrac{3\sqrt{6}}{24} - \dfrac{\sqrt{6}}{12}$

  J. $\dfrac{(2 - \sqrt{5})(2 + \sqrt{5})}{4 - 5} - \dfrac{3\pi}{7\pi}$

  K. $\dfrac{3 - \pi}{4} + \dfrac{8\pi^{2}}{32\pi}$

83. In a certain school district, the average annual salary for its 1,698 teachers is \$54,100. If the district's annual budget for education is \$500 million, what percent, to the nearest hundredth, of the education budget do teachers' salaries account for?

  A. 18.24%
  B. 18.37%
  C. 18.50%
  D. 18.64%
  E. 19.01%

84.

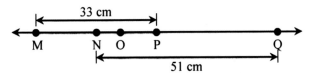

On the number line above, each line segment has an integer length, in centimeters. If it is true that 2(OP) = 3(NO) and PQ = 2(MN), what is the length of $\overline{NO}$?

  F. 3 cm
  G. 5 cm
  H. 6 cm
  J. 7.5 cm
  K. 9 cm

CONTINUE ▶

85.

6-Day Sales Statistics for E-Z Sales Store

Customers Served	Day
202	1
176	2
103	3
119	4
231	5
123	6

The table above shows the number of customers E-Z Sales Store served over a period of 6 days. What is the difference between the mean number of customers served and the median number of customers served?

A. 9
B. 9.5
C. 10
D. 10.5
E. 48

86. Albert has $\frac{3}{13}$ as many marbles as he and Jeamine have combined. After giving Albert 16 marbles, Jeamine now has twice as many marbles as Albert has now. How many marbles do they have combined?

F. 36
G. 72
H. 144
J. 156
K. 192

87. Jacie owns a coffee shop and charges $2.25 per cup. If running the store costs $560.00 per week, not including 1) coffee beans, which cost $0.75 per cup, and 2) cream and sugar, which, combined, cost $0.15 per cup, what is the minimum number of cups Jacie needs to sell every week, to break even?

A. 413
B. 414
C. 415
D. 416
E. 418

88. Rhonda accidentally dropped 6 marbles of equal size into a cylindrical cup of water. The opening of the cup had a radius of 4 inches, and the water level in the cup rose 1 inch. What is the volume of one marble?

F. $\frac{\pi}{16}$ in.^{3}

G. $\frac{8\pi}{3}$ in.^{3}

H. $\frac{11\pi}{4}$ in.^{3}

J. 8π in.^{3}

K. 16π in.^{3}

89. Fay kayaked upstream in a river that is flowing at a rate of 2.5 meters per second. It took her 4 **minutes** to travel three-fifths of a kilometer. How much less time would it have taken her to travel the same distance downstream, if the only thing that differed was the direction in which she was kayaking?

A. 80 seconds
B. 160 seconds
C. 200 seconds
D. 240 seconds
E. 300 seconds

90. The sum of three consecutive even numbers is the sum of the two smallest distinct prime numbers greater than 35. What is the greatest of the three consecutive even numbers?

F. 22
G. 24
H. 26
J. 28
K. 30

CONTINUE ▶

91. A sphere with a radius of 10 centimeters is placed into a square box that has an internal volume of 8,000 cubic centimeters. How many milliliters, where 1 milliliter equals 1 cubic centimeter, of water need to be added to the box so that no empty space remains? (Assume that the sphere does not float in water.)

A. $4,000\left(2-\dfrac{\pi}{3}\right)$

B. $8,000\left(1-\dfrac{3\pi}{2}\right)$

C. $8,000\left(\dfrac{4}{3}\pi-1\right)$

D. $500\left(16-\dfrac{\pi}{3}\right)$

E. $100(4-\pi)$

92.

A   B   C

-7   1 x

(Figure not drawn to scale.)

On the number line above, B is the midpoint of segment $\overline{AC}$, where A is located at -7, B at 1, and C at x. F (not shown) is the midpoint of $\overline{AB}$, and G (also not shown) is the midpoint of $\overline{BC}$. If y represents the range of values on the number line, which of the following absolute value expressions would properly express the range of values from F to G?

F. $|y-1|\le 4$
G. $|y+4|\le 1$
H. $|y-5|\le 1$
J. $|y-1|\le 5$
K. $|y-4|\le 1$

93. A store sells nuts for $0.95 per pound, chocolates for $1.30 per pound, and dried berries for $0.40 per pound. The store also sells its own trail mix by combining the nuts, chocolates, and dried berries in a ratio of 2 to 3 to 1, respectively, by weight. If the price of the trail mix represents the proportionate prices of each of the ingredients, how much trail mix could a customer buy for $1.55?

A. 0.75 pounds
B. 1 pound
C. 1.5 pounds
D. 1.8 pounds
E. 3.2 pounds

94. To visit his relatives' house, Amos drove 450 miles at an average speed of 75 miles per hour. On the way back, his average speed was 60 miles per hour. What was Amos's approximate average speed for the entire trip, if the distance to and from his relatives' house was the same?

F. 65
G. 66.67
H. 67.5
J. 67.75
K. 68.33

95. z is an element of Set Z, which is comprised of all unique and real values of x and y, where $-6\le \dfrac{3}{2}x\le 9$ and $-4\le \dfrac{2}{3}y\le \dfrac{4}{3}$. Which of the following expresses the range of possible values for z?

A. $-4\le z\le 2$
B. $-5\le z\le 4$
C. $-6\le z\le 6$
D. $-10\le z\le 8$
E. $-2\le z\le 4$

CONTINUE ▶

96. At the local stationery store, 3 pens and 8 pencils cost $3.05, while 4 pens and 3 pencils cost $3.07. What is the price of 1 pen and 1 pencil?

　F. $0.13
　G. $0.26
　H. $0.67
　J. $0.80
　K. $0.93

97.

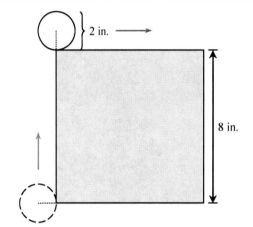

In the figure, lines *m* and *n* are parallel, and lines *s* and *t* are transversals that intersect at the center of circle *O*, which is tangent to both *m* and *n*. If the angle measures are as shown, what fraction of circle O is trapped between the lines *s*, *t*, and *m*?

　A. $\dfrac{23}{216}$

　B. $\dfrac{5}{24}$

　C. $\dfrac{1}{4}$

　D. $\dfrac{5}{12}$

　E. $\dfrac{5}{6}$

98. If a square has an area of 96 yd², what is the perimeter of a square that has half the area?

　F. $8\sqrt{6}$ yd
　G. $16\sqrt{6}$ yd
　H. $24\sqrt{2}$ yd
　J. $8\sqrt{3}$ yd
　K. $16\sqrt{3}$ yd

99. The price of concrete is ordinarily $96.00 per cubic yard, but the price is discounted by 15% when at least 1000 cubic yards of concrete is ordered. What would be the discounted price per cubic **foot**, to the nearest cent, if a customer orders 1,200 cubic yards of concrete?

　A. $3.02
　B. $9.07
　C. $27.06
　D. $54.12
　E. $363.67

100.

The diagram above shows two positions of a circle as it rolls around the edges of a square. If the dimensions of the circle and square are as shown, what is the distance traveled by the center of the circle, as the circle travels one circuit around the square?

　F. $32 + \dfrac{\pi}{2}$ inches

　G. $32 + 4\sqrt{2}$ inches

　H. $32 + 2\pi$ inches

　J. $32 + 4\pi$ inches

　K. 136 inches

STOP. THIS IS THE END OF THE TEST. IF TIME PERMITS, YOU MAY REVIEW YOUR ANSWERS TO PARTS 1 AND 2 OF THE TEST.

SHSAT
NYC EDITION
TEST 2

PART 1 — VERBAL

Suggested Time — 75 Minutes
45 QUESTIONS

SCRAMBLED PARAGRAPHS

PARAGRAPHS 1-5

DIRECTIONS: The purpose of this section is to organize sentences into the best six-sentence paragraphs possible. For each paragraph, the first sentence is provided, but the remaining five are presented in random or no particular order. Re-order and organize these five sentences, if necessary, to create the **most** logical paragraph. Each paragraph is worth **two** points, whereas every other question type in this test is worth one. Partial credit will not be given.

Blanks have been provided to help you keep track of the position of each sentence in the paragraph. For instance, if you think a sentence follows the first, given sentence, write "2" in the blank next to it; write "3" next to the sentence that you believe follows "2"; and so on. When you believe you have arranged the sentences correctly, transfer your response to your answer sheet.

Paragraph 1

On December 5, 2006, New York City's Board of Health voted to ban *trans* fats in the city's restaurants; eateries in the city had until July of 2007 to strike this artificial fat from their list of ingredients.

_____ **Q.** If it weren't for chemist Paul Sabatier's development of the hydrogenation process, for which he won the Nobel Prize for Chemistry in 1912, we may never have had *trans* fats; in 1902, Wilhelm Normann patented a process by which to hydrogenate liquid oils.

_____ **R.** Normann thus paved the way for *trans* fats, the first ever artificial food to become integrated into our food supply and the food many people love to eat but also love to hate.

_____ **S.** The first milestone victory came when the Food and Drug Administration (FDA) began requiring, as of January 1, 2006, all packaged foods, including dietary supplements, to list the amount of *trans* fats on their Nutrition Facts labels.

_____ **T.** Prior to the FDA's labeling requirement, there wasn't as much public awareness of the risks and dangers of *trans* fats because these sinister fats were rather inconspicuously listed as "partially hydrogenated oils" under the list of the food item's ingredients.

_____ **U.** This was the second monumental victory in a string of victories for health activists and for healthy living as a whole.

CONTINUE ▶

Paragraph 2

Cancer has not yet been cured, but one species of mushrooms—the turkey tail mushroom, to be exact—may provide some scintillating insight into how cancer may be battled.

_____ **Q.** All cells secrete cytokines, which are chemical messengers that help to regulate key biological processes by directing certain cells and substances to to encourage cell growth and destroy unneeded and harmful cells, including cancer cells.

_____ **R.** Furthermore, the mushroom excretes antiviral compounds that combat such viruses as the human papillomavirus and the oncovirus hepatitis-C, which can induce liver cancer.

_____ **S.** This is where the turkey tail mushroom could step in—a recent study showed that this mushroom can boost the presence of natural killer cells, which target tumors and viruses, and cytotoxic T cells, which kill off cells that are damaged, anomalous, or infected.

_____ **T.** Cancer, which starts when a rogue cell breaks away from its normal restraints on cell replication, develops in part when cancer cells exploit a "flaw" in our body's defense and repair mechanisms.

_____ **U.** But, unfortunately, cancer cells secrete a type of cytokine that signals T helper cells in the immune system to stop working; in this way, cancer cells avoid detection for destruction.

Paragraph 3

Starring action hero Gerard Butler, *300* grossed over $210 million, on an estimated budget of $65 million.

_____ **Q.** While uncertainty as to the size of the Persian army remains—ancient scribe and chronicler Herodotus put that estimate at over 1 million strong, while modern scholars figure between 30,000 and 120,000—it is undisputed that the Greeks were vastly outnumbered.

_____ **R.** In the end, with some help from the Greek traitor Ephialtes, who revealed to the Persians about a mountain pass around Thermopylae, the narrow coastal pass through which the Persians had intended to pass, the Persians prevailed.

_____ **S.** It told the tale of an elite group of 300 Spartans who led a group of several thousand Greeks in an effort to halt the massive Persian onslaught they faced in 480 B.C.

_____ **T.** Their victory, however, came at a price; historians believe that as many as 20,000 Persians were killed to the 2,000 Greeks killed in battle, and even with this victory, the Persians later proved unable to capture all of Greece.

_____ **U.** This movie, which premiered in 2006, was a modern, cinematographic take on the Battle of Thermopylae, an actual event in ancient Greek history.

CONTINUE ▶

Paragraph 4

Many of you have undoubtedly heard of the United States being referred as "Uncle Sam," the fictitious personification of the federal government, but why Sam and not Simon or Steven?

_____ **Q.** The soldiers who ate Wilson's food began calling it "Uncle Sam's," and after a newspaper ran a story about this, the moniker gained in popularity, eventually giving rise to the familiar tall, white-haired man dressed in patriotically colored garb—the rest is history.

_____ **R.** No one knows the answer with absolute certainty, but it would not be unreasonable to believe that the nickname of the world's greatest superpower would be traceable to a citizen of great societal prominence, perhaps a senator or corporate mogul.

_____ **S.** Instead, Samuel Wilson was a meatpacker who supplied beef to the United States Army during the War of 1812.

_____ **T.** And several different theories have, in fact, been posited to explain the eponymous origin of the nickname, as it refers to the United States, but one of the more popular theories attributes the "Uncle Sam" to someone who did not belong to the socioeconomic elite.

_____ **U.** As was custom at the time, Wilson stamped "U.S." on each of the barrels of beef he provided to the army—contractors were required to stamp onto the food's packaging their names and the location from where the food was being sent.

Paragraph 5

Perhaps it was inevitable that word would get out about the discovery of gold at Sutter's Mill in California, despite James Wilson Marshall and John Sutter's efforts to contain the news of their discovery.

_____ **Q.** Within a few months, nearly 75% of the males in San Francisco had departed to seek their fortunes in the gold mines; by August, the number of gold miners had risen to 4,000.

_____ **R.** By mid-March of 1848—Marshall had discovered flakes of gold on January 24 earlier that year while he was building a water-powered sawmill for Sutter—at least one newspaper reported that gold was being turned up at Sutter's Mill.

_____ **S.** They did, after all, want to maximize their own wealth, not share it with myriads of others; with such a discovery and consequent fantasies of abundant wealth, however, comes an infectious giddiness that is nigh impossible to contain.

_____ **T.** Reports of findings of gold continued making their way across the nation and even overseas, but the gold rush of 1849 only commenced in full force—partly due to the skepticism that the faced reports—after President James K. Polk acknowledged California's abundance of gold in his inaugural address of December 1848.

_____ **U.** Initially, and understandably, there was much doubt and skepticism about this report; when storekeeper Sam Brannan paraded through town with a vial of gold obtained from Sutter's Creek, that skepticism very quickly gave way to frenzied excitement.

CONTINUE ▶

Logical Reasoning
QUESTIONS 11-20

DIRECTIONS: For each question, read the information provided and select the **best** answer choice, based **only on the information given.** In other words, even if you know more about a particular set of facts than is provided, do not use your knowledge of the facts to aid your decision-making process.

When dealing with logical reasoning questions, be on alert for certain placement or position and order words and phrases, such as **to the right of**, **above**, **before**, and **next to**. "The puppy is **between** the kitten and duckling," for instance, is not necessarily the same as "The puppy is **between and next to** the kitten and duckling"; one or more other objects may separate the puppy from the kitten or from the duckling.

11. A comedian is someone who performs stand-up routines; the funnier a comedian is, the more people he makes laugh, on average, during his routines. Moreover, on average, professional comedians make more people laugh during their stand-up routines than amateur comedians do. The funniest professional comedian makes an average of 80 people laugh per night during his or her stand-up comedy routines. On Thursday night, Jerry the comedian made 100 people laugh during his stand-up routine.

   Based only on the information above, which of the following **must** be true?

   A. Jerry is the funniest professional comedian, since no other comedian could make more than 80 people laugh per routine.
   B. If Jerry was not already the funniest professional comedian, he became the funniest professional comedian with his Thursday night stand-up routine.
   C. If Jerry is not the funniest professional comedian and occasionally makes 100 or more people laugh during his stand-up routines, then there are other times that Jerry makes fewer than 80 people laugh during his stand-up routines.
   D. No one is funnier than Jerry.
   E. Jerry deserves to be paid more than the funniest professional comedian, if he is not the funniest professional comedian already.

12. Whenever Won is at home, he either writes or relaxes. Whenever he writes, he does research. Whenever he relaxes, he hums.

   Based only on the information above, which of the following **must** be true?

   F. If Won relaxes, he hums at home.
   G. If Won is at home and doing research, then he is also writing.
   H. If Won is at home, he is also either doing research or humming.
   J. If Won isn't relaxing, he isn't humming.
   K. If Won isn't writing, he isn't researching.

13. Sunnie studied art using four different media. She studied charcoal for three years, pastels for five, pen for five, and water colors for six. She never studied more than three art media in any given year.

   What is the **least** number of years Sunnie could have studied the different art media?

   A. 6
   B. 7
   C. 8
   D. 9
   E. 10

CONTINUE ▶

14. Seven students got in line—Jacob, Phillip, Sanders, Danielle, Cassie, Henry, and Beth, in that order—to buy school lunch.

1) None of the students who bought spaghetti stood immediately next to each other.
2) The two students who bought hamburgers stood next to each other.
3) Of the two students who bought pizza, one stood third in line.

Based only on the information above, which of the following **must** be true?

F. Jacob and Phillip both bought pizza, while Sanders bought spaghetti.
G. Henry and Jacob bought spaghetti, while Danielle and Cassie bought hamburgers.
H. Phillip bought pizza, while Jacob bought spaghetti.
J. Phillip bought spaghetti, while Jacob bought pizza.
K. Danielle and Beth both bought spaghetti, while Cassie and Henry both bought hamburgers.

15. Some of Birch School's field hockey players also play lacrosse. Those who play lacrosse also play either basketball or soccer.

Based only on the information above, which of the following **must** be true?

A. All Birch School athletes play four sports.
B. Some Birch School athletes play field hockey, lacrosse, and soccer.
C. Every basketball player at Birch School also plays lacrosse.
D. Some Birch School athletes play at least three sports.
E. No field hockey player at Birch School plays more than a total of three sports.

16. Five children—Jackson, Pierce, Stephen, LaToya, and Antoinette—each has a favorite classic game: chess, checkers, go, backgammon, and solitaire.

1) Pierce's favorite game is solitaire.
2) LaToya's favorite game is either chess or checkers.
3) Jackson does not play go.
4) Antoinette's favorite game is neither backgammon nor go.
5) No two children share the same favorite game.

Which of the following additional pieces of information, if true, would yield an exact determination of everyone's favorite game?

F. Jackson's favorite game is not checkers.
G. Antoinette's favorite game is checkers.
H. Jackson's favorite game is backgammon.
J. Stephen only plays go.
K. LaToya does not play backgammon.

17. The captains of six teams, each represented by a different color, are sitting around a regular hexagonal table such that each captain is directly facing only one other captain.

1) The lavender team's captain is sitting directly to the purple team's captain's right.
2) The magenta team's captain is sitting directly across from the turquoise team's, who in turn sitting immediately to the left of the burgundy team's captain.

What are the colors of the teams whose captains the gold team's captain is sitting directly in between?

A. burgundy and lavender
B. burgundy and magenta
C. turquoise and purple
D. turquoise and magenta
E. lavender and purple

CONTINUE ▶

45

18. At a luncheon, four prepackaged meals are available. Because the meals are prepackaged, the luncheon patrons are not able to mix and match meal components. Each meal has three components: an entrée (with a choice of a sandwich, chicken, macaroni, or fish), beverage (with a choice of juice, root beer, iced tea, or lemonade), and dessert (with a choice of a brownie, potato chips, fruit, or yogurt).

   1) The sandwich comes with juice.
   2) The brownie comes with the chicken.
   3) The fish comes with the iced tea.
   4) The root beer does not come with fruit.
   5) The yogurt comes with neither the macaroni nor the juice.

   Which of the following additional pieces of information, if true, would yield an exact determination of the available prepackaged lunches?

   F. The sandwich comes with fruit.
   G. The chicken comes with the root beer.
   H. The macaroni comes with lemonade.
   J. The macaroni comes with fruit.
   K. The fish comes with yogurt.

Questions 19 and 20 refer to the following information.

In the code below, (1) each letter always represents the same word, (2) each word is represented by only one letter, and (3) in any given sentence, the position of a letter is **never** the same as that of the word it represents.

Y	Q	W	M		means
"Are	we	going	today?"		

J	H	Y	M	Z	means
"We	will	be	going	later."	

Q	X	J	T	B	means
"Later	today	or	another	day."	

19. Which letter represents the word "we"?

   A. M
   B. J
   C. Y
   D. Q
   E. Cannot be determined from the information given.

20. Which word does the letter J represent?

   F. today
   G. going
   H. later
   J. another
   K. Cannot be determined from the information given.

CONTINUE ▶

READING

QUESTIONS 21-50

DIRECTIONS: Each passage below has five questions associated with it. After reading a passage, answer the questions, based **only on the information provided** by the passage; even if you have a deeper knowledge of the contents of the passage, do not base your answers on any outside knowledge.

We have come to expect our phones today to be more than phones. In fact, smartphones, as advanced, internet-ready phones are now called, are capable of handling many of the tasks that
5 could only have been reserved for computers even in the late 1990s. From providing internet access to offering entertainment and productivity applications, smartphones are indispensable companions to many people worldwide and have
10 already begun consolidating other now increasingly antiquated gadgets, such as mp3 players. We take for granted how much progress has been made technologically, but just 41 years ago, in 1973, a completely wireless phone—or
15 cell phone, as it were, was in and of itself a technological marvel.

On April 3, 1973, Martin Cooper, then the general manager of Motorola's Communications Systems division, placed a call to the head of re-
20 search at Bell Labs, which had been competing against Motorola to devise the first ever cellular phone. The cell phone Cooper called from did not resemble any modern telephone. It weighed as much as or more than most contemporary ul-
25 trabook laptops do, although there is some discrepancy as to the weight of the original incarnation of a cell phone—some sources claim it weighed 2.5 pounds, while others claim it weighed 30 ounces, two ounces shy of two
30 pounds. The original cell phone was so heavy that Cooper purportedly jested that calls necessarily had to be short—after all, "who had the strength to hold it to an ear for very long?"

It took Motorola 10 years before it released its
35 DynaTAC phone for public consumption in 1983, with each phone costing $3,500 and weighing 16 ounces. (Though the decade's worth of development and refinement led to a

halving of the phone's weight, the original Dy-
40 naTAC was a behemoth by today's standards; most cell phones today weigh in between four and six ounces, and some weigh as little as three.) And on October 13th, 1983, Ameritech executive Bob Barnett made history by fittingly
45 calling Alexander Graham Bell's grandson with the DynaTAC 8000X, giving Barnett the distinction of having made the first ever commercial cell phone call.

The motivation for cell phones was simple
50 enough: people didn't want to be tethered to a location. They wanted to be able to communicate with other people, not with a building or structure, even if that location could often move with a person (car phones were available at the
55 time), but it would take some more time before that autonomy and independence could and would be realized. It took nearly 7 years for global cell phone subscriptions to hit the million mark. Since then, however, the rate of cell phone
60 adoption has grown astronomically, as prices went down and the versatility of cell phones went up—by the end of 2011, there was a global total of 5.9 billion cell phone subscriptions, and this figure will only keep increasing. The cost of
65 producing phones will continue to plummet, and manufacturers will thus deploy more units, including smartphones, to more emerging markets and economies, where cell phones aren't nearly as ubiquitous.

CONTINUE ▶

21. What is the main purpose of the passage?

    A. to discuss the complications that arose in the development and invention of the first cell phones
    B. to persuade readers that cell phones were invented to allow people from being tethered to locations
    C. to suggest that cell phones are going to be become more ubiquitous around the world over time
    D. to compare and contrast the first cell phones, especially their size and weight, to current cell phones
    E. to explain the motivation behind cell phones and provide a brief history about early cell phones

22. The author assumes the reader knows which of the following pieces of information in using the phrasing "by fittingly" in line 44?

    F. Alexander Graham Bell's grandson's age at the time of the phone call
    G. Alexander Graham Bell's grandson's role in developing the DynaTAC cell phone
    H. Alexander Graham Bell's grandson's role in Bell Labs
    J. Alexander Graham Bell's significance
    K. Alexander Graham Bell's father's importance

23. Which of the following statements would the author most likely agree with?

    A. Bob Barnett worked for Motorola before being named as an Ameritech executive.
    B. Motorola changed its name to Ameritech.
    C. Alexander Graham Bell's son was the head of research at Bell Labs.
    D. The first cell phone weighed up to ten times the amount some cell phones weigh today.
    E. Martin Cooper changed his name to Bob Barnett.

24. Which of the following can be inferred by the statements made in the passage?

    F. In 2011, over 84% of the world's population had at least one cell phone subscription.
    G. Cell phones will get cheaper in all available markets.
    H. There were at least 6.5 billion cell phone subscriptions by the end of 2012.
    J. The majority of modern ultrabooks weigh 2.5 pounds or fewer.
    K. Eventually, everyone in the world will have at least one cell phone each.

25. Based on the passage, which of the following would the author most likely *disagree* with?

    A. Mp3 players are as relevant as they used to be.
    B. Bell Labs never released a cell phone because Motorola beat it to the market.
    C. It would have been difficult to hold the original cell phone up to one's ear for an extended period of time.
    D. Smartphones today can do many of the things computers in the late 1990s could do.
    E. The DynaTAC 8000X was far less affordable than cell phones today are.

26. What can be inferred from the passage about how much the DynaTAC 8000X weighed?

    F. It weighed between 1.8 and 2.5 pounds.
    G. It weighed between 0.9 and 1.25 pounds.
    H. It weighed more than five times the weight of most cell phones today.
    J. Its weight was too much for children to pick up.
    K. Its weight led to fatigue after more than 40 minutes of use.

CONTINUE ▶

Until relatively recently, it was widely believed that neurogenesis, the process by which new neurons are created, ceases once the brain reaches maturity. But in 1998, a team of scien-
5 tists provided the first true evidence of neuro- genesis in the adult hippocampus, a region of the brain that is involved in the processing and de- velopment of memories. Unfortunately, their re- sults could not be replicated because of safety
10 concerns associated with their methodology— the scientists had used chemical markers that permanently integrated into the DNA of the di- viding brain cells of their subjects. Moreover, their method could not shed light on the extent
15 to which adult neurogenesis occurs. Thus, for over a decade many questions about adult neuro- genesis lingered.

Then, in the June 6, 2013, issue of the journal *Cell*, an article was published that not only af-
20 firmed the existence of adult neurogenesis but also provided insight into the extent of adult neurogenesis; the researchers were able to do all of this by taking the innovative approach of studying the after-effects of the series of above-
25 ground atomic bomb tests that were conducted between 1945 and 1963, over half a century ago.

When atomic weapons detonate, they release ra- dioactive isotopes into the atmosphere. (Isotopes are variations of a chemical element that host
30 different numbers of neutrons in their nuclei. And except for the most stable nuclear configu- rations, which occur when the numbers of pro- tons and neutrons of an atom are equal, most isotopes are unstable and therefore undergo a de-
35 cay process that causes them to break down.) Among the isotopes released by atomic weapons detonations is carbon-14—carbon-12 is the sta- ble and most commonly recurring isotope of car- bon—which assimilates into the ecosystem and
40 ultimately integrates into our chromosomes dur- ing DNA replication.

By measuring the ratio of carbon-14 to carbon- 12 in the dentate gyrus (a region of the hippo- campus where adult neurogenesis was believed
45 to occur) of 55 post mortem brains belonging to people whose ages ranged from 19 to 92, the re-

searchers found that an estimated 700 new neu- rons are created per day in adults, with that num- ber decreasing modestly as people age. And un-
50 like the vast majority of non-renewing neurons, of which there are over 100 billion in a mature brain, these regularly renewing subpopulation of neurons live much shorter lives. What this means is that no new neurons are added in the
55 rest of the brain, including in the rest of the hip- pocampus, after one has reached the age of two.

Many questions about the human brain remain, but with this research, we are one major mile- stone closer to understanding what might be the
60 most biologically complex system in existence. It is possible that the dentate gyrus plays a sig- nificant role in the process of learning, including memory formation and development of person- alities, and it is quite the ironic twist that what is
65 arguably the single greatest force of mass de- struction served to provide the radioactive mat- ter necessary for a better understanding of the brain, without which we could not survive.

27. What is the main purpose of this passage?

   A. to illustrate that, with the discovery of the role of the dentate gyrus, the ques- tion of how the human brain exactly works is now answered
   B. to argue that, without nuclear weapons, it would not have been possible for sci- entists to understand how the dentate gyrus works
   C. to explain how radioactive isotopes of carbon helped scientists piece together the mystery of how the dentate gyrus works
   D. to discuss a recent development in a cer- tain scientific field and to provide back- ground information about that develop- ment
   E. to highlight how much there is still left to understand about the inner workings of the human mind and brain

CONTINUE ▶

28. What can be inferred from the passage about the brain's development process?

F. By the time a person is 92 years old, the dentate gyrus probably produces fewer than 500 neurons per day.
G. Neurons produced by the dentate gyrus can probably permanently replace non-renewing neurons in the rest of the brain, as long as the brain does not sustain serious injury.
H. Because there are 100 billion neurons in the mature brain, an addition of 700 neurons per day probably is probably insignificant to one's learning process.
J. The dentate gyrus is formed after the brain has fully matured in order to be able to produce fresh neurons for the brain.
K. Aside from the neurons that are created by the dentate gyrus, the brain is fully grown by age two.

29. Which of the following statements is the most logically valid?

A. Approximately 0.000007% of all neurons in the brain are created in the dentate gyrus.
B. It is possible that an extremely small number, relatively speaking, of all neurons in the brain play a very significant role in the development of the human mind.
C. One of the primary flaws with the approach that the researchers took while studying neurogenesis was that they chose to study isotopes that there released into the atmosphere over half a century ago.
D. The rate of neurogenesis in the dentate gyrus of the average 92-year-old is the same as that of the average 19-year-old.
E. The researchers who studied adult neurogenesis measured the ratio of carbon-13 to carbon-12 to draw the conclusions they did.

30. What was one of the limitations of the applicability of the research conducted by the team of scientists who provided the first true evidence of adult neurogenesis?

F. The team could not find enough willing test subjects or participants.
G. Safety concerns with the team's methodology prohibited the team from continuing its research.
H. The extent of adult neurogenesis could not be determined using the team's approach.
J. The team's research only led to more questions than answers for a long time.
K. It was impossible for the team to continue using the chemical markers that became permanently integrated into the DNA of dividing cells.

31. Which of the following does the author believe to be most ironic?

A. that adults can create new neurons
B. that 700 neurons could be just as important as the other 100 billion neurons
C. that it took over a decade for research into adult neurogenesis to start up again because of unverified safety concerns
D. that a weapon of mass destruction was the key to understanding more about something essential to life
E. that radioactive fallout from more than 50 years ago can be absorbed by our bodies

32. What is the author's overall tone throughout the passage?

F. informative and objective
G. condescending and indifferent
H. zealous and presumptuous
J. objective and aggravated
K. curious but ill-informed

CONTINUE ▶

According to the Centers for Disease Control and Prevention, an estimated 35.7% of adults and 17% of children and adolescents 2-19 years old in the U.S. are said to be obese. Obesity, which for adults has been defined as having a body mass index (BMI) of greater than or equal to 30—in children, a BMI percentile ranking is used to determine obesity—is thus a big problem because it can, and often does, pose serious health risks; coronary heart disease, hypertension, type 2 diabetes, and certain cancers are some of the conditions that obesity puts people more at risk for. To better understand obesity, one must first have at least a rudimentary understanding of saturated fats.

Saturated fats are solid at room temperature and are much more prone to clustering together in solid clumps, whereas unsaturated fats are generally liquid at room temperature. Fatty acids are comprised of two main parts: a carboxylic acid head and an aliphatic tail or tails. Biochemically speaking, the aliphatic hydrocarbon chains—hydrocarbons are molecules comprised entirely of hydrogen and carbon atoms—of saturated fatty acids are as fully loaded with hydrogen atoms as possible to produce relatively geometrically flat and straight chains, at least as flat and straight as they can possibly be. The relative flatness and straightness of the aliphatic chains permit other saturated fatty acids to come close together physically in proximity.

Unsaturated fatty acids, on the other hand, are not as saturated with hydrogen atoms as the number of carbon atoms on their aliphatic chains will theoretically permit because the double bonds of unsaturated fatty acids alter the fatty acids' stereoscopic structure. As such, the hydrocarbon chains of unsaturated fatty acids prevent ready clustering. And because they can't clump together as easily, unsaturated fats are more likely to stay in liquid form. (If you've ever seen the terms *monounsaturated fats* and *polyunsaturated fats* on nutrition labels, these terms are referring to the number of double bonds that the unsaturated fatty acid chains contain, where a monounsaturated fat contains fatty acids with one double bond in each of the aliphatic chains and a polyunsaturated fatty acid's aliphatic chains contain more than one double bond.)

Though a difference in the aliphatic chains of saturated fats and unsaturated fats may not seem to be a reason for excitement, it is the clustering ability of saturated fatty acids that serves as the culprit behind saturated fat's virulence as a health threat. Saturated fats contribute to the formation of arterial plaque—cholesterol and calcium are two of the other components of this plaque—which clogs arteries. And when arteries get clogged, the heart works harder to get blood to the body because it has to pump blood harder to ensure the same rate of blood flow, but through tighter spaces; increased blood pressure also leads to weaker arterial walls, since increased blood pressure leads to a faster wearing down of the arteries, and thereby increases the risk of hemorrhaging. Moreover, if the arteries become too clogged, insufficient blood flow will lead to oxygen deprivation to certain organs or body parts. There are many other physiological consequences saturated fats have on the body, but suffice it to say that it is beneficial to minimize the intake of saturated fats.

33. What is the main idea of this passage?

A. If people minimized their intake of saturated fats, obesity would not be a problem anymore.
B. Obesity poses many significant health risks.
C. Molecular geometry is an extremely important part of chemistry.
D. There are significant geometrical differences between saturated fats and unsaturated fats.
E. The properties of fats dictate the physiological effects fats have on people.

CONTINUE ▶

34. Which of the following is NOT mentioned in the passage as a health risk posed by obesity?

F. coronary heart disease
G. hypertension
H. type 1 diabetes
J. type 2 diabetes
K. certain types of cancer

35. Which of the following is not necessarily a difference between saturated fatty acids and unsaturated fatty acids?

A. state of matter, i.e., solid, liquid, or gas, at room temperature
B. number of aliphatic chains
C. stereoscopic structure of the aliphatic chains
D. hydrogen saturation rate or level per aliphatic chain
E. relative flatness of the aliphatic chains

36. What is the primary difference between monounsaturated fatty acids and polyunsaturated fatty acids?

F. Each aliphatic chain of monounsaturated fatty acids is shorter than each aliphatic chain of polyunsaturated fatty acids.
G. Monounsaturated fatty acids have one carboxylic acid head whereas polyunsaturated fatty acids have two or more.
H. Monounsaturated fatty acids have one aliphatic chain whereas polyunsaturated fatty acids have two or more.
J. Each aliphatic chain of monounsaturated fatty acids has one double bond whereas each aliphatic chain of polyunsaturated fatty acids has at least two.
K. Monounsaturated fatty acids are half as likely to cluster with other fatty acids as polyunsaturated fatty acids are.

37. Which statement can be inferred from the passage?

A. Unsaturated fats never pose any health risks.
B. *Trans* fats are the most dangerous kinds of fats ever discovered, so stay away from them.
C. The clustering ability of saturated fatty acids allows for the development of arterial plaque.
D. Eating saturated fats inevitably leads to cancer, hypertension, and other serious health risks.
E. More than 35.7% of the people in the United States are considered obese.

38. Which of the following is NOT mentioned in the passage as being triggered by the ingestion of saturated fats, whether directly or indirectly?

F. a buildup of arterial plaque
G. an increased risk of hemorrhaging
H. oxygen deprivation to some body parts
J. a weakening of arterial walls
K. the increased production of cholesterol and calcium

CONTINUE ▶

In 1977, the Convention on International Trade in Endangered Species (CITES) banned the sale of rhinoceros parts in an effort to bring rhinos back from the brink of extinction—by 1910, the
5 population of white rhinos was down to 100 in South Africa, and in 1995, even after the ban, only 2,410 black rhinos were left. The purpose of the CITES ban was to counteract all of the poaching that had been going on as a result of
10 the widespread belief that the rhinoceros horn was a panacea capable of treating all manners of ailments, from fevers and measles to epilepsy. But because the demand for these prized horns remains extremely high, with rhino horns fetch-
15 ing as much as $65,000 per kilogram (approximately 2.2 pounds) on the black market in 2012, up from $4,700 in 1993, poaching has continued rampantly. Rather interestingly, and ironically, the most effective way to protect rhinoceros
20 populations may be to legalize the trade of rhino horns.

The restriction on the free trade and sales of rhino horns by CITES was tantamount to limiting the easy supply of rhinoceros horn available
25 to the public, thus driving up the price of rhino horn. And in the face of constantly increasing demand, the prices have only gone up, as we have seen from the astronomical jump in price in a span of fewer than 10 years. With demand, and
30 consequently prices, so high for rhino horn, poachers have been more incentivized to hunt rhinoceroses; neither the law nor safety risks have been deterring poachers—poaching has more than doubled every year for the past five
35 years; in 2012, 668 rhinoceroses were poached, and extrapolations of current poaching estimates foresee rhinoceroses becoming extinct within two decades.

But if the trade of rhino horn were tightly regu-
40 lated, the rhino population could feasibly be saved because rhinoceros horns can be cut or shaved without any physical repercussion to the animal, since rhino horns grow back over time. Furthermore, if rhino horns could be acquired le-
45 gally to meet the market demands, the prices for horns would be driven down, and poachers would have less incentive to continue slaughter-

ing rhinos. Given that not even attempts to educate the public about the truths of rhino horns
50 have suppressed demand for this exotic commodity—rhino horns are keratin, the same material that comprises human fingernails—legalizing the harvesting and sale of rhinoceros horns may be the most viable way of preserving these
55 endangered beasts.

But if we are to act to protect these beasts, whatever protective measures we decide to implement, we must act now. As of November 6, 2013, the Western black rhino, a subspecies of
60 the black rhinoceros—the black rhinoceros species itself is currently listed as "critically endangered"—was officially declared extinct by the International Union for Conservation of Nature (IUCN), which pointedly blamed poachers and
65 the lack of proper conservation efforts. The last Western black rhino was seen in 2006, and according to the IUCN, the Northern white rhino is "teetering on the edge of extinction" as well.

39. Which of the following best tells what this passage is about?

    A. This passage is about the dire situation of rhinoceroses and one possible unconventional solution that could help prevent the extinction of rhinoceroses.

    B. This passage is a plea to the readers to donate more time and funds to the preservation of rhinoceroses.

    C. This passage is an explanation of what caused the Western black rhinoceros's extinction.

    D. This passage is a news piece designed to show how the value of rhinoceros horn has gone up over the years and why this is contributing to the endangerment of rhinoceroses.

    E. This passage is about the need to outright ban the trade of rhino horn and to impose severe consequences for those caught breaking the law.

CONTINUE ▶

40. What is the best definition of the word "panacea" (line 11), as it is used in this passage?

    F. a miracle drug that promotes eternal life
    G. a medicine that cures fevers, measles, and epilepsy
    H. a topically applied analgesic that relieves skin conditions and fevers
    J. a cure-all that can treat many different ailments and illnesses
    K. a drug that boosts immune system health

41. According to the passage, why has poaching continued to increase over the years?

    A. Improved technology has made it easier for poachers to hunt rhinoceroses and make a living from hunting rhinoceroses.
    B. Rhinoceroses are becoming rarer to find, so hunting rhinoceroses has become more of an extreme sport for poachers, with each successful hunt giving a tremendous boost to the poacher's reputation.
    C. Rhinoceroses are projected to go extinct within the next two decades, so many poaches believe that they need to poach now before there is no more rhinoceros horn left to poach.
    D. The price that a poacher can fetch from selling rhinoceros horns has gone up astronomically within the past decade, so poachers are willing to take greater risks to fetch rhinoceros horns.
    E. No government is actively policing the poaching of rhinoceros horns, thus effectively giving poachers free rein.

42. Which of the following can be inferred from the passage?

    F. A lower supply of a product leads to an increase price of that product.
    G. One rhinoceros horn will bring a poacher at least $65,000.
    H. A greater supply of a product leads to a lower price for that product.
    J. Increased demand of a product leads to lowered prices of that product.
    K. People's willingness to risk injury and to break the law increases as a reward's monetary value increases.

43. What innovative way might stop the poaching of rhinoceros horns?

    A. establishing wildlife preserves for rhinoceroses, at least until their population numbers can go back up
    B. drastically lowering the prices that can be fetched for rhinoceros horns
    C. legalizing and tightly regulating the trade of rhinoceros horns
    D. shutting down the black markets in which rhinoceros horns are being sold
    E. prosecuting those involved in the buying of rhinoceros horns, as well as those involved in the poaching of the horns

44. With which of the following statements would the author agree, regarding rhinoceros horns?

    F. The rhinoceros must be killed for its horn to be extracted.
    G. The species and subspecies of rhinoceros alters the value of the horn.
    H. Rhinoceros horns have been scientifically proven to have curative properties.
    J. Rhinoceros horns can be harvested without any physical harm to the animal.
    K. Without their horns, rhinoceroses are very vulnerable and defenseless.

CONTINUE ▶

To say that Cornelius Vanderbilt was a self-made man would be to make quite the understatement. Born on May 27, 1794, to a poor and illiterate seaman, Vanderbilt would forge a path
5 for himself that would destine him to become one of America's most successful businessmen.

As a child, Vanderbilt spent much of his youth working for his father—he dropped out of school at age 11 to help his father when one of
10 his siblings died. And when he turned 16, he used the hundred dollars he had earned from landscaping for his father to buy a sailboat and used that one boat to begin a passenger ferry business in New York Harbor. Between his skill
15 as a sailor and his aggressive pricing schemes to undercut his competition, Vanderbilt grew his business, enabling him to grow it even further— during the War of 1812, he was even commissioned by the military to deliver supplies to forts
20 along the Hudson River.

With the advent of the steamboat and the rise in popularity of the steamboat as a means of waterway travel, however, Vanderbilt had to make a decision. He perceived that clinging on to his
25 tried and true formula for success with sailboats would be financially detrimental; the steamboat, which rendered the sailboat obsolete, allowed passengers to be transported more quickly, reliably, and cost efficiently, and there was no way
30 he could compete. Thus, he made the decision, demonstrating perspicacious business acumen and savvy, to retire his sailboat business in 1817 and to focus on assuring his continued success, this time in the steamboat industry, by obtaining
35 employment as a steamboat operator. He continued working as a steamboat operator until he was in his mid-30s, when he launched his own steamboat business with the same business principles he used to succeed with his sailboats. His
40 strategy paid off. By 1946, Vanderbilt was a millionaire, commanding a fleet of over 100 steamboats.

Cornelius Vanderbilt did not stop there. He knew there was more he could accomplish, so he
45 leveraged his success in his steamboat operations and invested into various ventures in Central America, paving the way for his entry into

the transatlantic steamship industry in 1855. Moreover, when the railroad industry began tak-
50 ing shape, Vanderbilt took advantage of his presence in the steamboat industry to acquire railroads to allow him to connect his passengers who needed passage between waterway and railway. And from there, he proceeded to leave his
55 indelible mark on U.S. history as a railroad tycoon with his acquisitions of a number of railroads, such as the Lake Shore and Michigan Southern Railway, Michigan Central Railroad, and Canada Southern Railway, among others.

60 By opting to embrace the changing times and capitalize on the situations and opportunities presented to him, Vanderbilt built an unprecedented fortune, having amassed by the time he died a fortune valued at over $100 million or
65 roughly 1.15% of the national GDP at the time, in a nation of approximately 46.4 million people.

45. Which of the following would be the best title for the passage?

   A. "The Rise and Fall of the Steamship Industry"
   B. "What It Takes to Succeed"
   C. "Cornelius Vanderbilt, Richest Man of All Time"
   D. "The Life and Legacy of an American Icon"
   E. "America, The Land of Opportunity"

46. Which of the following was NOT one of the myriad vocations, as are mentioned in the passage, that Vanderbilt had in his lifetime?

   F. landscaper
   G. military supplies procurement officer
   H. sailboat passenger ferry operator
   J. railroad tycoon
   K. steamboat fleet owner

CONTINUE ▶

47. Which of the following is the best substitute for *perspicacious* (line 31), as it is used in the context of the passage?

    A. astoundingly fortunate
    B. keenly perceptive
    C. subtly cunning
    D. deceitfully manipulative
    E. impossibly brilliant

48. What can be inferred about how Vanderbilt succeeded with his steamboat fleet?

    F. He charmed his passengers with humorous and engaging conversation so that they would keep riding with him.
    G. He knew the waterways better than anyone else did, so he could ferry passengers more quickly than other steamboat operators could.
    H. He undercut all of his competitors by at least 10%, even when his competitors started offering discounted rates.
    J. He offered extreme discounts and also spread malicious rumors about other steamboat operators so that his passengers would not feel good about using his competitors' services.
    K. He priced his fares aggressively so that passengers would likely choose his steamboats over those of his competitors.

49. Which of the following most directly allowed Vanderbilt to gain his initial foothold in the railroad industry?

    A. his expansion into the transatlantic steamship industry
    B. his acquisition of more than half of the startup railroads in the United States, such as the Michigan Southern Railway
    C. the construction of the Panama Canal
    D. his decision to learn how to be a steamboat operator so that he could get into the steamboat industry
    E. his ability to adapt to the times and capitalize on opportunities

50. According to the passage, how did the steamboat render the sailboat obsolete as a ferry vehicle?

    F. The steamboat was quicker and less reliable than the sailboat was.
    G. The steamboat could hold between 10 and 20 times more people than the sailboat could.
    H. The steamboat couldn't operate in smaller bodies of water, although the sailboat could.
    J. The steamboat was quicker, more reliable, and more cost efficient than the sailboat was.
    K. The steamboat was much more expensive than the sailboat was, so it was more cost efficient than the sailboat was.

CONTINUE ▶

PART 2 — MATHEMATICS

Suggested Time — 75 Minutes
QUESTIONS 51-100

GENERAL INSTRUCTIONS

Answer or solve each question or problem. Once you have arrived at the correct answer or come up with a satisfactory answer choice, mark your answer sheet accordingly. **DO NOT MARK ON YOUR ANSWER SHEET OTHER THAN TO FILL IN YOUR ANSWER CHOICES.**

IMPORTANT NOTES:
   (1) Formulas and definitions of terms and symbols are **not** provided.
   (2) Diagrams may not have been drawn to scale. Do not make any assumptions about any relationship in a diagram unless it can be figured out or derived from the given information.
   (3) Assume that all diagrams are drawn in one plane, unless the problem specifies otherwise.
   (4) Graphs have been drawn to scale. Unless the problem states otherwise, you can assume relationships based on how they appear. For instance, if lines look perpendicular on a graph, you may assume they are perpendicular; the same goes for concurrent lines, straight lines, collinear points, right angles, etc.
   (5) Reduce all fractions to simplest terms.

---

51. What is the quotient when the least common multiple of 84 and 189 is divided by the greatest common factor of 84 and 189?

   A. 2×2
   B. 2×3
   C. 3×3
   D. 6×6
   E. 9×9

---

52. $(\sqrt{24})(\sqrt{6}) =$

   F. $6\sqrt{2}$
   G. $6\sqrt{3}$
   H. 12
   J. 72
   K. $72\sqrt{2}$

53. Three investors, Bella, Damien, and Lucius, plan to invest a total of $42 million into a new shopping center. If Bella plans to invest 150% of what Damien plans to invest, and Damien plans to invest twice what Lucius will invest, how much does Damien plan to invest?

   A. $6 million
   B. $7 million
   C. $9 million
   D. $14 million
   E. $21 million

CONTINUE ▶

54. {140, 141, 142, …, 298, 299, 300}

How many numbers in the set above are multiples of 7 but not of 14?

- **F.** 10
- **G.** 11
- **H.** 21
- **J.** 22
- **K.** 23

55. What is the best approximation of the fraction $\frac{1}{17}$ as a decimal number expressed in scientific notation?

- **A.** 5.88×10^{-3}
- **B.** 5.88×10^{-2}
- **C.** 5.89×10^{-2}
- **D.** 58.8×10^{-4}
- **E.** 58.8×10^{-3}

56. For what positive value of x does

$$\frac{25}{8} = \frac{(x+1)^2}{72}?$$

- **F.** 4
- **G.** 5
- **H.** 8
- **J.** 14
- **K.** 15

57. Today, Richard ate 7 fewer than twice the number of candies his brother Carlos ate yesterday. If Carlos ate 5 more candies today than he did yesterday, how many candies did Carlos eat today if Richard ate 13 candies today?

- **A.** 7
- **B.** 10
- **C.** 13
- **D.** 15
- **E.** 20

58. The product of four different positive integers is 42. How much greater is the greatest integer than the median of the smaller three integers?

- **F.** 1
- **G.** 3
- **H.** 5
- **J.** 7
- **K.** 9

59.

A B   C   D

$$CD : BC = 3 : 2$$
$$BC : AB = 4 : 1$$

If the length of every segment in the figure above has an integer value, and the ratios of the segments as indicated, which of the following could be the length of BD?

- **A.** 36 units
- **B.** 121 units
- **C.** 125 units
- **D.** 128 units
- **E.** 130 units

60. What values of m satisfies the equation $m^2 - 5m = 36$?

- **F.** -1 and 5
- **G.** 2 and -3
- **H.** 4 and -1
- **J.** 6 and -6
- **K.** 9 and -4

61. Evaluate the expression $xy(x + 2)(y - 3)$ when $x = 7$ and $xy = 91$.

- **A.** 990
- **B.** 1200
- **C.** 1800
- **D.** 8190
- **E.** 9990

CONTINUE ▶

62. $\left(\dfrac{4}{9} - \dfrac{7}{15}\right) \div \dfrac{13}{10} =$

- **F.** $-\dfrac{5}{13}$
- **G.** $-\dfrac{2}{117}$
- **H.** $\dfrac{82}{117}$
- **J.** $\dfrac{533}{450}$
- **K.** $\dfrac{13}{585}$

63.

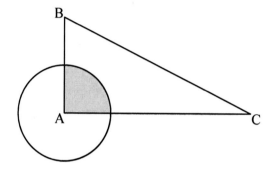

In the figure above, point A is the center of the circle and a vertex of the right triangle, which has an area of 12 square units and where $\angle BAC$ is the right angle. Point D (not shown) is the point of intersection of the perimeter of circle A and segment AB. The ratio of AB to AC is 2 to 3, and the ratio of AD to AB is 1 to 2. What is the area of the shaded region, in square units?

- **A.** π
- **B.** 2π
- **C.** 4π
- **D.** 16π
- **E.** 36π

64. Fernando is 5 years older than Alexa. In 9 years, Fernando will be 3 times as old as Alexa is now. How old is Alexa now?

- **F.** 5 years old
- **G.** 7 years old
- **H.** 9 years old
- **J.** 11 years old
- **K.** 13 years old

65. Tanner skied 32 hours in 5 days. He skied 4 hours on the 1st day, 6 hours each day on the 2nd and 3rd, and 9.5 hours on the 4th. For how long did he ski on the 5th day?

- **A.** 5.5
- **B.** 6
- **C.** 6.5
- **D.** 7
- **E.** 7.5

66. M and N are distinct elements of Set A, which consists of the natural numbers from 3 to 16, inclusive. If $\dfrac{M}{N} = P$, where P is an integer, how many unique values of P exist?

- **F.** 1
- **G.** 2
- **H.** 3
- **J.** 4
- **K.** 5

67.

14 bwoks = 9 jleps
27 jleps = 35 amooks

According to the conversion rates above, how many bwoks are 100 amooks worth?

- **A.** 85
- **B.** 100
- **C.** 120
- **D.** 140
- **E.** 155

CONTINUE ▶

68. 16 workers will build a house; they can do so in 144 days. If all workers work at the same rate, how many more workers would be needed to build the same house in 96 days?

    F. 8
    G. 16
    H. 24
    J. 32
    K. 48

69. Solve the following equation for x, when y equals 2: $3|x+2| = 5y + 7$

    A. $x = -\dfrac{23}{3}, \dfrac{11}{3}$
    B. $x = -\dfrac{11}{3}, \dfrac{11}{3}$
    C. $x = -\dfrac{23}{3}, \dfrac{23}{3}$
    D. $x = -\dfrac{19}{3}, \dfrac{15}{3}$
    E. $x = -5, 5$

70. The area of an equilateral triangle with side lengths of 10 cm can be expressed in the form $x^2\sqrt{y}$ cm², where x and y are integers. If a circle's radius is xy cm, what is the circle's area?

    F. 25π sq cm
    G. 45π sq cm
    H. 75π sq cm
    J. 105π sq cm
    K. 225π sq cm

71. $-3 + 6 + -9 + 12 + \ldots + 48 + -51 =$

    A. -51
    B. -27
    C. -24
    D. -6
    E. -3

72. At a stationery store, 5 pencils and 5 erasers cost \$5.75, and 7 pencils and 4 erasers cost \$6.76. What is the cost of an eraser?

    F. \$0.39
    G. \$0.40
    H. \$0.41
    J. \$0.42
    K. \$0.43

73. Marlon has an exam tomorrow morning at 10:30 am. It takes him 30 minutes from the time he leaves home to get to his classroom and 45 minutes for him to leave home from the time he wakes up. If he wants to sleep 8.25 hours before his exam, how much time does he have to study, if he begins studying now, at 11 am?

    A. 9 hours
    B. 9 hours and 30 minutes
    C. 13 hours and 50 minutes
    D. 14 hours
    E. 15 hours and 15 minutes

74. $50(3 + 0.4)^2 - 100(1 - 0.7)^2 =$

    F. 46.2
    G. 80
    H. 488
    J. 569
    K. 578

75. a is an integer such that $15 < a < 27$. b is an odd integer $35 < b < 44$. What is the mean of the greatest possible and least possible sums of a and b?

    A. 56
    B. 59
    C. 60
    D. 60.5
    E. 61

CONTINUE ▶

76. To prepare for a race, Phyllis runs laps around a quarter-mile track. Her goal is to run 40 laps at an average pace of 9 minutes per mile. If she starts at 2:45 pm and manages to beat her goal by 7 minutes, at what time did she finish running?

    F. 8:52 pm
    G. 8:45 pm
    H. 8:38 pm
    J. 4:22 pm
    K. 4:08 pm

77. How many integer values of x satisfy the absolute value inequality $|x+17| \leq 33$?

    A. 63
    B. 64
    C. 65
    D. 66
    E. 67

78. Quentin is making a batch of cake batter. He mixes in 4 grams of butter for every 5 grams of flour, and 8 grams of raw eggs for every 3 grams of flour. If he makes 402 grams of cake batter in total, how much of its total mass is comprised of raw eggs and butter?

    F. 284 grams
    G. 312 grams
    H. 344 grams
    J. 362 grams
    K. 387 grams

79. A basketball team captain must select 5 players out of 6 students who tried out. Because all 6 students were equally good, he decides to select the 5 randomly. How many different groups of 5 could he pick?

    A. 6
    B. 12
    C. 18
    D. 24
    E. 30

80.

If point B is placed on the number line above such that the length of segment AB is one-fifth the length of segment BC, what are the possible values for B?

    F. -4.5 and -22.5
    G. -4.5 and -10.5
    H. -3 and -10.5
    J. -1 and 17
    K. 3 and 14.5

81. A group of students is planting tree saplings on Earth Day. The first tree the students plant is 263 centimeters above ground and 11 centimeters below ground. The second tree is 317 centimeters tall, and 246 centimeters of it are above ground. How many more centimeters below ground is the second tree than the first?

    A. 17
    B. 28
    C. 43
    D. 60
    E. 71

82. Clara has a collection of 352 stamps, of which 154 are nature-themed, 110 are sports-themed, and the rest are architecture-themed. If she picks 64 stamps at random, how many more nature-themed stamps than architecture-themed stamps is she likely to pick?

    F. 3
    G. 9
    H. 12
    J. 20
    K. 24

CONTINUE ▶

83.

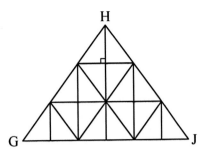

Triangle GHJ above is comprised of 18 smaller, congruent right triangles that are oriented in the same direction, as shown above. If the non-hypotenuse sides of each of these smaller triangles have lengths of 3 centimeters and 4 centimeters, which of the following represents a possible perimeter of triangle GHJ?

A. 36 centimeters
B. 48 centimeters
C. 96 centimeters
D. 108 centimeters
E. 126 centimeters

84.

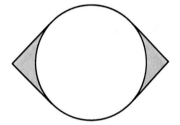

The figure above shows a circle overlaid on two shaded, congruent squares. The center of the circle is also a vertex point for each of the squares, and two of the sides of each square are radii of the circle. If the length of a side of both of the squares is 10 feet, what is the area of the shaded region above, in square feet?

F. $4 - \pi$
G. $10 - 4\pi$
H. $100 - 25\pi$
J. $200 - 50\pi$
K. $400 - 75\pi$

85. A class of 47 students was surveyed to determine how many students played which instruments. It was found that 24 students play cello, 22 play guitar, 17 play violin, 5 play all three instruments, and 5 do not play any instruments at all. How many students play exactly two instruments?

A. 5
B. 6
C. 11
D. 17
E. 22

86. A carnival sold x adult admissions tickets at $12 per ticket and y junior admissions tickets at $9 per ticket, where x and y are positive integers. It sold $5n$ times as many adult tickets as it did junior tickets, where n is also a positive integer. Which of the following could be the revenue generated by ticket sales?

F. $316
G. $930
H. $1,161
J. $1,563
K. $2,130

87. What is the average of the smallest and second smallest of the fractions $\frac{17}{3}$, $\frac{28}{5}$, $\frac{45}{8}$?

A. $\dfrac{169}{15}$

B. $\dfrac{271}{24}$

C. $\dfrac{169}{30}$

D. $\dfrac{449}{40}$

E. $\dfrac{449}{80}$

CONTINUE ▶

88. An empty swimming pool that can hold x gallons of water will be filled by 2 hoses simultaneously. The first hose outputs water at 5 gallons per minute, while the second hose outputs water at 3 gallons per minute. Both hoses are turned on at the same time at 12:20 pm, but there is a series of cracks that collectively drain 2.5 gallons of water per minute. After an hour, the pool is filled to 60% of its maximum capacity. If the first hose is turned off after the hour, how much longer will it take to fill the remainder of the pool?

- **F.** 330 minutes
- **G.** 420 minutes
- **H.** 440 minutes
- **J.** 575 minutes
- **K.** 624 minutes

89.

Value of Goods Transported

Value of Goods Transported by a Vehicle	Number of Vehicles That Transported the Listed Value of Goods
$1,000	55
$2,000	20
$3,000	15
$4,000	10

According to the table above, what is the total value of the goods that were transported?

- **A.** $180,000
- **B.** $144,000
- **C.** $139,500
- **D.** $130,500
- **E.** $126,750

90. $(3x - 5y) - (7 + 8x - y) =$

- **F.** $-5x - (4y - 7)$
- **G.** $-5x - 6y - 7$
- **H.** $-7 - (5x + 2y)$
- **J.** $11x + 6y - 7$
- **K.** $-(5x + (4y + 7))$

91. Stem-and-Leaf Plot of the Height of Tomato Plants, in Inches

```
2 | 5 6 7 8 9 9
3 | 0 0 2 2 2 3 5 6 7
4 | 1 1 1 2 3 3 4 4 5 6 6
5 | 0 2 3 3 4
6 | 1 4
```

According to the plot above, what was the median height of the sampled tomato plants?

- **A.** 35 inches
- **B.** 36 inches
- **C.** 39 inches
- **D.** 40.5 inches
- **E.** 41 inches

92. David receives a coupon to take 25% off a shirt's list price, if he buys the shirt online. At the mall, the same shirt sells for 80% of its list price. David is a store club member, so he receives 5% off the discounted in-store price. How much more does David save by buying the shirt online with the coupon than in-store, in terms of percent of the shirt's list price?

- **F.** 0%
- **G.** 1%
- **H.** 1.75%
- **J.** 2%
- **K.** David would save more buying in-store.

93.

If the pattern of shading was continued in the figure above, which of the following squares would be shaded?

- **A.** 123rd
- **B.** 256th
- **C.** 312th
- **D.** 474th
- **E.** 569th

CONTINUE ▶

94. Trains A and B depart their respective stations, which are 450 miles apart, at the same time and head towards each other along parallel tracks. Train A travels at 60 miles per hour, and train B travels at 90 miles per hour. From the time that the trains initially pass each other, how long does it take train A to reach the train station B?

- **F.** 2 hours
- **G.** 3 hours
- **H.** 3.75 hours
- **J.** 4.5 hours
- **K.** 5 hours

95. Kip has 7 cards. 4 are labeled with one letter each, while 3 are labeled with one number each. No two cards share the same number or letter. If Kip arranges the cards so that the first and last cards cannot be numbered cards and the cards must alternate between lettered and numbered cards, how many ways can he arrange the 7 cards?

- **A.** 12
- **B.** 16
- **C.** 96
- **D.** 144
- **E.** 5040

96. A taxi company is holding a 3-day promotion, from Monday to Wednesday, whereby a passenger can hire a taxi for $2.50 plus $0.05 per mile driven, for any one-way trip. If Ellie lives 40 miles from work, and gas costs her $4.00 per gallon, and her car has a fuel efficiency of 30 miles per gallon, how much would she save by using the taxi service to commute to and from work during the promotional period? Assume she doesn't have any other car-related expenses for the 3-day period, if she drives.

- **F.** $5.00
- **G.** $12.50
- **H.** $12.75
- **J.** $20.00
- **K.** $22.50

97. What is the average of all of the two-digit numbers that are evenly divisible by 8?

- **A.** 52
- **B.** 56
- **C.** 112
- **D.** 312
- **E.** 624

98.

1-Year Investment Returns

Account Type	Amount Invested or Deposited	Returns on Investment
Savings	$2,500	$50.00
Stock	$4,730	$283.80
Mutual Fund	$5,770	$634.70

The table above shows how much Franklin invested into various account types and how much money he made from them in a year. If Franklin had instead invested all of his money into the mutual fund, how much more money would he have made after the same one-year period? Assume the rates of returns on the account types would have stayed the same.

- **F.** $460.00
- **G.** $460.75
- **H.** $461.00
- **J.** $461.50
- **K.** $465.00

99. What is the smallest real number value of x that satisfies the equation $\sqrt{36+x^2}=6.5$?

- **A.** -4
- **B.** -3.5
- **C.** -2.5
- **D.** 0.5
- **E.** 2.5

CONTINUE ▶

100. Hardison drives his 6-wheeled truck 7,700 miles in 20 days. (There are 5,280 feet in a mile.) If each of the 6 wheels of his truck has a radius of 12 inches, approximate the number of revolutions each tire made per day, on average, by using $\frac{22}{7}$ for π.

    F. 53,900
    G. 323,400
    H. 646,800
    J. 1,940,400
    K. 6,468,000

STOP. THIS IS THE END OF THE TEST. IF TIME PERMITS, YOU MAY REVIEW YOUR ANSWERS TO PARTS 1 AND 2 OF THE TEST.

SHSAT
NYC EDITION
TEST 3

PART 1 — VERBAL
Suggested Time — 75 Minutes
45 QUESTIONS

SCRAMBLED PARAGRAPHS
PARAGRAPHS 1-5

DIRECTIONS: The purpose of this section is to organize sentences into the best six-sentence paragraphs possible. For each paragraph, the first sentence is provided, but the remaining five are presented in random or no particular order. Re-order and organize these five sentences, if necessary, to create the **most** logical paragraph. Each paragraph is worth **two** points, whereas every other question type in this test is worth one. Partial credit will not be given.

Blanks have been provided to help you keep track of the position of each sentence in the paragraph. For instance, if you think a sentence follows the first, given sentence, write "2" in the blank next to it; write "3" next to the sentence that you believe follows "2"; and so on. When you believe you have arranged the sentences correctly, transfer your response to your answer sheet.

Paragraph 1

When we think of history, we tend to think of the rise and fall of societies and the various roles wars and religions have played in the development and progression of humankind.

_____ **Q.** But because natural history tends to be more "honest" than human history, as long as we have accurate means of determining the past, we can be reasonably confident in our analyses of Earth's retrospectives.

_____ **R.** We think of writings and artifacts that have survived the tests of time; very rarely do we consider the history beyond that of our own, the history of the natural world around us.

_____ **S.** The trick has been and will always be devising such accurate means, which require ingenuity, astute perceptiveness, and the ability to draw logical conclusions.

_____ **T.** Humanity, though, has repeatedly proven itself up to the task of employing these mental faculties; from the relatively simple dendrochronology to the more complex radiocarbon dating, we have developed highly reliable methods to help us understand the past.

_____ **U.** This natural history, unfortunately, often proves to be difficult to ascertain because direct evidence to support theories of the sequence of events has not always existed, unlike human history, which is rife with evidence, albeit the evidence is often distorted and biased.

CONTINUE ▶

Paragraph 2

The northeastern coast of Australia is home to the picturesque Great Barrier Reef, the world's largest coral reef and one of the seven wonders of the natural world.

_____   **Q.** This massive coral reef system is larger than the Great Wall of China; despite its grandeur in both beauty and size, the Great Barrier Reef is not invulnerable—no reefs are.

_____   **R.** The other major threat to coral reefs is the warming of the oceans, as reefs also depend on heat-sensitive symbionts, i.e., zooplankton and zooxanthellae, for sustenance.

_____   **S.** Carbon dioxide, which accounted for several billion metric tons of these greenhouse gas emissions in the United States alone, is one of the biggest threats to coral reefs, which depend on acid-sensitive calcium carbonate for structure.

_____   **T.** Thus, to prevent the dual threats of ocean acidification and warming from wreaking irreversible havoc global ecological havoc, we must immediately effect changes to our industrial and consumption habits and practices.

_____   **U.** And in the coming years, coral reefs around the world will likely be irreparably damaged from anthropogenic abuse, should humans continue their current industrial and consumer consumption trend of generating massive quantities of greenhouse gases.

Paragraph 3

If your 63-year-old grandmother made the declaration that she would ride in a barrel over Niagara Falls, you'd probably think she was kidding.

_____   **Q.** From 1901 to 1955, 15 people attempted the stunt, with 10 surviving the fall, and on June 15, 2012, Nikolas Wallenda became the first person to walk a tightrope across the falls.

_____   **R.** Taylor was not the first person to go over Niagara Falls—that distinction belongs to Sam Patch, who, famously known as the Yankee Leaper, jumped over the edge in 1829 and survived—but she was the first to do so in a barrel and survive.

_____   **S.** But on October 24, 1901, one woman, 63-year-old schoolteacher Annie Edson Taylor, decided she would try her hand at obtaining instant fame, which she hoped would help to improve her financial situation, as the first person to go over Niagara Falls in a barrel.

_____   **T.** Having survived the fall, Taylor unfortunately did not achieve the level of fame she had sought, although she did become a minor celebrity, but her legacy as a daredevil lived on.

_____   **U.** You might even think she was losing her mind and possibly going senile; not many people in their right minds would attempt to accomplish such a daunting feat, especially not people in their 60s.

CONTINUE ▶

1

Paragraph 4

The product of a joint venture between the British and French governments, the Concorde jet began its commercial service in January 1976 and continued its operation for 27 years.

_____ **Q.** For one, people who lived under the flight paths of the jets complained of the extreme noise they produced as they flew.

_____ **R.** Another problem was that the jet was not fuel efficient, given the extreme power it needed to fly as fast it did; as such, the craft had to be smaller in size and could not hold enough passengers to be cost effective for the airlines that operated these jets.

_____ **S.** Operated by British Airways and Air France, this engineering marvel served as a symbol of luxury and speed, capable of flying from New York City to London in 3.5 hours while traveling at 1,350 miles per hour, or roughly double the speed of sound.

_____ **T.** While the idea of reducing travel time by half—typical commercial jets fly the same route in a tad over 7 hours—was amazing, the Concorde jet was not free from criticisms.

_____ **U.** And after an Air France jet crashed after takeoff on July 25, 2000, killing 113 people in the process, all Concorde jets were grounded for a year; three years and some months after the accident, rising operational costs and lower ticket sales forced the jet into retirement.

Paragraph 5

The first self-propelled, heavier-than-air aircraft took flight on December 17, 1903, when Wilbur and Orville Wright's gasoline-powered biplane covered 120 feet in 12 seconds.

_____ **Q.** It had been widely theorized before this historic attempt that supersonic flight was not possible because transonic wave drag rise—simply speaking, the amount of resistance experienced by aircraft traveling near the speed of sound—would eviscerate the aircraft.

_____ **R.** This remarkable milestone in aviation technology history was achieved by Air Force Captain Chuck Yeager, who was a test pilot in the experimental *X-1* rocket plane, which was built by Bell Aircraft company to see whether supersonic flight was possible.

_____ **S.** On October 14, 1947, Yeager proved these theorists wrong; he flew the *X-1* over Rogers Dry Lake and exceeded the 662 miles per hour needed to go supersonic.

_____ **T.** Since that historic first flight, inventors, engineers, and aviators have worked to continually fly aircraft faster, more efficiently, and for longer periods of time.

_____ **U.** Fast forward to over a century later, and it is now common to fly at tremendous speeds—the unmanned Falcon HTV-2 drone, for example, reached a top speed of 13,000 miles per hour before losing control and crashing into the Pacific Ocean on August 11, 2011—but it took almost 44 years for man to fly faster than the speed of sound.

CONTINUE ▶

71

LOGICAL REASONING
QUESTIONS 11-20

DIRECTIONS: For each question, read the information provided and select the **best** answer choice, based **only on the information given.** In other words, even if you know more about a particular set of facts than is provided, do not use your knowledge of the facts to aid your decision-making process.

When dealing with logical reasoning questions, be on alert for certain placement or position and order words and phrases, such as **to the right of, above, before,** and **next to.** "The puppy is **between** the kitten and duckling," for instance, is not necessarily the same as "The puppy is **between and next to** the kitten and duckling"; one or more other objects may separate the puppy from the kitten or from the duckling.

11. If my car is broken, I will ride the bus. If I am limping, I will ride the bus.

Based only on the information above, which of the following **must** be true?

A. If I am limping, my car is broken.
B. If I am limping, I cannot drive, and that is why I will ride the bus.
C. If I ride the bus, my car is broken.
D. If I do not ride the bus, my car is not broken and I am not limping.
E. If my car is broken, I am limping.

12. Larry prepares his meals for the week ahead. He will eat at least one meal, but not more than three meals, per day. He doesn't eat the same meal more than once per day.

Larry will eat beef five times, fish four times, salad five times, and pasta once. What is the least number of days he can eat three meals?

F. 0
G. 1
H. 2
J. 3
K. 4

13. School X is the only place game Z is played. No student at school X hears of game Z before entering the school. Joshua has just heard of game Z.

Which of the following is a valid conclusion from the statements above?

A. Joshua is a first year at school X.
B. Joshua heard of game Z from his school X friends.
C. Joshua is a student at school X.
D. Game Z has spread to other schools.
E. None of the above.

14. Four boys traveling together come to a river, which they must cross. Luckily, they find a rowboat that can hold two of them at a time. If the boat always needs to have at least one person in it to cross the river, how many times must the boat cross the river to transport all four boys across?

F. 3
G. 4
H. 5
J. 6
K. 7

CONTINUE ▶

15. Everyone in Huntsville knows how to shoot rifles. Some Huntsville residents can score a bull's-eye every time they shoot. Everyone who hits a bull's-eye with every shot is also good at bowling. Trey knows how to shoot rifles and is good at bowling.

Based only on the information above, which of the following **must** be true?

A. Trey can score a bull's-eye every time he shoots.
B. Some people in Huntsville are good at bowling.
C. Trey lives in Huntsville.
D. If Trey doesn't live in Huntsville, then he can hit a bull's-eye with every shot.
E. Most people in Huntsville can score a bull's-eye with every shot.

16. Daisy, Edgar, Fannie, Greta, and Hobart each made a sketch, and each sketch had a different theme. They submitted their work to be sold at an auction. Each sketch was presented and sold one at a time.

1) The nature sketch was sold second.
2) Hobart's culture sketch was sold before Fannie's architecture sketch.
3) Daisy's sketch was sold immediately after Greta's.
4) The space sketch was sold before the architecture sketch.
5) The inventions sketch was sold last.

Based only on the information above, which of the following **cannot** be true?

F. Greta's sketch was sold third.
G. The culture sketch was sold third.
H. The nature sketch was sold before the culture sketch.
J. Greta created the space sketch.
K. Edgar created the inventions sketch.

17. Five students, Jamie, Kris, May, Nick, and Omar, stood in line to get tickets.

1) Jamie was second in line.
2) Kris was immediately before Omar in line.

Based only on the information above, which of the following **must** be true?

A. May was either third or fourth in line.
B. If Omar was fourth, then Nick was last.
C. Kris was either first, third, or fourth.
D. If May was third, then Oscar was last.
E. Nick was either first or last in line.

18. Baxter, Janice, Luke, Margo, and Sally wanted to see who could hold their breath the longest. The person who held his or her breath the longest won.

1) Margo held her breath longer than Luke did.
2) Janice held her breath the third longest.
3) Baxter lost his breath immediately before Sally did.

If Luke was not in last place, then who was?

F. Janice
G. Sally
H. Baxter
J. Margo
K. Cannot be determined from the information given.

CONTINUE ▶

73

Questions 19 and 20 refer to the following information.

In the code below, (1) each letter always represents the same word, (2) each word is represented by only one letter, and (3) in any given sentence, the letters may or may not be presented in the same order as the words.

H	M	L	P	T	means
"Chuck	talked	with	the	manager."	

N	H	T	K	X	means
"Abby	spoke	with	the	waiter."	

T	F	Q	L	H	means
"Dirk	talked	with	the	server."	

H	K	P	Z	B	means
"Abby	yelled	at	the	manager."	

19.   Which letter represents the word "talked"?

A. L
B. T
C. H
D. P
E. Cannot be determined from the information given.

20.   Which word is represented by the letter Q?

F. server
G. with
H. the
J. Dirk
K. Cannot be determined from the information given.

READING
QUESTIONS 21-50

DIRECTIONS: Each passage below has five questions associated with it. After reading a passage, answer the questions, based **only on the information provided** by the passage; even if you have a deeper knowledge of the contents of the passage, do not base your answers on any outside knowledge.

Nitrogen, like oxygen, is a double-edged sword. Without enough of it, life cannot be sustained. Too much nitrogen, on the other hand, can lead to a wide range of ecological and human health 5 complications. The solution seems simple: make sure just the necessary amount of nitrogen is being used and applied. Reality is far from that simple, though.

Nitrogen is the most abundant element in our at-10 mosphere, comprising 78.09% of the atmosphere. (By comparison, oxygen, which is also essential to life, comprises only 20.95%.) Quite the opposite is true of the relative availability of soil-based nitrogen, which is an essential macro-15 nutrient for the sustenance of plant life—the other two macronutrients essential to vegetative growth are potassium and phosphorous. If scientists had not been able to synthesize fertilizer by converting atmospheric nitrogen (N_2) into the 20 ionic compound ammonium nitrate (NH_4NO_3) through the process of nitrification—both ammonium (NH_4^+), which is a positively charged cation, and nitrate (NO_3^-), which is a negatively charged anion, contain nitrogen—our planet 25 would currently not be able to support our current population of nearly 7 billion. So far, so good; we can see just how important nitrogen is. Unfortunately, this is where the problem begins, too.

30 Ordinarily, when farmers and other agriculturalists apply fertilizer, soil microbes convert the ammonium found in the fertilizer to more nitrate, which is water-soluble and provides nourishment for plants. When an excess of fertilizer 35 is applied, however—and this is often the case, as crops, on average, use less than half the nitrogen found in fertilizers—the unused nitrate ions leach into groundwater, lakes, and streams. This process consequently can lead to the asphyxia-40 tion of the aquatic life in the affected bodies of water. Moreover, the excess nitrate run-off has led to the contamination of drinking water and consequently the increased prevalence of health complications, especially in infants under 6 45 months of age that drink water that contains nitrate in excess of the federally regulated levels.

The maximum contaminant level (MCL), as established by the United States Environmental Protection Agency under the Safe Drinking Wa-50 ter Act to control the maximum amount of contaminants that can be found in public water systems, for nitrate is 10 milligrams per liter (mg/L). If infants consume water containing nitrate in excess of the 10 mg/L MCL, they could 55 develop a potentially fatal blood disorder called methemoglobinemia or "blue-baby" syndrome. This disorder arises because nitrate interferes with the ability of red blood cells to carry oxygen. In mild to moderate cases, the infant may 60 experience diarrhea, vomiting, and lethargy. And in more serious cases, the infant will show symptoms of cyanosis, which is how the expression "blue-baby syndrome" arose; the infant will experience a shortness of breath, and his skin, 65 lips, or nail beds may turn a grayish or bluish hue.

Because the balance of nitrogen, along with its amino and nitric derivatives, in our ecosystem is a delicate one, we must be judicious in our use 70 of synthetic nitrogen-based products.

CONTINUE ▶

21. What is the main idea of this passage?

  A. Nitrogen is more harmful than it is helpful.
  B. Nitrogen is an incredibly important element.
  C. Excess exposure to nitrogen leads to illnesses in infants.
  D. Nitrogen is at once vital to our survival and detrimental to our ecosystem with excessive use.
  E. There is more nitrogen in our atmosphere than there is oxygen, which indicates just how much of an influence it has in our society.

22. What does the passage imply about the process of nitrification?

  A. Since ammonium is a positively charged ion and nitrate is a negatively charged ion, they can be used together as a magnet.
  B. Ammonium nitrate is an essential component of fertilizer.
  C. Because ammonium contains more atoms than nitrate does, ammonium has a greater magnitude of charge.
  D. Potassium and phosphorous, two other elements essential to fertilizer, are found in abundance in the soil.
  E. Nitrogen is more important to our survival than oxygen is because there is almost four times as much nitrogen in the atmosphere as there is oxygen.

23. What role do soil microbes play in the application of fertilizer to soil?

  A. They convert ammonium to nitrate.
  B. They help regulate the amount of nitrate ions that leach into groundwater.
  C. They allow plants to take in more ammonium more efficiently.
  D. They assist in releasing nitrogen trapped in the soil back into the atmosphere.
  E. They play no part in the application of fertilizer to soil.

24. Which is NOT listed in the passage as a symptom of methemoglobinemia?

  F. diarrhea
  G. vomiting
  H. high fever
  J. cyanosis
  K. lethargy

25. What was the purpose of the Safe Drinking Water Act?

  A. to prevent public water systems from being excessively contaminated
  B. to make sure all water found in the United States was safe for drinking
  C. to ensure that drinking water in the United States had contaminant concentrations of no greater than 10 mg/L, per contaminant
  D. to experiment on people to find out what level of contamination was considered safe for drinking and what level was not
  E. to protect infants from the possibility of drinking contaminated water

26. Which of the following statements is most strongly supported by the passage?

  F. If the concentration of nitrate in the water that an infant drinks is greater than 10 mg/L, the infants will develop "blue-baby syndrome," which is fatal.
  G. The nitrate run-off that leaches into groundwater does not harm the aquatic ecosystems it affects.
  H. The amount of nitrogen found in soil is about the same as the amount of nitrogen found in the atmosphere.
  J. If farmers applied less fertilizer, we'd have zero nitrate run-off and still have the same bounty of crops that we enjoy.
  K. Nitrogen is essential to our survival because it is essential to the survival of plant life, which we depend on.

CONTINUE ▶

Caffeine, a xanthine alkaloid, is an important part of many people's daily routines. In fact, so many people consume caffeine that the annual global consumption of caffeine itself, not the to-
5 tal number of fluid ounces of caffeinated beverages, exceeds 120,000 metric tons, or 120 million kilograms. And since a cup of coffee usually contains between 95 to 200 milligrams of caffeine, 120,000 tons of caffeine is the caffeine
10 equivalent of between 600 billion and 1.26 trillion cups of coffee is consumed globally per year. For many people, however, caffeine helps them stay alert and focused by fighting off drowsiness. That explains why people drink caf-
15 feinated beverages, but why would the plants from whose leaves caffeine is extracted need this stimulant?

Even though caffeine doesn't wake plants up, it does give a jolt—to the insects and bugs that try
20 to eat the leaves of those plants, that is, so to speak. So while caffeine defends us humans from falling asleep on the job and risking unemployment, it defends its host plants from predators by acting as a natural pesticide that para-
25 lyzes and kills many insects that feed on the plants. And it's not just the adult insects that caffeine impacts. Studies involving powdered tea and coffee, as well as pure caffeine and related compounds, have found that caffeine disturbs
30 the behavior and development of numerous insects and their larvae.

In tobacco hornworms, mealworms, milkweed bugs, and butterfly and mosquito larvae, caffeine was found to distort the insects' behavior, de-
35 press food consumption, and, in some cases, inhibit reproduction. A test conducted with mosquito larvae showed that caffeine could cause them to become so uncoordinated that they would drown because they could not swim to the
40 surface of the water for air. Furthermore, in sufficiently high doses, caffeine makes for a killer drug, literally, as it has been shown to kill exposed insects within hours or days. (The same is true of caffeine's lethality towards humans, too.
45 The only difference is that much larger doses are needed to kill humans—more than 10 grams, or approximately 170 milligrams of caffeine per kilogram of bodyweight, is generally fatal—

which is understandable, given the size discrep-
50 ancy between humans and insects.) And when caffeine is coupled with other naturally occurring insecticides, the combined potency is far greater than the sum of the combinations' parts.

The discovery of caffeine's potency against in-
55 sects raised many interesting questions, chief among them being, "Can we use caffeine to replace our pesticides and insecticides?" Unfortunately, more time may be needed before caffeine can, if ever, be used as an alternative to more
60 commonly used pesticides that have been proven to be harmful to human health. For while caffeine is relatively harmless to humans, it is lethal enough to the rest of our ecosystem that it could decimate populations of vegetation-friendly
65 earthworms and other animals needed for the upkeep of healthy soil. And yet another problem is the possibility that excess caffeine may seep into groundwater and be carried off, potentially harming marine life as well.

27. What is the main idea of the passage?

    A. Caffeine is an extremely important commodity in global commerce.
    B. Caffeine not only wakes people up but also harms more diminutive life forms.
    C. Caffeine will most likely eventually replace other pesticides and insecticides.
    D. Caffeine is about as potent, if not more so, as artificial pesticides are.
    E. Productivity would decrease significantly without caffeine.

28. Which of the following is NOT listed by the passage as a way caffeine can affect living organisms?

    F. death
    G. paralysis
    H. seizures
    J. interference with reproduction
    K. depression of food consumption

CONTINUE ▶

29. How does caffeine help its host plants?

    A. It prevents pests from coming near the plants, meaning that the plants are safe from being eaten.

    B. It provides plants with a bitter taste that repels insects and other pests.

    C. It causes plants to produce a more potent toxin that kills or paralyzes pests.

    D. It protects the plants by acting as a natural pesticide or insecticide.

    E. It allows plants to regenerate the eaten portions of their leaves faster because caffeine is a stimulant and thus stimulates and accelerates healing in plants.

30. Which of the following assumptions is made by the passage in lines 40-50?

    F. Caffeine is never lethal to humans because it is impossible for humans to drink enough cups of coffee or tea in a short enough period of time to consume the caffeine required to be lethal.

    G. It is safe for people over 60 kilograms to consume more than 10 grams of caffeine.

    H. An organism's body mass plays a significant role in determining how lethal caffeine is to the organism.

    J. Age plays an important role in the lethality of caffeine in humans; older people are generally less likely to be affected by caffeine's potency in high doses.

    K. Caffeine as a global commodity generates more revenue than any other.

31. The passage expresses which of the following concerns about caffeine's use as a pesticide?

    A. Manufacturers of artificial pesticides would be driven out of business, and that would result in a depressed economy.

    B. Caffeine will be too efficient at killing the pests farmers and growers do not want amongst their crops.

    C. The use of caffeine as a pesticide may harm crops more than it helps them, as well as cause other ecological damage.

    D. If caffeine seeps into our groundwater, not only might it harm marine life, but it could end up in our drinking water, too, and that could lead to widespread cases of inadvertent caffeine addiction.

    E. The passage expresses no such concerns because caffeine is completely fine to use as a pesticide, since it takes a very large dose to be lethal to humans.

32. Lines 32-40 imply which of the following?

    F. Mosquitos are hatched on the surface of a body of water.

    G. Mosquito larvae alternate between living underwater and living on land.

    H. Mosquito larvae's gills allow the larvae to breathe perfectly underwater.

    J. Mosquitos alternate between living underwater and on land throughout their lives.

    K. Mosquito larvae cannot breathe indefinitely underwater.

CONTINUE ▶

The word *empire* conjures up images of vast stretches of land that extend beyond the limits of human vision, rulers donned in silken robes with servants and slaves at their beck and call, and

5   powerful, armor-clad warriors marching to either conquer more territory or do battle against an invasive threat. But empires were more than just about glamor and power; they were also about the advancements mankind made as the

10 empires expanded, stabilized, and flourished. They represent hallmarks of human achievement in artistry, technological and intellectual innovation, and law and order. Many of the earliest empires began alongside or near rivers that allowed

15 for the assured sustenance of the peoples—cases in point, Rome rose to prominence near the Tiber River in Italy, Egypt had the Nile, and China had the Yellow and Yangtze. It is no surprise, then, that the earliest recorded empire was also

20 along a river—or two, for the Akkadian Empire.

Founded by King Sargon around 2330 B.C., in Mesopotamia, which is the region of fertile land between the Tigris and Euphrates Rivers—or what is now present-day Iraq, Syria, and por-

25 tions of several other countries—the capital of the Akkadian Empire, Akkad, lay just north of the region of Sumer, which the Sumerians had already developed into a civilization a thousand years before Sargon's time, showcasing city-

30 states in which ziggurats, or monolithic mud-brick temples, commanded great attention, irrigation techniques that made formerly parched lands arable, and a writing system comprised of wedge-shaped characters called cuneiform.

35 There was much the Akkadians could learn from the Sumerians, so that's what they did; they intermingled with the Sumerians, learning from them and eventually outdoing them.

Conflict has always been a part of human his-

40 tory, and the Akkadians and Sumerians were no stranger to treachery and war. Before Sargon took power by deposing the king of Kish, which was an Akkadian city, he was the king's trusted cupbearer. Once he overthrew the king, Sargon

45 led troops against Lugalzagesi, the great Sumerian leader who had brought all of Sumer under his command. Unfortunately for Lugalzagesi, however, the lingering animosity between the

city-states of Sumer did not aid him in his de-

50 fense against Sargon. Having captured Lugalzagesi and thus the Sumerian city-states, Sargon sent Akkadian governors to those city-states to impose his laws and orders, among the first of which was to tear down the walls around the cit-

55 ies to allow for a greater unification of his realm.

Furthermore, by razing these barriers, Sargon was better able to promote intra-Mesopotamian commerce as well as commerce between Mesopotamia and more distant lands. Consequently,

60 mercantilism thrived through maritime trade, as merchants traded pearls, ivory, and other luxury items for olive oil and wood. As the concept of coinage and currency had not yet been formally developed and implemented, merchants used

65 copper, silver, and other precious metals as a rudimentary form of currency. The merchants' increasing prosperity also increased Sargon's, through his collection of taxes, which he used to fund his military might and support royal artists

70 and scribes, who glorified him in their sculptures and inscriptions. Sargon ruled for over 50 years and founded a dynasty that lasted through the reign of his grandson.

33. What was the author's main purpose for writing this passage?

    A. to show how Sargon overthrew the king of Kish

    B. to provide an overview of how the earliest empire came to be

    C. to illustrate the precedent that Sargon set for all subsequent emperors in history

    D. to explain how Sargon unified the city-states of Sumer and incorporated them into the Akkadian Empire

    E. to hypothesize that Akkad only succeeded because the Sumerians did not come to Lugalzagesi's aid

CONTINUE ▶

34. Which of the following statements best captures the entire significance of empires, as discussed in the passage?

    F. Empires served to showcase all manners of human achievement in their time.
    G. Empires served as the basis for modern systems and methods of governance, such as democracy.
    H. Empires served as hubs for commerce and trade and so flourished as a result.
    J. Empires were significant because they represented the luxury and power that the citizens of empires enjoyed.
    K. Empires were significant because their ziggurats unified multitudes of people under the banner of a single religion.

35. Which of the following is NOT mentioned in the passage as being true of Sumer?

    A. Sumer's monolithic mud-brick temples commanded great attention.
    B. Irrigation techniques helped Sumer's city-states to flourish.
    C. Sumer was at one point more advanced than Akkad was in at least some ways.
    D. Sumer used cuneiform, a writing system comprised of wedge-shaped characters.
    E. Akkadians planned to learn as much from the Sumerians as possible so they could one day outdo their southern counterparts.

36. Which of the following statements can be inferred from the passage?

    F. The system of laws in the civilization of Sumer was far more advanced than that of the region of Akkad, at least initially.
    G. All of the earliest empires were founded along rivers.
    H. Sargon wouldn't have become emperor if the king of Kish hadn't trusted him.
    J. Lugalzagesi forced at least some Sumerian city-states under his command.
    K. Cuneiform was the most advanced writing system of its time.

37. What was the significance of Sargon razing the city walls of former Sumerian city-states?

    A. By doing so, Sargon was able to prevent his Akkadian governors from plotting covertly against him in an effort to overthrow him, since they were still disgruntled by being forced under his command.
    B. By doing so, Sargon was ultimately able to collect more tax revenue, which in turn allowed him to increase his power as an emperor in various ways.
    C. By doing so, Sargon was able to eliminate costly wall maintenance fees and thus increase the amount of money he saved; in turn, he used this money to increase his power as an emperor in various ways.
    D. By doing so, Sargon promoted greater happiness amongst the people of his empire, as they were allowed to move more freely between cities.
    E. By doing so, Sargon made it easier for individual city-states to deploy reserve military forces more quickly to Sargon's side whenever his main armies needed reinforcements.

38. Which of the following was NOT specifically listed in the passage as a commonly traded commodity in the Akkadian Empire, under Sargon's rule?

    F. gold
    G. ivory
    H. pearls
    J. wood
    K. olive oil

CONTINUE ▶

80

Theft crimes come in all forms and magnitudes, from misdemeanor larcenies of a few dollars' worth of another's personal belongings to felonies involving armed robberies of banks. Many
5 steal out of perceived necessity; others steal for sport, to see if it could be done and how much profit could be made; former-surfing-champion-turned-jewel-thief Jack Roland Murphy comes to mind with his 1964 theft of the Star of India, a
10 563-carat blue star sapphire, the 116.75-carat Midnight Star Sapphire, and the 100.32-carat Delong Star Ruby, among other gems, from the American Museum of Natural History in New York City. Among the worst thieves, however,
15 are entire governments that themselves perpetrate thefts and thus threaten to erase a valuable part of human history—Nazi Germany was one of the most egregious.

After World War I officially ended on Novem-
20 ber 11, 1918, the German economy, which was already in shambles from the debt brought on by the expenditures of World War I, further plummeted into a seemingly inescapable abyss when Germany was forced to pay substantial repara-
25 tions to France and Great Britain as a result of the Treaty of Versailles, which was signed on June 28, 1919, and it did not help that the tariffs placed on German exports by foreign powers crippled Germany's ability to make the repara-
30 tion payments. Unwittingly and rather ironically, the countries that were trying to punish Germany were instead fueling the flames of the next war—by placing the tariffs on German goods, they depressed Germany's economy even further
35 and opened up the ripe opportunity for Adolf Hitler to rise to power; in spite of, and in significant portion because of, Germany's poor economic situation, Adolf Hitler was able to manipulate Germany into uniting under his lead and
40 becoming his war machine for the launch of World War II.

While Hitler marginalized the significance of establishing a sound economic policy that would permit Nazi Germany to thrive, claiming that
45 "the economy is something of secondary importance," even he realized that money was necessary for him to build up and continue building up a devastating military presence. He was also

intelligent enough to realize that Germany's cur-
50 rent state of economic affairs would prevent him from actualizing his militaristic ambitions. His solution to Germany's financial troubles, since Germany was not in a position to help itself out of its dire economic straits, was simple: as the
55 Nazi forces conquered their neighbor countries, they would also loot the gold, jewelry, art, and other riches from the conquered. And although the Germans did not win the war, their piratical modus operandi was, by many metrics, ex-
60 tremely successful, with estimates of their war-time loot and plunder exceeding $400 million in gold from occupied countries and another $140 million from individuals. It has also been projected that the Nazi forces illicitly took as much
65 as 20 percent of the Western fine artworks.

To this day, much of what the Nazis stole is still at large. Some of the stolen gold has been recovered—we have General George Patton to thank for that—but over 100,000 paintings and other
70 pieces, such as china, crystal, and silverware, have still to be returned to their rightful owners.

39. What is the main idea of the passage?

    A. Theft crimes come in all forms and magnitude, from misdemeanors to felonies.

    B. Nazi Germany was one of the most egregious theft crime perpetrators in history.

    C. Many pieces of art, jewelry, and china stolen by Nazi Germany are still at large.

    D. Thieves steal for various reasons, some out of necessity, while others for sport.

    E. Germany's dismal economic conditions compelled Hitler to trigger the second World War.

CONTINUE ▶

40. How did the Treaty of Versailles cause Germany's already poor economy to become even worse?

  F. The Treaty of Versailles required Germany, whose economy had already taken a significant hit because of war expenditures, to pay significant reparations.
  G. The Treaty of Versailles not only required Germany, whose economy had already taken a significant hit because of war expenditures, to both pay significant reparations but also imposed significant export tariffs on German goods.
  H. The Treaty of Versailles caused Germany to go bankrupt.
  J. The Treaty of Versailles forced Germany to pay more reparations to Britain and France than to any other country.
  K. The Treaty of Versailles pushed Germany down into an inescapable economic abyss.

41. Which of the following statements would the author most likely agree with?

  A. Jack Roland Murphy stole the largest gems ever crafted by mankind from the American Museum of Natural History.
  B. If Germany had maintained much of its wealth after signing the Treaty of Versailles, which ended World War I, Hitler would not have been able to rise to power.
  C. Germany would have been able to make its reparations without much difficulty if foreign nations had not imposed export tariffs on German goods.
  D. Eventually, all of the valuables that had been stolen by Nazi Germany will be returned to their rightful owners.
  E. Nazi Germany's looting of other countries was especially problematic because it resulted in the loss of a valuable part of human history.

42. Why was it ironic that countries imposed tariffs on German exports?

  F. The countries that imposed the tariffs on German exports were in actuality limiting their own potential revenues.
  G. The countries that tried to punish Germany were probably expecting Germany to feel even more humbled and broken.
  H. The countries that imposed the tariffs were trying to collect more money from Germany to help themselves recover economically, as World War I left many countries economically unstable.
  J. The countries that tried to punish Germany for its actions in World War I were in actuality providing Germany with a reason to go to war again.
  K. The countries that tried to punish Germany felt no sympathy for Germany.

43. About how much total gold did the Nazis loot and plunder during World War II?

  A. $140 million
  B. $280 million
  C. $400 million
  D. $420 million
  E. Over $500 million

44. Which of the following can be inferred from the passage?

  F. The 20% of the Western fine art the Nazis stole equates to exactly 100,000 pieces of art.
  G. Even Hitler didn't believe that economy was insignificant.
  H. General George Patton recovered almost all of the gold that the Nazis had stolen.
  J. Jack Murphy would have stolen larger gems if such gems had been available.
  K. Germany's piracy didn't provide it with the funds needed to win the war.

CONTINUE ▶

The Bill of Rights, which was adopted on December 15, 1791, is comprised of the first ten amendments to the Constitution. The first and foremost of these amendments protects the fol-
5 lowing rights and freedoms of United States citizens: freedom of religion, freedom of speech, freedom of the press, the right to assemble peaceably, and the right to petition the government for a redress of grievances. The boundaries
10 of these rights and freedoms become obfuscated, however, when the safety, well-being, or freedoms of other people or parties must be evaluated. For better or worse—for the better in the vast majority of cases—the Supreme Court issues
15 decisions to help delineate these boundaries, and the landmark case of *Tinker v. Des Moines Independent Community School District*, 393 U.S. 503, is one of them.

John Tinker, his younger sister Mary Beth, and
20 Christopher Eckhardt, three public school students in Des Moines, Iowa, were suspended for wearing black armbands to school in protest of the Vietnam War. In December of 1965, a group of adults and students alike met at the Eckhardt
25 home to come up with a way to express their discontent with the government's involvement in Vietnam. Their plan involved wearing black armbands during the holiday season and fasting on December 16 and on New Year's Eve. The
30 principals of the Des Moines schools were alerted to this plan and, on December 14, agreed to ask any student wearing such an armband to remove it, lest the student be suspended from school until they would come back without
35 wearing his or her armband. The students were aware of their principals' policy, but that didn't deter them from wearing the armbands to school. On December 16, Mary Beth and Christopher wore their armbands to school, while
40 John wore his to school the next day. All three were suspended, and none of them returned to school until after New Year's Day, when the planned duration for wearing armbands was over.

45 After being approached by the Iowa Civil Liberties Union and securing the legal support of the American Civil Liberties Union, the children's fathers filed a complaint in the United States District Court, seeking nominal damages and an
50 injunction against the principals' adopted regulation regarding armbands. After losing in District Court, which dismissed the complaint and held that the regulation of the armbands was within the school board's power on the ground that the
55 regulation was reasonable in order to prevent disturbance of school discipline, the plaintiffs appealed the decision to the U.S. Circuit Court and lost there, too, leaving them with no other option but to appeal to the Supreme Court if they
60 wanted any chance of vindication.

The Supreme Court of the United States was much more favorable to the plaintiffs' cause, overturning the lower courts' decisions seven to two—there are nine Supreme Court justices—
65 and held that 1) the children were not being disruptive in their wearing of armbands to publicize their opinions, and 2) First Amendment rights cannot be denied in schools when there is no evidence to establish that the rights were denied in
70 order to prohibit the interference with school discipline or the rights of others.

45. What was the author's purpose for writing this passage?

   A. to illustrate how much authority the Supreme Court of the United States has
   B. to show how easily it is for rights and freedoms to be obfuscated
   C. to argue that it is unfair for schools to prohibit peaceful methods of war protest
   D. to promote absolute freedom of speech, no matter what the situation may be
   E. to discuss a case that went before the Supreme Court and how it was resolved

CONTINUE ▶

46. According to the passage, why did John and Mary Beth Tinker and Christopher Eckhardt wear black armbands to school?

   F. to introduce a new fashion concept
   G. to protest the limitations certain schools were placing on students' right to freedom of speech
   H. to indicate to others that they were observing a religious holiday by fasting
   J. to peacefully express their anti-war sentiments
   K. to promote support for the Vietnam War

47. Which of the following questions remains unanswered by the passage?

   A. Who helped the children's fathers file their complaint against the principals of the Des Moines schools that banned the black armbands?
   B. Which amendment protects the freedom of speech?
   C. How long did it take for the children's fathers' suit to get to the Supreme Court?
   D. How many justices serve on the Supreme Court?
   E. When was the Bill of Rights adopted?

48. From the information presented in the passage, what happened immediately after the decision laid down by the United States District Court?

   F. The case was appealed to the Supreme Court of the United States.
   G. The case was appealed to the U.S. Circuit Court.
   H. The case was dropped altogether.
   J. The case was appealed to the Iowa state supreme court.
   K. The case was appealed to the Iowa circuit court.

49. What was outcome of the children's fathers' lawsuit in the United States District Court?

   A. The District Court ruled in favor of the principals, holding that the schools could not ban armbands to prevent the disturbance of school discipline.
   B. The District Court ruled in favor of the fathers, holding that the schools could not ban the armbands in order to prevent the disturbance of school discipline.
   C. The District Court ruled in favor of the principals, holding that the schools could ban the armbands to prevent the disturbance of school discipline.
   D. The District Court ruled in favor of the fathers, holding that schools may limit students' freedom of speech when such limitations are necessary.
   E. The District Court ruled in favor of the principals, holding that schools may absolutely limit students' freedom of speech.

50. Which of the following statements would the author agree best represents the Supreme Court's ruling on the case?

   F. Schools cannot reasonably enforce dress codes because dress codes limit the students' ability to express themselves, since mere clothes don't disrupt discipline.
   G. Schools can limit any Amendment rights as long as the limitations are justified.
   H. Students do not have any privacy rights in schools because the safety of other students always takes first priority.
   J. Schools cannot limit First Amendment rights without evidence that the exercise of the rights will lead to a disruption in school discipline.
   K. Students are allowed to communicate however they want in school, so long as they do not resort to physical acts that would disrupt the discipline in schools.

CONTINUE ▶

PART 2 — MATHEMATICS

Suggested Time — 75 Minutes
QUESTIONS 51-100

GENERAL INSTRUCTIONS

Answer or solve each question or problem. Once you have arrived at the correct answer or come up with a satisfactory answer choice, mark your answer sheet accordingly. **DO NOT MARK ON YOUR ANSWER SHEET OTHER THAN TO FILL IN YOUR ANSWER CHOICES.**

IMPORTANT NOTES:
(1) Formulas and definitions of terms and symbols are **not** provided.
(2) Diagrams may not have been drawn to scale. Do not make any assumptions about any relationship in a diagram unless it can be figured out or derived from the given information.
(3) Assume that all diagrams are drawn in one plane, unless the problem specifies otherwise.
(4) Graphs have been drawn to scale. Unless the problem states otherwise, you can assume relationships based on how they appear. For instance, if lines look perpendicular on a graph, you may assume they are perpendicular; the same goes for concurrent lines, straight lines, collinear points, right angles, etc.
(5) Reduce all fractions to simplest terms.

---

51. What is the difference between the greatest common factor and the least common multiple of 10 and 15?

    A. 15
    B. 25
    C. 55
    D. 85
    E. 145

---

52. If $6y - 3 = 2x + 5$, what is the value of $3x + 4$ in terms of y?

    F. $9y - 4$
    G. $9y - 8$
    H. $9y - 16$
    J. $6y - 4$
    K. $6y + 9$

---

53. $8y(3z - 7zu) =$

    A. $-32yz$
    B. $11yz - 15yzu$
    C. $24yz - 56yzu$
    D. $-32yu$
    E. $11yz + yzu$

---

54. S is 15% of T, and T is 150% of 800. What is the value of S?

    F. 12
    G. 132
    H. 225
    J. 180
    K. 1320

CONTINUE ▶

55. To qualify for a race, each runner must run five trial laps and post a mean lap time of 1 minute, 8 seconds. Kyle ran four laps in 64, 72, 74, and 66 seconds. What is the slowest time he can run the last lap and still qualify?

    A. 59 seconds
    B. 1 minute
    C. 1 minute, 4 seconds
    D. 1 minute, 7 seconds
    E. 1 minute, 11 seconds

---

56. $\dfrac{7}{35} \times \dfrac{5}{24} \div \dfrac{3}{7} =$

    F. $\dfrac{1}{56}$

    G. $\dfrac{8}{7}$

    H. $\dfrac{7}{8}$

    J. $\dfrac{5}{8}$

    K. $\dfrac{7}{72}$

---

57. Hernando is now 13 years old. 8 years ago, he was half as old as his cousin was then. How old is will his cousin be 7 years from now?

    A. 25
    B. 28
    C. 17
    D. 12
    E. 31

58. If x and y are positive integers, which of the following **must** be true?

    I. $(x+y)^2 = x^2 + y^2$

    II. $(x-y)^2 = (y-x)^2$

    III. $2xy = 0$

    F. I only
    G. II only
    H. III only
    J. II and III
    K. I, II, and III

---

59. Simplify the expression

$$\frac{mn}{n^2 + m}\left[\left(\frac{m + n^2}{n - m}\right)\left(\frac{m - n}{n}\right)\right], \text{ where}$$

$m \neq n,\ m \neq -n^2,$ and $n \neq 0$.

    A. n
    B. $n^2 + m^2$
    C. $m - n$
    D. $m^2 - n^2$
    E. $-m$

60.

What is the difference between the sum and product of the lengths of $\overline{LM}$ and $\overline{MN}$?

    F. 0
    G. 3
    H. 7
    J. 11
    K. 17

CONTINUE ▶

61.

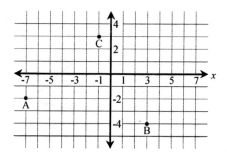

What is the area of the triangle that would result when line segments are drawn from point A to points B and C and from point B to C?

A. 30 square units
B. 31 square units
C. 32 square units
D. 32.75 square units
E. 33.5 square units

---

62. If $3x - 5y + 4 = 16 + y$, what is the value of y in terms of x?

F. $0.5x - 2$
G. $0.5x - 12$
H. $2x - 12$
J. $2x - 8$
K. $0.75x - 3$

---

63. If x equals 5.49 rounded down to the nearest whole number, and y equals 5.51 rounded up to the nearest whole number, how much greater is 60 divided by x than 60 divided by y?

A. 0
B. 1
C. 2
D. 3
E. 5

---

64. If t and u are positive integers, what is one possible value of $t + u$, if $t^2 - u^2 = 115$?

F. 5
G. 17
H. 23
J. 28
K. 31

65.

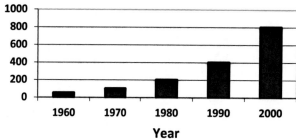

In the figure above, lines m and n are parallel. If $x = 3y$, what is the value of $5y$?

A. 195
B. 225
C. 275
D. 300
E. 335

66.

Population of Urbantown over the Decades

Based on the graph, when will Urbantown's population be 400% of its population in 1990?

F. 2000
G. 2005
H. 2010
J. 2015
K. 2020

CONTINUE ▶

67. Martin plans to giftwrap a rectangular box. If the edges of the box measure 0.5 **ft.**, 7 in., and 3 in., how many square inches of wrapping paper are needed to wrap the box?

   A. 162
   B. 126
   C. 81
   D. 52
   E. 10.5

68. If $\dfrac{3(j+k)}{4}$ is an integer, where j and k are both positive and $j = 14$, what is the smallest possible value of k?

   F. 1
   G. $1\dfrac{1}{3}$
   H. $\dfrac{1}{2}$
   J. $\dfrac{2}{3}$
   K. $2\dfrac{1}{4}$

69. Let $m \,\Phi\, n = \dfrac{m+n}{3}$, for all values of m and n.
What is the value of $(m \,\Phi\, n) \,\Phi\, m$, when $m = 7$ and $n = 8$?

   A. 2
   B. 4
   C. 5.25
   D. 6.33
   E. 9

70. Cheryl ate d pieces of candy. If her friend Cassidy ate $d + 4$ pieces of candy, and they ate a total of 14 pieces, how many did Cassidy eat?

   F. 2
   G. 5
   H. 8
   J. 9
   K. 10

71. When x is divided by 7, the remainder is 4. What is the remainder when 7 divides $2x$?

   A. 1
   B. 2
   C. 4
   D. 5
   E. 6

72. A goldsmith created a brick of gold that was 9 centimeters wide, 10 centimeters long, and 0.003 meters tall. If the density of gold is about 19.30 grams per cubic centimeter, which of the following best approximates the mass of the brick of gold?

   F. 0.513 grams
   G. 54.2 grams
   H. 272 grams
   J. 521 grams
   K. 540 grams

73. If the numeral M,NOP,QRS,TU7.14 is divided by 10,000, which letter or digit will be in the ten thousands place?

   A. M
   B. N
   C. O
   D. 7
   E. 1

CONTINUE ▶

74. Magnus enjoys playing role-playing board games. His favorite one requires players to use a 20-sided die, numbered from 1 to 20. What is the probability of Magnus rolling a multiple of 3 but not of 4 on his next turn?

F. $\dfrac{1}{10}$

G. $\dfrac{1}{5}$

H. $\dfrac{1}{20}$

J. $\dfrac{3}{10}$

K. $\dfrac{1}{4}$

75.

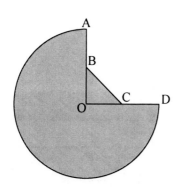

In the figure above, a quarter of circle O, which has a radius of 6, was removed and replaced by triangle BOC. If points B and C are the midpoints of radii $\overline{OA}$ and $\overline{OD}$, respectively, what is the perimeter of the new figure?

A. $9\pi + 3(2 + \sqrt{2})$

B. $12\pi + 6 + 3\sqrt{2}$

C. $9\pi + 6 + 2\sqrt{2}$

D. $27\pi + 4.5$

E. $27\pi - 4.5$

76. What is the sum of 50% of 7 and 7% of 50?

F. 100% of 7
G. 57% of 50
H. 157% of 7
J. 50% of 57
K. 100% of 57

77. Jessie jumped $\dfrac{7}{6}$ times as far as Jarvis did. If Jessie jumped 21 feet, what was their combined jumping distance, in feet?

A. 18
B. 21
C. 24.5
D. 39
E. 42.5

78. Roger plants a tree sapling every 15 yards along a 300-yard stretch, including one at the very beginning of the stretch. After he plants these saplings, he has left over exactly one more than half of the number of saplings he set out with. How many saplings did he start out with?

F. 20
G. 21
H. 40
J. 43
K. 44

79. If $m^2 - n^2 > 0$ and $m + n < 0$, which of the following **must** be true?

A. $m - n > 0$
B. $n - m > 0$
C. $n - m < 0$
D. $m - n < 0$
E. $n^2 - m^2 > 0$

CONTINUE ▶

80. A 9-sided polygon has 2 sides of *s* inches each, 2 other sides of $2s - 1$ inches each, and 3 sides of $s + 4$ inches each. The final 2 sides have lengths of 11 and 13 inches. If the polygon's perimeter is 196 inches, what is *s*?

F. 14
G. 15
H. 18
J. 20
K. 21

81.

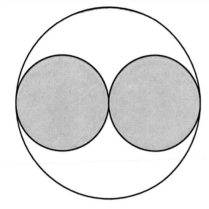

In the figure, two congruent circles are inscribed in a larger circle, as shown. What is the ratio of the area of shaded region to that of the unshaded region, if the radius of the larger circle is double that of the smaller circles?

A. 1 : 4
B. 1 : 2
C. 1 : 1
D. 2 : 3
E. 3 : 4

82. Marsha scored 93, 89, and 92 on three tests. After her fourth, her average for the four tests was a 94. What is the difference between her highest and lowest scores on the four tests?

F. 4
G. 5
H. 7
J. 13
K. 25

83.

ICE CREAM SALES

Day	1	2	3	4	5	6	7
# of Sales	199	178	185	206	177	166	191

What is the difference between the median and mean of the number of ice cream sales for the days shown above?

A. 0
B. 1
C. 2
D. 3
E. 4

84. Betty is *k* years old now and Lacey is 16 years older. In 12 years, Lacey will be twice as old as Betty is then. How old is Lacey now?

F. 17
G. 20
H. 23
J. 27
K. 28

85.

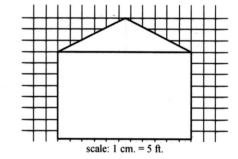

scale: 1 cm. = 5 ft.

The figure above was drawn on a grid comprised of 1-cm squares. What is the approximate area of the full-sized figure?

A. 93.5 sq ft
B. 1674 sq ft
C. 2330 sq ft
D. 2615 sq ft
E. 5250 sq ft

CONTINUE ▶

86. A roller coaster car holds 52 people, and the ride finishes in 140-second intervals. If 613 people are waiting in line right when the roller coaster ride opens, how long will it be before the last person finishes riding the ride?

  F. 25 minutes, 40 seconds
  G. 28 minutes
  H. 32 minutes, 35 seconds
  J. 560 minutes
  K. 1680 minutes

87.   Set A = {2, 4, 6, ..., 48, 50}
          Set B = {1, 3, 5, ..., 47, 49}

If the sum of the numbers in A is x, and the sum of the numbers in B is y, what is $x - y$?

  A. 0
  B. 25
  C. 50
  D. 75
  E. 100

88. Carlos has some flashcards. Among them are 6 white, 5 yellow, 4 blue, 3 red, and 2 green cards. If he picked two cards at random, without replacement, what is the probability that both are yellow?

  F. $\dfrac{1}{19}$

  G. $\dfrac{1}{10}$

  H. $\dfrac{2}{9}$

  J. $\dfrac{3}{13}$

  K. $\dfrac{9}{380}$

89. A species of moth has two subspecies in a particular forest: one dark gray, the other ivory white. Of 450 moths a biologist catches, 270 are dark gray. If there are an estimated 20,000 moths in the forest, about how many more gray moths are there than white ones?

  A. 3,500
  B. 4,000
  C. 8,000
  D. 10,000
  E. 12,000

90. If the boundary of a circle whose diameter is 10 units passes through the coordinate (5, 0), which of the coordinates **cannot** also lie on the circle's boundary, if the center of the circle must have integer coordinates?

  F. (5, 10)
  G. (0, 5)
  H. (0, 0)
  J. (10, 5)
  K. (-5, 0)

91. There are 48 students in Mrs. Henderson's class. If the ratio of girls to boys is 7:5, how many more girls are there in the class?

  A. 2
  B. 4
  C. 6
  D. 8
  E. 14

92. Which of the following is probably the best approximation of $\sqrt{11^2 + 12^2}$?

  F. 12.6
  G. 13.9
  H. 14.7
  J. 16.3
  K. 18.1

CONTINUE ▶

93. Kaylee started out with x pens. She gave half to Lou, who started out with two fewer than Kaylee started out with. Lou then gave half of his new total to Ilene, who started out with three fewer pens than Lou started out with. Ilene in turn gives a third of her new total to Kaylee. If Kaylee ends up with 37 pens, what is x?

A. 36
B. 30
C. 24
D. 20
E. 18

94. On Kathy's property's blueprint, ¼-inch represents 2 meters. If her garage is 96 square meters, how many square inches will the garage take up on the blueprint?

F. 1.5
G. 8
H. 24
J. 32
K. 64

95.

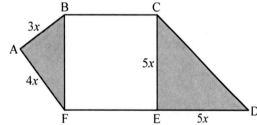

The figure above was constructed with a square and two right triangles, with side lengths as shown. Which of the following could **not** be the area of the shaded regions if x is an integer?

A. 18.5 sq cm
B. 37 sq cm
C. 74 sq cm
D. 166.5 sq cm
E. 1,850 sq cm

96. Bill plans to have 187 friends and family members at his wedding reception. Each table can sit 13, and each table will be filled completely before the next table is opened up for seating. How many people will sit at the last table to open up?

F. 3
G. 4
H. 5
J. 7
K. 11

97. Set $L = \{1, 3, 5, \ldots, 83, 85, 87, 89\}$

How many numbers in L have 3 as a factor, but do not have 9 as a factor?

A. 22
B. 21
C. 20
D. 19
E. 17

98. Young McDonald keeps only ducks and cows on his farm. There are exactly three ducks for every two cows. What is the least number of animals that could be on his farm if the total number of legs is a perfect square?

F. 14
G. 49
H. 64
J. 70
K. 196

CONTINUE ▶

99. There are 16.5 feet in one rod, and 4 rods in one chain. If there are 5280 feet in one mile, how many chains are in one mile?

    A. 1760
    B. 320
    C. 52
    D. 66
    E. 80

100. If the radius of the base of a regular right cylinder is tripled, but the height divided by two, to create a new cylinder, what percent of the original cylinder's volume is the volume of the new cylinder?

    F. 300%
    G. 450%
    H. 600%
    J. 750%
    K. 900%

**STOP. THIS IS THE END OF THE TEST.
IF TIME PERMITS, YOU MAY REVIEW
YOUR ANSWERS TO PARTS 1 AND 2
OF THE TEST.**

ANSWERS
& EXPLANATIONS

SHSAT
NYC EDITION
TEST KEY 1

Answer Key – Test 1

VERBAL

SCRAMBLED PARAGRAPHS

Paragraph 1
TRQUS

Paragraph 2
QUTSR

Paragraph 3
RTSQU

Paragraph 4
SUQRT

Paragraph 5
RTQSU

LOGICAL REASONING

11. D
12. H
13. D
14. K
15. A
16. J
17. C
18. K
19. A
20. K

READING

21. D
22. K
23. B
24. G
25. D
26. J
27. C
28. H
29. C
30. J
31. C
32. J
33. B
34. K
35. D
36. H
37. D
38. F
39. A
40. K
41. B
42. H
43. D
44. K
45. C
46. G
47. E
48. J
49. D
50. F

Answer Key – Test 1

MATHEMATICS

51. E			**76.** G	
52. G			**77.** E	
53. C			**78.** F	
54. J			**79.** B	
55. B			**80.** F	
56. K			**81.** B	
57. D			**82.** H	
58. F			**83.** B	
59. B			**84.** H	
60. J			**85.** B	
61. A			**86.** J	
62. G			**87.** C	
63. C			**88.** G	
64. J			**89.** B	
65. D			**90.** J	
66. J			**91.** A	
67. B			**92.** F	
68. J			**93.** C	
69. E			**94.** G	
70. H			**95.** C	
71. D			**96.** J	
72. G			**97.** B	
73. C			**98.** K	
74. G			**99.** A	
75. C			**100.** H	

VERBAL EXPLANATIONS ▶

Answer Explanations – Verbal
Practice Test 1

SCRAMBLED PARAGRAPHS

Paragraph 1 (TRQUS)

The lead sentence introduces the word *fracking* and what it is not, to clear up any potential confusion for the reader and to be humorous.

Sentence T follows the lead because it defines what fracking is. Specifically, it defines fracking as the process of hydraulic fracturing. Without T, none of the other sentences would make sense because the rest of the paragraph is about the differences between hydraulic fracturing and traditional drilling.

R comes after T because it compares fracking to traditional methods of drilling and that fracking allows more oil and gas to be extracted. Q comes after R by generally explaining the general limitation of traditional drilling. U comes after R because U describes what fracking does differently from traditional drilling to overcome the limitation traditional drilling. S comes last because it follows up by finishing the explanation that U began.

Note: It may be tempting to select S after Q because S discusses wellbores, after the idea of wellbores is introduced in Q. The problem is that S also discusses how pressurized fluids are used, but the idea of pressurized fluids is brought up by U.

Paragraph 2 (QUTSR)

The lead sentence mentions a very powerful solar flare that took place in 1859. Q comes after the lead because it identifies the solar flare as the Carrington Event and puts into perspective just how powerful the solar flare was, in contrast to other solar flares.

U follows Q because U is the transition between the discussion of the Carrington Event and solar flares in general, which the remaining sentences are about.

T comes after U because U explains that a solar flare is the result of the sudden release of the magnetic energy that has been accumulating in the Sun's atmosphere and T defines just how much energy can comprise a solar flare. S comes after T by further relating the amount of energy in a solar flare in terms that more people are able to appreciate and understand. R wraps up the paragraph by relating the energy output of a solar flare to the energy output of the Sun.

Easy Clusters: TSR is an easy cluster to make because T leads to S, which then leads to R. QU is also an easy cluster to make. It should be apparent that Q is the first sentence after the lead, so then it should be easy to figure that the correct ordering is QUTSR.

Paragraph 3 (RTSQU)

The lead sentence introduces the goliath bird-eating spider as possibly the most massive spider in existence.

R follows the lead because it specifies how large the goliath bird-eater can get and further specifies that it is the largest known tarantula alive. T follows R because it touches on the massiveness of the goliath bird-eater again. T also proceeds to discuss the variety of prey that the goliath bird-eater eats.

S comes after T because it explains how the goliath bird-eater, like other tarantulas, feeds on its prey. Q continues to describe the feeding process for tarantulas, so Q follows S naturally. U follows Q because the phrase "this entire feeding process" is referring to the feeding process that was just described.

Note: It might seem to make more sense for U to come before the entire feeding process is described, since sequentially, a tarantula must capture its prey before consuming it, and U describes how the goliath captures and bites its prey, but the explanation above explains why it must come after the feeding process is described.

Paragraph 4 (SUQRT)

The lead sentence mentions the introduction of the iPhone as a pivotal moment in communications history, in particular with regard to the wider adoption of smartphones.

S follows the lead because it clarifies that the iPhone wasn't the smartphone and that it wasn't even the first popular smartphone. U comes after S because "that distinction" must have an antecedent to which it is referring and because U states that the Blackberry line of smartphones led the market for several years as the exceedingly popular smartphone option. Q follows U; while Blackberry was the smartphone market leader, it no longer is so.

R follows Q because R explains Blackberry's decline from its position as the smartphone market leader, explaining that the fall of Blackberry can be attributed to the rise of the iPhone and Android platforms. T follows R and acknowledges the dominance that Apple and Google have in the smartphone market.

Tip: Because T suddenly introduces a brand new idea that is not discussed in any of the other sentences—that the line between smartphones and traditional computers has been irreversibly blurred—it is possible to conclude that T is the final sentences of the paragraph.

Paragraph 5 (RTQSU)

The lead sentences briefly defines and describes the concept of game theory.

R follows the lead because it bridges the gap between the lead sentence and the remaining sentences, all of which focus on elucidating the concept of game theory by explaining what the prisoner's dilemma scenario entails. T follows R by providing the general background information needed to construct the rest of the paragraph.

Q comes after T. T states that two suspects are brought in for interrogation; Q further elaborates on the interrogation process and what it entails. S then follows Q because it shows how the police make it more difficult for the suspects to adhere to their original agreement of never betraying each other by not revealing that each suspect could get off with no sentence at all, which is what leads them to fink on each other. The fear of being backstabbed or betrayed is what drives each accomplish to try to cheat to come out on top, and this is where U comes in to wrap the paragraph up.

Clusters: TQ and SU are the easiest clusters to make, for the reasons stated above. If you can reason that R comes first, it becomes a matter of figuring out whether T or S comes after R. Since it would not make much sense for S to come after R, T must. This leads to the correct ordering of RTQSU.

LOGICAL REASONING

11. (D) To solve this problem, we can see that there can only be at most two columns of stacked dishes because the red and green dishes must be in the same column and the blue, yellow, and orange dishes must be in the same column, leaving no other dishes to begin a third.

Moreover, if there are two columns of dishes, there is only one possible configuration for the two columns, since the relative positions of the columns do not matter for this problem:

Column 1	Column 2
	B
G	Y
R	O

This chart eliminates A and E as answer choices because it shows that they can be true.

Answer choices B, C, and D focus on a single column of dishes, so it is most time efficient to look for any discrepancies between the orderings presented in the answer choices and the conditions rather than to draw out every possible way the dishes could be stacked in one column. Mainly, what we are looking for is to see if the order contradicts the following statements: 1) yellow is immediately beneath blue, 2) yellow is someplace between blue and orange, 3) green is immediately on top of red, and 4) orange is at the very bottom of its column.

First, we can see that B does not seem to contradict any of the conditions, so we skip over that. The same is true for C. Looking at D, we can see that it does contradict one of the conditions. In D, orange is not at the very bottom of its column, thus the statement cannot be true, and D is the correct choice as a result.

12. (H) To solve this problem, draw a diagram or chart that will illustrate the order in which Martha exercised and listened to music.

From the first condition, we know that Martha bikes before she runs and runs before she lifts weights. From the third and fourth conditions, we can conclude that Martha plays tennis the day after she lifts weights. Thus, we see that Martha bikes, runs, lifts weights, and plays tennis, in that order, with yoga coming somewhere in between, since it is on a Thursday.

Because she plays tennis the day after she lifts weights, we can conclude Martha doesn't lift weights on Wednesday. Thus, it must be true that Martha lifts weights on Friday and plays tennis on Saturday, which is what H expresses.

Below are the charts for the possible schedules for Martha:

Martha's Exercise & Music Schedule

Mo	Tu	We	Th	Fr	Sa
Bikes	Runs		Yoga	Weights	Tennis
Pop	?		Jazz	Country	Rock

Martha's Exercise & Music Schedule

Mo	Tu	We	Th	Fr	Sa
Bikes		Runs	Yoga	Weights	Tennis
Pop		?	Jazz	Country	Rock

Martha's Exercise & Music Schedule

Mo	Tu	We	Th	Fr	Sa
	Bikes	Runs	Yoga	Weights	Tennis
	Pop	?	Jazz	Country	Rock

As we can see, F is wrong because Martha cannot listen to pop on Wednesday. Martha cannot run on Mondays, either, which rules G out. It is possible that Martha takes a break on Tuesday, but she may also take a break on Wednesday, ruling out J. The same reasoning applies to why K is the wrong answer.

13. **(D)** Use the process of elimination to arrive at the correct answer. But first it must be understood that each boy participates in exactly two sports, since the facts state that the boys participate in more than one sport, but not all three.

Answer choice A cannot be the correct answer because it contradicts the statement that the three boys participate in only one sport in common. B is incorrect because there is not enough information to conclude that all three boys play football; furthermore, there is not enough information to conclude that Art and Lou participate in soccer and track. Similarly, C is incorrect because there is not enough evidence to conclude that the boys all run track. E is incorrect because, according to it, the three boys would not participate in any sport in common.

The correct answer is therefore D. To see why D actually is the correct answer, let's construct a sample chart—multiple charts are possible, so this is just an example to illustrate the point.

Student 1	Student 2	Student 3
Football	Football	Football
Track	Soccer	Track/Soccer

The chart shows one sport in common by all three, which means that exactly one of the students is playing a different second sport than the other two, since it is not possible for all three students to participate in two sports in common. And since a sport is offered once per season, a student cannot repeat the same sport during the school year. This means that exactly two of the students must participate in exactly two of the same sports per school year.

Study tip: Make charts to see that the example chart works for all sports combinations.

14. **(K)** To solve this problem, construct a chart or table. We know Stacy attends the first two, Randy attends the last two, and Kim attends one session with Stacy and one with Randy.

Since Kim attends three sessions, though, we know for sure that she attends the third session. The base chart or table looks as shown below, with information still missing:

Sessions & Attendance

	1	2	3	4	5
Stacy	X	X			
Randy				X	X
Kim			X		
Aaron					

Without having to do more work than this, we can go down the list of answer choices to see if any of them fit.

We can see that A is wrong because it is possible attends the first session, but it is not a must. The same is true for G and J. H is wrong because Kim must attend the third session, so the statement made in H is necessarily wrong.

Thus, K is the correct answer. The conditions did state that Aaron will never attend a session Kim attends. So if it's the case that Kim must attend the third session, Aaron will not.

15. **(A)** To solve this problem, draw a diagram or chart that illustrates the order in which the zoologist visited the animals. First, fill in the penguin and tiger.

First Visited

1.	
2.	Tiger
3.	
4.	Penguin
5.	
6.	
7.	

Last Visited

Because we know that the lion was visited immediately after the elephant was, the lion was visited either last or second to last, since the chart won't permit the lion to be visited first, third, or fifth. Moreover, we know that the zoologist visits the crocodile before she visits the gorilla and the gorilla before the iguana. Thus, we can construct the following charts:

First Visited

1.	Crocodile
2.	Tiger
3.	Gorilla
4.	Penguin
5.	
6.	
7.	

Last Visited

Since the lion has to be immediately behind the elephant, the elephant can either be fifth or sixth, and the lion can be either sixth or seventh, accordingly. This means that the iguana can either be fifth of seventh. Thus, all three of these animals can be visited in two time slots, which is the statement expressed by choice A.

16. **(J)** This problem tests logic statements. We can rearrange the statements to conditional statements to make them easier to process, according to the rules of logic:

$$P \rightarrow \sim F$$
$$F \rightarrow S$$

Note: ~ means "not." As such, the first conditional statement should be read, "If S, then not F." Of course that in itself is an abbreviated form of "If my parents are home, then I will not go to my friend's house." The other statement is an abbreviation for, "If I go to my friend's house, then it is sunny outside."

If a conditional statement is true, then only its contrapositive is also true. In other words, the only valid statements that can be derived from the above conditional statements:

$$F \rightarrow \sim P$$
$$\sim S \rightarrow \sim F$$

Choice F is wrong because it is possible that I didn't go to my friend's house for another reason that doesn't include the sunniness outside or whether my parents are home. G draws an invalid conclusion because there may be other reasons, and follows the reasoning as to why F is wrong. H is wrong because even though it is always sunny and my parents aren't home when I go to my friend's house, it's not necessarily the case that I always go to my friend's house whenever it is sunny or when my parents aren't home. K is wrong because it is based on the logic of $\sim S \rightarrow \sim F$ and $\sim F \rightarrow P$. But because the latter statement is not necessarily true, as it is the converse of the statement $P \rightarrow \sim F$. Further remember that only the contrapositive of a true conditional statement is also true.

17. **(C)** What we can conclude from the facts of the problem is that everyone is good at math in Edutopia, but everyone who is also good at writing in Edutopa becomes a journalist, novelist, or blogger. If Henderson is an engineer, three possible conclusions exist: 1) Henderson is good at writing, but he isn't living in Edutopia; 2) Henderson lives in Edutopia, but he is not good at writing; and 3) Henderson does not live in Edutopia, and he is not good at writing. Only choice C is in line with these possible conclusions.

Use the process of elimination. Choice A is incorrect because, as we can see, Henderson could be good at writing. B is incorrect because the passage does not link proficiency at math with being able to be an engineer. D is incorrect because Henderson can live in Edutopia, as we saw above. E is incorrect because the facts state that Henderson is an engineer. Thus, we see that C is the correct answer.

18. **(K)** To solve this problem, draw a chart or diagram. We know that the history, math, and economics books cannot be on the same shelf as the geography book, thus we can come up with the following baseline diagrams:

Books on Shelf

H, M, E
G

or

Books on Shelf

G
H, M, E

There are many possible configurations, but notice that we're looking for which of the answer choices cannot be true. It is possible for the psychology book to be on the top shelf, so F is incorrect. And if the psychology book can be on the top shelf, then the art book can be on the middle shelf, since there's no condition stating that the art book cannot be on the same shelf as the geography book. Thus, we can eliminate G. As we saw from the baseline diagrams, the math book can be on the bottom shelf, so H is incorrect. J is incorrect because the psychology book can be on the middle shelf, as long as the history, math, and economics books are on the top shelf. This leaves K as the correct answer. Because the history, math, and economics books are together on the same shelf, and each shelf can hold at most three books, it is not possible for them to share a shelf with the geography book, or any other book for that matter.

19. **(A)** To solve problems such as this, it is important to see which words and corresponding letters overlap among the sentences. In this way, it is possible to narrow down or deduce which letters are assigned to which words.

We see that "Curt" does not appear in any sentence but the first, but "fixes," "cars," "and," and "boats" do appear in multiple sentences. Since the only letter that does not appear in any other sentence besides the first is N, we can deduce that "Curt" is represented by N. Thus, choice A is the correct answer.

20. **(K)** In order to solve this problem, we have to first decode as many of the sentences as possible. We can see that the word "and" appears in three sentences and the letter P also appears in three sentences, which means P represents "and". "Cars" only appears in the first and third sentences, and the first and third sentences share no other words or letters, so we can figure that the letter T represents "cars".

By using a similar process of matching words and letters between sentences, it should be pretty easy to figure out that "boats" is represented by the letter U, which means that the word "fixes" is represented by the letter O. By comparing the third and fourth sentences, we see that "bikes" is represented by the letter R. The second and fourth sentences reveal that "planes" is represented by the letter S. At this point, we can see that in the fourth sentence, we're left with "Sue" and the letter K, so the fourth sentence is completely solved.

We are left with "Meg" and "flies" in the second sentence, along with the letters L and V, and with "Lee," "drives," and "or" in the third sentence, along with the letters M, X, and W. Because we cannot at this point figure out which letters are assigned to which words, given that the instructions indicate that the letters may or may not be presented in the same order as the words, we are left with five words that might be representable by more than one letter.

READING ▶

READING

(Aposematic Coloration)

21. **(D)** This passage is about how various species of animals employ or take advantage of aposematic coloration, which is a warning mechanism based on an animal's color scheme or pattern to ward off predators from attempting to eat the animal.

Choice A may appear to be a true statement, but it is subtly, but significantly, different from the first two lines. Top or apex predators are only relatively safe from predation; they are not safe from predation. B is a true statement, but there is significantly more to the passage than just harmless animals benefitting from aposematic coloration. C is incorrect because, while the passage does use butterflies, snakes, and frogs as the primary examples of aposematic coloration, the passage does not indicate that these animals benefit the most from aposematic coloration. In other words, just because they're used as the examples doesn't make them the greatest possible examples of animals that benefit from aposematic coloration.

D is correct. Aposematic coloration is a significant evolutionary development and various animal species, including the harmless ones, take advantage of the existence of aposematic coloration through mimicry. Thus, the entire passage is about how aposematic coloration is beneficial to animals. E is incorrect. While it may be the case that it is hard to tell mimics apart, this is not the focus of the passage.

22. **(K)** It can be inferred from the passage in lines 29-31 that Müllerian mimics share similar coloration schemes as well as unpleasantness as prey. Thus, a Müllerian mimic would be at least somewhat unpleasant or noxious to a predator.

F is incorrect because it is not supported by the passage. Moreover, even if being a Müllerian mimic does not confer a significant advantage against those predators that can tolerate the primary prey's toxicity, that doesn't necessarily mean a Müllerian mimic is going to be at a disadvantage overall, or even against those specific predator. Perhaps if the prey wasn't toxic at all, the predator would eat even more of the prey.

G is unsupported by the passage. While the first part of the statement may be true to an extent, there's no indication that Müllerian mimics are equally toxic to predators. H is incorrect because the conclusion drawn in it is too strong. While it may be the case that Müllerian mimics draw their source of unpleasantness or toxicity from different sources, as is the case with Viceroy and Monarch butterflies, it is not stated in the passage that the sources of unpleasantness must come from different sources. J is also unsupported by the passage. It is not known whether one Müllerian mimic is more potent or unpleasant to predators than the others are.

23. **(B)** The last paragraph of the passage mentions that the coral snake is deadly and that the milk snake is harmless. Both species possess transverse bands of red, black, and yellow. On the coral snake, the red and black bands are separated by a yellow band. On the milk snake, the red and yellow bands are separated by a black band. The only answer choice that works here is B, which correctly states the coloration pattern of coral snakes: "Red on yellow will kill a fellow, but red on black is a friend of Jack."

A is incorrect because Jack should prefer red next to black. C is incorrect because red next to black indicates that the venom will lack. D is incorrect because red next to yellow indicates the poisonous coral snake. Moreover, there's no indication in the passage of a white band on either the coral snake or the milk snake. E is incorrect because red on yellow will kill a fellow and red on black will not kill Jack.

24. **(G)** In lines 22-25, the passage indicates that a significant portion of the monarch butterfly population is eaten every year by animals that can tolerate the monarch's toxins. Thus, it is proper to conclude that aposematic coloration may be a deterrent, but not one against every predator.

F is incorrect because it states in lines 45-47 that even harmless animals that do not employ aposematic coloration can benefit from aposematic coloration. The subsequent lines establish that these harmless animals are called Batesian mimics. Batesian mimicry takes advantage of and is based on aposematic coloration but is not itself a form of aposematic coloration, as aposematic coloration is defined. H is incorrect because there is nothing to indicate that the smaller a species of poison dart frog is, the more toxic it is going to be. J is incorrect because the first four lines only indicate apex predators' relative safeness, not their absolute safeness. K is incorrect because there's no indication in the passage of how quickly the golden poison arrow frog's poison can kill a human.

25. **(D)** D is correct because a Batesian mimic copies the appearance of a species of animal that is known to be toxic or potent. Thus, a con artist posing as a dangerous criminal that law enforcement officers do not want to go after is the most parallel to what Batesian mimics do.

A is incorrect because there is no mimicry involved. B is incorrect the owl butterfly isn't itself copying the appearance of a species of animal that uses aposematic coloration; the butterfly's wings make it appear to not be prey. C is incorrect because the child is not mimicking anything for protection. E is incorrect because there is no mimicry involved here.

26. **(J)** J is most likely what the author meant by the phrase "sequestering of salicylic acid" because the bitterness of the butterfly comes from salicylic acid. Thus, it makes sense that the butterfly would use a method or process

that makes itself even more bitter to predators. In fact, the word "sequester" means to isolate. But even without knowing what sequester means, J makes the most sense.

F doesn't work because this question is about the butterfly, not the food source. G is unsupported by the passage, as there is no mention of another potent substance. H is also unsupported by the passage; it's an overstatement of the information presented in the passage. There's no support to indicate that the butterfly concentrates salicylic acid so much that it will kill a predator within seconds. K is incorrect because the passage is about the effect of salicylic acid to the predator. There's no indication of what sort of internal damage, if any, that the butterfly sustains, so the statement in K is not supported by the passage.

(Rosalind Franklin)

27. **(C)** The purpose of the passage is to discuss Rosalind Franklin's life and her contributions to the discovery of the double helical structure of DNA using x-ray crystallography. This is best represented by choice C.

Choice A is incorrect. Although the passage does mention that Watson and Crick used Rosalind's work to complete their understanding of the structure of DNA, this in itself does not necessarily mean that Rosalind was a better scientist. B is incorrect because it is feasible that with more time Watson and Crick would have been able to figure out everything they needed to know to determine the structure of DNA. D is incorrect because its scope is too narrow for the passage. While it is true that x-ray diffraction played an important role in the discovery of the structure of DNA, that's not the emphasis of this passage. E is incorrect because this passage only briefly touches on the tension between Rosalind and Maurice Wilkins.

28. **(H)** Lines 31-37 indicate that Maurice Wilkins had assumed that Rosalind had been

hired as a technical assistant, not as a lead researcher. Thus, it is probable that he treated her as a subordinate rather than a colleague.

Choice F is not as strong as H is. Though it is feasible that Wilkins assumed Rosalind did not have the educational background necessary to be a lead researcher, the passage focuses on the role Wilkins thought Rosalind was supposed to play. G is incorrect because there is no indication in the passage that Rosalind boasted at all.

J is incorrect because it assumes too much. While the passage does mention differences in personalities, it does not say that Wilkins and Rosalind disagreed about every little detail of their work. K is incorrect because it is completely unsupported by the passage; there is no indication that Rosalind tried to boss Wilkins around or that she thought he was a technical assistant.

29. **(C)** C is the correct answer because Rosalind Franklin did not work as a lead research manager and officer for the British Coal Utilisation Research Association; she worked as an assistant research officer. The other answer choices are incorrect because they state accurate facts that took place in Rosalind Franklin's life.

30. **(J)** Rosalind Franklin was not included as a recipient of the 1962 Nobel Prize in Physiology or Medicine because she had passed away before she could receive the award, and the Nobel Prize is not awarded posthumously (lines 11-14). Thus, J is the correct answer.

F is incorrect because it is factually incorrect. Lines 14-15 state that Rosalind Franklin passed away four years before she could be included as a recipient of the Nobel Prize, not five years before. G is incorrect because there is no proof in the passage that Maurice Wilkins prevented Rosalind from obtaining the Nobel Prize. H is incorrect because it is not supported; the passage does not mention if there is a limit to the number of people who

can receive a Nobel Prize. K is incorrect because it is also unsupported by the passage. Nowhere in the passage is there mention of Photograph 51's value to the discovery of the structure of DNA being discredited.

31. **(C)** Lines 44-45 indicate that there are two forms of DNA, a dry 'A' form and a wet 'B' form. Photograph 51 was of the 'B' form, which means that it was of the wet form of DNA. Thus, C is the correct answer.

Choice A is incorrect because there is no mention in the passage of what DNA form Photograph 50 was of; there is no mention in the passage of Photograph 50 at all. B is also unsupported by the passage; there is no way to infer that Rosalind got her lead research position through the wealth of her family.

D is incorrect; while Cambridge University certainly seemed to be a leader in the understanding of DNA, there's no comparison between Cambridge and any other university to justify D. E is incorrect because it is unsupported by the passage; certainly, Watson and Crick are revered, as evidenced by lines 1-5. There is not enough evidence, however, to claim that they are the most revered names in biology today.

32. **(J)** Lines 59-64 indicates that Watson and Crick published the paper about the structure of DNA in *Nature* in 1953, so it can be reasoned that this is when the structure of DNA was officially revealed publicly. At the very least, this is the date that makes the most sense.

(Reciprocal Altruism)

33. **(B)** The focus of this passage is altruism and why it might appear to be strange as an evolutionary mechanism, but the passage also uses Vervet monkeys and vampire bats to explain how altruism can make sense as an evolutionary mechanism. Thus, choice B best represents the author's primary purpose for writing the passage.

Choice A is incorrect. This choice is a trap. Though the author does heavily focus on explaining altruism by using Vervet monkeys and vampire bats as examples, this is not the purpose of the passage. The purpose of the passage is to explain altruism and reciprocal altruism in general. C is incorrect because this passage is not to discuss Charles Darwin's take on the theory of evolution. D is incorrect because there's no evidence in the passage that indicates that a portion of Darwin's book was about altruism. E is incorrect because it is too narrow in scope. While it is true that sounding warning calls or sharing food can benefit an individual in the long run, this isn't the main purpose of the passage; like A, E is also a trap.

34. **(K)** Altruism, as it is defined and described in the context of the passage, is the increasing the fitness of another while concurrently reducing one's own fitness. Thus, K is the only true example of altruism. The neighborhood watchman, who is a volunteer, risks his life to protect the neighborhood.

F is not a true example of altruism because leaving an orphanage a fortune does not decrease the philanthropist's fitness. G is not an example of altruism because a father's children represent his fitness; they are what will survive him genetically. It could be argued that H is an example of altruism because the lion is decreasing his fitness by not eating the gazelle. The act of sparing the gazelle's life does not put the lion in harm's way or does not risk his immediate ability to survive; there's not enough context—perhaps the lion was already full. J is not an example of altruism because the mercenary is being paid, so he is not displaying "generosity".

35. **(D)** The fourth paragraph makes it apparent that altruism works in the context of reciprocal altruism, which is when other members of a species or group will also display altruistic behaviors. The major assumption here is that the altruistic behaviors will be demonstrated by more than just one individual. Thus, D is the correct answer.

A is incorrect because altruism has nothing to do with societal happiness and gratitude; altruism is about survival. B is incorrect because there are other methods of displaying altruism other than sharing food. C is incorrect because it is not supported by the passage; it could be the case that some animals survive without any charity. E is incorrect because it is not known whether altruism would work even when every member of a group is selfish. In fact, the passage implies that altruism would not work if every other member of the group was selfish, in lines 53-58.

36. **(H)** Lines 34-42 discuss the curious phenomenon of vampire bats sharing food, despite the fact that vampire bats have extremely fast metabolisms. It is curious that they share food for because they can die within 36 hours of not having food, so sharing food poses a high risk for bats. Thus, it may appear to be counterintuitive that they share food. All of this is expressed by answer choice H.

F is incorrect because sharing food with those not of immediate kin is not counterintuitive by itself. It is only counterintuitive when taking into account the extreme metabolism of vampire bats. Thus, F is incorrect because it does not encompass the entire reason sharing food with kin might be counterintuitive. G is incorrect because the word "food" is not defined in the passage as solid foods. J is incorrect because the passage directly states that vampire bats do share food. K is incorrect because it is not known, based on the passage, whether vampire bats have to expend more energy than other mammals do because they fly (in fact, bats are the only mammals that can fly); furthermore, and perhaps more importantly, even if vampire bats do have to expend more energy than other mammals because they fly, their expenditure of more energy to fly is not hinted in the passage as why it doesn't make sense for vampire bats to share food. Thus, K is wrong because, even if it is true, it is not direct enough to be the correct answer; it is a trap.

37. **(D)** The engine driving evolution in line 14 is survival and the promulgation of one's genetic material. We are looking for an example of behavior that goes against survival and the promulgation of one's genes. D is the correct answer because an untrained driver looking for a thrill by driving recklessly in an extremely dangerous situation without anyone to watch him does not help or promote his survival.

A is incorrect because the tiger believes that the piglets are her cubs, so she is behaving in a way that is conducive to survival and the promulgation of her genes. B is incorrect because a soldier cowering and then fleeing is acting to ensure his chance for survival. C is incorrect because the victor lion is attempting to ensure his own genetic line by taking over a pride; he does not care about the offspring of over male lions. E is incorrect because the bear is acting to protect its cubs, which will ensure the survival and promulgation of its genes.

38. **(F)** It can be inferred from the passage that natural selection is fundamentally different from artificial selection; the phrase "in stark contrast to" in lines 9-10 indicate that artificial selection does not entail nature weeding out the weakest and least fit traits for survival.

G is incorrect because there is no indication in the passage that artificial selection is the process by which people breed animals for traits they find desirable. This choice is a trap because this is actually what artificial selection is; it is not, however, something that can be inferred from the passage. H, J, and K are all incorrect for the same reason that they cannot be inferred from the passage due to the lack of evidence or information presented by the passage.

(Graphene)

39. **(A)** This passage is about graphene and its various properties and traits and their potential commercial and industrial implications. Thus, A is the best choice, despite the fact that the word "substance" is a generic word; however, graphene is a substance, so "substance" is not an inaccurate descriptor for graphene.

Choice B is incorrect because the passage was written to discuss the properties of graphene and their potential implications, not to urge the immediate adoption of graphene. Furthermore, the last paragraph mentions that graphene is not yet ready for commercial deployment. C is incorrect because the main purpose of this passage is not about giving the discoverers of graphene their due credit. D is incorrect because the passage was not written to reveal an obscure fact to the public. E is incorrect because the passage is not about how graphene is currently being used around the world; if anything, the passage is about how graphene *may* be used eventually, not currently.

40. **(K)** The passage does not make any mention of graphene's reactivity to gases, but it does mention all of the other properties listed as properties in the other answer choices.

Choice F is incorrect because graphene's impermeability is mentioned in lines 34-35. G is incorrect because graphene's elasticity is discussed in lines 28-31. H is incorrect because graphene's conductivity is discussed in lines 19-21. J is incorrect because graphene's structural strength is mentioned in lines 11-19.

41. **(B)** Lines 34-41 indicate that graphene may be used in ultrasensitive gas sensors because graphene's impermeability can block out even helium atoms, and helium is the second smallest element, next to hydrogen. But because the passage does not state that graphene's lattice structure could block out hy-

drogen atoms, it's a possibility that graphene's lattice structure may permit hydrogen atoms to pass through.

Choice A is wrong because the passage does not state that graphene could be used in gas sensors to detect all gases, since the passage specifically omits hydrogen as a gas that graphene can detect. C and D are incorrect because lines 35-44 are about graphene's impermeability only. E is incorrect because even though graphene might be used in ultrasensitive gas sensors in the future, that does not mean it will be used in all gas sensors, or even all ultrasensitive gas sensors; factors like price could impact how widespread the use of graphene becomes.

42. **(H)** Lines 2-5 discuss the shape and structure of graphene; it is comprised of carbon atoms arranged in a lattice of hexagons, similar to the patterns found in honeycombs. Thus, it can be inferred that honeycombs are arranged in a lattice of hexagons.

Choice F is incorrect because there is not enough information to support it. Graphene is currently the strongest substance discovered, but that does not mean it will always be the strongest substance. G is incorrect because there is no indication by the passage that the hexagon lattice is the most perfect shape to ever be created. J is incorrect because there is not enough information to justify the notion that a hexagon lattice of titanium atoms is even possible, let alone stronger than graphene. K is incorrect because graphene is not necessarily impermeable to all gases; it may be permeable to hydrogen.

43. **(D)** Lines 59-63 state that the practical integration of graphene into current electronics is a ways off because of the current limitations of graphene, such as the inability to properly control graphene's conduction properties. This implies that graphene's conduction properties are either not yet fully understood or unable to be controlled.

Choice A is incorrect. Perhaps people could use and need 40 GHz to 150 GHz clock-speeds. B is incorrect because the passage does not mention the price of replacing silicon with graphene. C is incorrect because the mass production of graphene is not cited as the reason graphene is not yet commercially available. E is also unsupported by the passage. For all we know, it may be possible to fit 900 million to 1.4 billion graphene transistors onto a modern CPU.

44. **(K)** In lines 45-49, the passage states that graphene was the focus of much academic and industrial research. Thus, it can be inferred that 3,000 research papers about a given subject matter are more than the average number of research papers written about other subjects.

F is unsupported by the passage. Just because the passage uses 2010 as an example, this does not mean that 2010 was the record-setting year for interest in graphene. G is also incorrect for a similar reason. H is incorrect because even if the interest in graphene hadn't been so high, it's possible that the professors could have won the Nobel Prize in 2010. It's true that it's a possibility that a lower level of interest in graphene may have influenced the professors' winning of the Nobel Prize, but it's also possible that a lower level of interest may not have impacted the outcome at all. J is incorrect because the passage does not give any indication as to the timeline of when graphene may be used commercially. While it is not infeasible that graphene will be used in commercial products in the next 10 years, it's could be the case that graphene won't see incorporation into commercial products for more than 10 years.

(Kay Cottee)

45. **(C)** This passage is about introducing Kay Cottee, briefly discussing her background, and applauding her for her grand feat of being the first woman to circumnavigate the globe. Thus, C is the best answer.

A is incorrect because the passage is not about chronicling Kay Cottee's personal and professional life. While the passage does discuss what inspired Kay Cottee to become a sailor, it does not go into much detail about Kay Cottee's entire life. Moreover, chronicling her life is not the purpose of the passage. B is incorrect because the passage's main purpose is not to explain how and why Kay Cottee became a sailor, even though the process of her becoming a sailor is certainly one aspect of the passage. D is incorrect because the author does not use any language to indicate to the readers that they should set loftier goals for themselves. E is incorrect for a similar reason that D is incorrect; the author does not emphasize that many feats are left to be accomplished.

46. **(G)** In lines 51-56, the passage indicates that the official recorded time for Kay Cottee's circumnavigation was 189 days, 0 hours, and 32 minutes; in actuality, however, Kay Cottee arrived in 187 days. Thus, as far as we can tell, there was about a two-day difference between Kay Cottee's official time and her actual time. Thus G is the correct answer.

47. **(E)** Lines 48-50 state, "she was only able to survive because she was harnessed to her boat by two safety lines," which implies that if she had not been harnessed, she would have died. Thus, E is the correct answer.

A is incorrect because there is not enough information in the passage to support the idea that 70-foot waves can only be generated by 100-knot or faster winds. B is incorrect because it may have been possible for Kay Cottee to survive if she had only been harnessed to her boat with one safety line; she may not have been able to, but there is not enough evidence in the passage to argue either side. C is incorrect because there is not enough evidence in the passage to justify the idea that a casual sailor would have definitely drowned. D is incorrect because we don't know if the capsizing was the worst obstacle Kay Cottee had to overcome. While it certainly would be reasonable to suspect that capsizing in 70-foot waves would have likely been one of the biggest obstacles for Kay Cottee, there's not enough support to justify the notion that it was by far the worst.

48. **(J)** Lines 39-43 define global circumnavigation. It requires the sailor to "span a distance of at least 21,600 nautical miles, cross the equator and every longitude, and finish in the same port." Only J accurately represents this. The other choices are either missing information or insert inaccuracies.

For instance, F omits the distance and equator and longitude crossing requirements. G is incorrect because it inserts a requirement that the sailor must cross every latitude, and it omits the equator crossing requirement and the distance requirement. H is incorrect because it inserts a latitude cross requirement. K is incorrect because it also inserts a latitude crossing requirement and omits the requirement of having to start and finish at the same port.

49. **(D)** Kay named her yacht *Jimmy Mac* in honor of her father. Lines 32-34 specifically state that she changed the name in order to get the sponsorship from Blackmores Laboratories. Thus, it can be inferred that she would not have changed the name to *Cinnamon Scrub* if she didn't need to get a sponsorship.

A is incorrect because the passage does not say that Blackmores Laboratories was Kay's only option for a sponsorship and that she had no chance of ever getting a sponsorship from anyone else. B is not correct. While Kay's father likely did play a role in her development as a sailor, there's not enough information to conclude she would not have gotten into sailing, if it weren't for him. C is incorrect because lines 27-31 indicate that Linda Wayman was Kay Cottee's partner for only the Two-Handed Trans-Tasman race. E is incorrect because it is unsupported by the passage; the passage does not state that Kay Cottee was the only woman to ever successfully complete a global circumnavigation.

50. **(F)**   The author clearly respects Kay Cottee. Words such as "exceptional" (lines 5-6) and "incredible" (line 63) indicate the author's admiration for Kay Cottee. It is also apparent the author feels bewilderment towards Kay Cottee's sponsor's decision to make her wait until Sunday to arrive in Sydney Harbor—lines 59-60 indicate the author's bewilderment and inability to understand Kay Cottee's sponsor's decision.

G is incorrect because "disgust" is too strong of a word. H is incorrect because the author does not use language to indicate skepticism about the reports that Kay could have survived 100-knot winds and 70-foot waves. J is incorrect because the author expresses admiration for Kay Cottee, not disdain. K is incorrect because the author is not completely objective. The author respects and admires Kay Cottee, so the author was not completely objective.

MATH EXPLANATIONS ▶

Answer Explanations – Mathematics
Practice Test 1

---

51. **(E)** To solve this problem, substitute 9 in for p and 16 in for n. You should get the following:

$$\frac{m}{45} = \frac{16}{9}$$

From here, we multiply both sides by 45. Since 45 divided by 9 equals 5, we get $m = 16 \times 5 = 80$, as shown below:

$$m = \frac{16 \times \cancel{45}^{\,5}}{\cancel{9}^{\,1}} = 16 \times 5 = 80$$

---

52. **(G)** Use the distributive property of multiplication to expand each side fully to get:

$5z + 12z + 15 = 4z - 24$, which is rewritten

$17z + 15 = 4z - 24$

Rearranging to get like terms on each side of the equation, we get:

$13z = -39 \rightarrow z = -3$

---

53. **(C)** If x is an even integer, it's not possible for $0.5(x + 1)$ to be even, since $(x + 1)$ is odd. Thus, one-half of an odd integer is necessarily a decimal number.

$2x + 1$ can be prime. If x is 1 or 2, or many other numbers, $2x + 1$ is prime. $x(x - 1)$ can equal 0, if $x = 0$. (Remember, 0 is an even integer.) $(x - 1)(x + 1)$ is always going to be odd, since $x - 1$ is odd and $x + 1$ is odd, if x is even. Finally, $x^2 + 6x + 9$ is odd because x^2 is even and $6x$ is even when x is even. Thus, $x^2 + 6x$ is even. The sum of an even number and an odd one (in this case, 9) is odd.

---

54. **(J)** Since 798 is a large number, the easiest way to approach this problem is to realize that 798 is even. Dividing 798 by 2 (a prime number), we get 399, which shouldn't be difficult to realize is divisible by 3 (a prime number). Dividing 399 by 3, we get 133. 133 is divisible by 7, which is prime, and 19, which is also prime.

Thus, the prime factors are 2, 3, 7, and 19. (Remember, 1 is not considered prime.)

Tip: It might be tempting to select H as an answer, since 133 isn't further divisible by 3, and it would take far too long to try dividing by 133 by guessed numbers. But since the other answer choices contain other numbers, and we're looking at prime factorization, try dividing 133 by the numbers available in the other answer choices.

---

55. **(B)** First, do the subtraction by finding the common denominator, which is 45:

$$\left(\frac{4}{9} - \frac{7}{15}\right) = \left(\frac{20}{45} - \frac{21}{45}\right) = -\frac{1}{45}$$

Next, do the fraction division to arrive at the correct answer:

$$-\frac{1}{45} \div \frac{13}{10} = -\frac{1}{{}_{9}\cancel{45}} \times \frac{\cancel{10}^{\,2}}{13} = -\frac{2}{117}$$

---

56. **(K)** First, find the values of the absolute value expressions. Then, make those positive and simplify the resulting fraction:

$$\frac{3|5 - 2 - 7|}{|(1 - 2) - \frac{1}{2}(10)|} = \frac{3|-4|}{|(-1) - 5|} = \frac{3(4)}{6} = \frac{12}{6} = 2$$

57. (D) Ahmed has 23 crayons. 7 are blue, 6 are green, and the rest are gray. This means that he has 10 gray crayons.

7 crayons are removed, meaning there are 16 crayons left in the box. The probability of picking a gray crayon out of these 16 crayons is now 0.25, which means that 4 of the 16 crayons are gray. This means that Ahmed had removed 6 gray crayons, which means that the final crayon that was removed was either a blue crayon or a green crayon.

Since there are 13 possible crayons that the other removed crayon could have been selected from, and 7 were blue and 6 were green, the probability that Ahmed removed a blue crayon from the box is 7 out of 13.

58. (F) The bar over the last three digits of the shown decimal number indicate that the decimal repeats those three digits infinitely. To figure out what improper fraction the decimal number is worth, we need to find a way to eliminate the fraction. We can do so by doing the following:

If $N = 3.462462...$, then $1000N$ would equal $3,462.462462...$

Subtracting N from $1000N$ would yield $999N = 3459$.

Dividing both sides by 999, we get

$$N = \frac{3459}{999} = \frac{1153}{333}$$

Tip: In this case, we can fairly easily see that 3459 is divisible by 3, since 3, 45, and 9 are all divisible by 3. But, in more ambiguous cases, it is helpful to know that if the sum of a digits of a number is a multiple of 3, then the number is divisible by 3.

59. (B) The union of Sets V and W is the range of numbers from 930 to 1113, inclusive. To find how many distinct numbers there are in this range of numbers, subtract 930 from 1113 and add 1. (The one has to be added to account for the first number you're starting with.) The answer is 184.

60. (J) Negative exponents flip fractions, so what we're actually dealing with is:

$$\left(-\frac{161^3}{23^4} \right)^{-1} = -\frac{23^4}{161^3}$$

Since 161 is divisible by 23 and 7, we can rewrite the above as:

$$-\frac{23^4}{161^3} = -\frac{23^4}{(23 \times 7)^3} = -\frac{23}{7^3} = -\frac{23}{343}$$

61. (A) Since E and F are midpoints of segments AD and CD, respectively, E's coordinates are (0, 4) and F's are (4, 0). To find the coordinates of the point of intersection of segments BE and AF, find equations for the lines of which the segments are parts.

The equation of the line containing BE is $y = \frac{1}{2}x + 4$, since $m = \frac{8-4}{8-0} = \frac{4}{8} = \frac{1}{2}$ and the y-intercept of the line is point E.

The equation of the line containing AF is $y = -2x + 8$, since $m = \frac{0-8}{4-0} = \frac{-8}{4} = -2$ and the y-intercept of the line is point A.

Next, set the equations of the lines equal to each other, as such: $\frac{1}{2}x + 4 = -2x + 8$

Solving for x yields $2.5x = 4$, which yields $x = \frac{4}{2.5} = \frac{40}{25} = \frac{8}{5} = 1.6$

Substituting in the value of x into the equation $y = -2x + 8$, for instance, we get $y = -3.2 + 8 = 4.8$, for (1.6, 4.8).

62. (G) To find the least common multiple of 510 and 1,122, first find the prime factors.

510's prime factors: $2 \times 5 \times 3 \times 17$
(Recognize 510 is divisible by 10 and 51.)

1,122's prime factors: $2 \times 11 \times 3 \times 17$
(First, recognize 1,122 is divisible by 11. $1,122 \div 11 = 102 = 2 \times 51 = 2 \times 3 \times 17$.)

Since 510 and 1,122 share 2, 3, and 17 as prime factors, those factors count once when finding the least common multiple.

$2 \times 3 \times 17 = 102$

Then, we multiply 102 by the factors that did not overlap, which are 5 and 11:

$102 \times 5 \times 11 = 5,610$

---

63. (C) There are 9 possible unique cones.

There are three possible cones that can be made without any toppings, one for each flavor of ice cream.

Then there are 6 possible cones that can be made with one topping, since two possible toppings exist for each flavor of ice cream.

---

64. (J) 1 cm on the blueprint represents 7 feet in actuality, so 1 cm^2 represents 49 ft^2 in actuality. Thus, 1×70 cm^2 represents 49×70 ft^2 in actuality, which is 3,430 ft^2.

---

65. (D) If Audrey scored a mean of 4 goals in 5 field hockey games, that means she scored 20 goals altogether in 5 games. If she scored a mean of 3 goals in 3 of those 5 games, that means she scored 9 goals in those 3 games. That leaves 11 goals she needs to score in 2 games. If she scored 8 in one of the other two games (since she can't score more than 8), the least she could have scored was 3 in either of those two games.

66. (J) First, get rid of all of the decimals to make the problem look like:

539 jings = 1540 hings
49 hings = 28 gings

Thus, 1 ging = $\dfrac{7}{4}$ hings.

1540 and 539 are also divisible by 7 to get 220 and 77, respectively, which we can express as 220 hings = 77 jings. Then, divide both sides by 11 to get 20 hings = 7 jings.

Thus, 1 hing = $\dfrac{7}{20}$ jings.

To find how many jings 1 ging is equal to, consolidate the two equations as such:

$$\frac{7}{4} \times 1 \text{ hing} = \frac{7}{4} \times \frac{7}{20} \text{ jings} = \frac{49}{80} \text{ jings}$$

---

67. (B) Since Lisanne is 42, and Sandra is 14, Lisanne is 3 times as old as Sandra is, which means n is 3. Lisanne is $2n + 3$ years older than Alexis is. Substitute 3 for n, and we see that Lisanne is 9 years older than Alexis is, which makes Alexis 33.

---

68. (J) When octane and ethanol are mixed together in a ratio of 9 to 1, the resulting volume is 80% of the sum of the individual volumes. Thus, to fill a 1,000-gallon container:

$1,000 = 0.8V$, where V is the sum of the volumes. Divide by 0.8 to get $V = 1,250$.

Since the octane and ethanol are mixed in a ratio of 9 to 1, the volume of ethanol is one-tenth of 1,250, or 125, gallons:

Thus, the volume of octane: $1,250 - 125 = 1,125$

69. **(E)** If Kon cuts out a square of side length 3x inches from each corner of the rectangular piece of cardboard and folds up the resulting flaps, he will have a box with a height of 3x inches, or 0.25x feet (dividing 3x by 12 to convert inches to feet), and side lengths of [3 − 2(0.25x)] and [4 − 2(0.25x)] feet. Thus, after simplifying, we get the following expression:

$$V = 0.25x(3 - 0.5x)(4 - 0.5x)$$

70. **(H)** Because 1.5 inches goes perfectly into 24 inches 16 times, 36 inches 24 times, and 18 inches 12 times, the box will fit 16 × 24 × 12 = 4,608 sugar cubes. A bag of 5,000 sugar cubes costs $25, so we can set up the following ratio to determine the value of the sugar cubes in the box:

$$\frac{4,608}{5,000} = \frac{x}{\$25}$$

Multiply both sides by $25 to get:

$$x = \frac{4,608 \times \$25^{1}}{_{200}5,000} = \frac{\$4,608}{200} = \frac{\$2,304}{100}$$

This is equal to $23.04.

71. **(D)** The population of the super colony is 45,000 ants. 2% of that is 900 ants, which represents the number of drones there are in the colony. To find the number of soldiers, we have to do the following operation:

45,000 − (9 + 36,000 + 900) = 8,091 soldier ants

To find what percent of the number of soldier ants is the number of drones:

$$\frac{900}{8,091} \times 100\% = 11.12\%$$

72. **(G)** The circumference of Car A's tires is 20π inches. It travels 16,000π feet, but we need to convert this to inches by multiplying by 12, which is 192,000π inches.

If Car B, whose tires have a radius that's x times the radius of Car A's tires, also traveled 192,000π inches, but did so after its tires spun 3,840 times, the circumference of each of its tires is:

$$\frac{192,000\pi}{3,840} = 50\pi \text{ inches}$$

Thus, the circumference of Car B's tires is 2.5 times (50π ÷ 20π) that of Car A's, which further means that the radius of Car B's tires is 2.5 times that of Car A's.

73. **(C)** The total fish population before any were sold was 650, of which there are 340 pink and yellow fish combined. A total of 85 pink and yellow fish were sold Thursday, which leaves 255 pink and yellow fish and a total fish population of 565. If the population of pink and yellow fish is to be five-sevenths of the total fish population, the total fish population needs to be:

$$255 = \frac{5}{7}x$$

$$x = \frac{7 \times 255^{51}}{_{1}5} = 357$$

Since the total fish population needs to be 357, 208 blue fish must be sold for the combined population of pink and yellow fish to be five-sevenths the total fish population.

74. **(G)** If (2, 3) is reflected over the y-axis, the result is (-2, 3). If (2, -3) is then shifted to the left by 3 units, you get (-5, 3).

When a point (a, b) is reflected over the line y = x, the new coordinates look like (b, a). When (a, b) is reflected over the x-axis, the result is $(a, -b)$, and when (a, b) is reflected over the y-axis, the result is $(-a, b)$.

If $(-5, 3)$ is reflected over $y = x$, the result is $(3, -5)$. If $(3, -5)$ is shifted up 8 units, the result is $(3, 3)$. If $(3, 3)$ is shifted to the left one unit, the result is $(2, 3)$. Thus, F is incorrect.

If $(-5, 3)$ is reflected over the y-axis, the result is $(5, 3)$. If this point is shifted right by 3 units, the result is $(8, 3)$. Thus, G is correct.

If $(-5, 3)$ is reflected over the x-axis, the result is $(-5, -3)$. If $(-5, -3)$ is shifted to the right by 7 units, the result is $(2, -3)$. If $(2, -3)$ is reflected over the x-axis again, the result is $(2, 3)$. Thus, H is incorrect.

If $(-5, 3)$ is shifted to the right by 7 units, you get $(2, 3)$. Thus, J is incorrect.

If $(-5, 3)$ is reflected over the y-axis, $(5, 3)$ results. If $(5, 3)$ is shifted left by 3 units, the result is $(2, 3)$. Thus, K is incorrect.

---

75. **(C)** Convert pounds to tons, as such:

$16,380 \div 2,000 = 8.19$ tons

Set up proportions to find how much food the larger battalion requires in 5 weeks:

$$\frac{x}{8.19} = \frac{520 + 780}{520} = \frac{1,300}{520}$$

Solving for x, we get

$$x = \frac{8.19 \times \cancel{1,300}^{5}}{{}_{2}\cancel{520}} = 8.19 \times 2.5 = 20.475$$

This number is represents the tons of rations the larger battalion needs for 3 weeks. To find how much it'll need for 5 weeks, multiply this result by 5/3 to get 34.125 tons.

76. **(G)** Since a is one-half of b, where a is a 2-digit number and b is a 3-digit number, a must be greater than 50, which leaves 5, 6, and 7 as possible choices for the first digit of a. Doubling any number greater than or equal to 50, but less than 100, leads to a 3-digit number greater than or equal to 100 but less than 200. Thus, b's first digit is 1.

Next, deduce that a's first digit cannot be 5. Doubling any number in the 50s leads to a 3-digit number that's greater than 100 but less than 120, or a number from the set $\{100, 102, \ldots 116, 118\}$. The problem is that 0 is not included in the original set of numbers we can choose numbers from and the 1 cannot be repeated. Thus, the first digit of a can either be 6 or 7.

If a's first digit is 6:

Because b is even, and digits don't overlap between a and b, b must end in 2 or 4. But if b's last digit is 2, that means a's last digit is 1 (since 6 cannot be repeated), which doesn't work, since 1 would have to be repeated between a and b.

If b's last digit is 4, the last digit of a has to be 7, to give $a = 67$ and $b = 134$.

If a's first digit is 7:

b's last digit can be 2, 4, or 6. If b's last digit is 2, a must be 71 or 76, and b must be 142 or 152. a cannot be 71, however, since 1 cannot repeat. $a = 76$ and $b = 152$.

If b's last digit is 4, a must be 72 (since a cannot be 77) and b must be 144. But, as we can see, 4 is repeated. Thus, this is not a possible solution, either.

If b's last digit is 6, a must be 73 (since a cannot be 78, as 8 is not an option) and b must be 146.

There are 3 possibilities for a and b: $a = 67$, $b = 134$; $a = 73$, $b = 146$; and $a = 76$, $b = 152$

77. **(E)** The ratio of girls to boys in the robotics club is 3 to 4, so that means there are $3x$ girls and $4x$ boys in the club. If there are 27 girls, that means x is 9. That in turns means there are 36 boys. $27 + 36 = 63$ club members.

78. **(F)** First, find Yoshi and Luigi's rates of mowing the smaller lawn:

$$\text{Yoshi's rate} = \frac{1\ \text{lawn}}{45\ \text{min}} = \frac{1\ \text{lawn}}{\frac{3}{4}\ \text{hr}} = \frac{4\ \text{lawn}}{3\ \text{hr}}$$

$$\text{Luigi's rate} = \frac{1\ \text{lawn}}{60\ \text{min}} = \frac{1\ \text{lawn}}{1\ \text{hr}} = \frac{1\ \text{lawn}}{\text{hr}}$$

$$\text{Combined rate} = \frac{4}{3} + 1\ \frac{\text{lawn}}{\text{hr}} = \frac{7\ \text{lawn}}{3\ \text{hr}}$$

Since the larger lawn is equivalent to 14 of the smaller lawn, use the following equation to find how much time is needed to mow the larger lawn:

$$14\ \text{lawns} = \frac{7\ \text{lawns}}{3\ \text{hrs}} \times t\ \text{hrs}$$

Solve for t: $t = \frac{14 \times 3}{7} = 6$ hrs

79. **(B)** After Juanita gives Connor one-fourth of her pens, Connor, who had y pens to start, now has $y + \frac{1}{4}x$ pens. Connor then gives Ramone two-fifths of his new pen total. Since Ramone is now up 30 more pens than he started out with, that means Ramone's new pen total is now:

$$z + \frac{2}{5}\left(y + \frac{1}{4}x\right) = z + 30$$

Thus, after converting the fractions to decimals, we see that the number of pens Ramone received is $0.4(y + 0.25x) = 30$.

80. **(F)** 1,000 millimeters = 1 meter, so if you square both sides, you get 1,000,000 square millimeters = 1 square meter. As such, 10,000 square meters equals 10,000,000,000 square millimeters, which equals 1 hectare. To find the hectare equivalent of 10 square millimeters, divide by 1 hectare by 1,000,000,000. Thus, 1 hectare = 10^{-9} square millimeters.

81. **(B)** Substitute 4 for x into the expression:

$$\frac{(4-6)(4+8)}{2(\frac{1}{2}(4)-3)(4+2)} = \frac{-2 \times 12}{2(-1)(6)} = \frac{-24}{-12} = 2$$

82. **(H)** A rational number is one that can be expressed in the form p/q, where p and q are integers.

F can be expressed as a rational number:

$$-(\sqrt{7} - \sqrt{13})^2(\sqrt{7} + \sqrt{13})^3(\sqrt{7} - \sqrt{13}) =$$
$$-(\sqrt{7} - \sqrt{13})^3(\sqrt{7} + \sqrt{13})^3 =$$
$$-((\sqrt{7} - \sqrt{13})(\sqrt{7} + \sqrt{13}))^3 =$$
$$-(7 - 13)^3 = -(-6)^3 = 216$$

G can be expressed as a rational number:

$$((1 - \sqrt{2})(1 + \sqrt{2})) = 1 - 2 = -1$$

J can be expressed as a rational number:

$$\frac{(2-\sqrt{5})(2+\sqrt{5})}{4-5} - \frac{3\pi}{7\pi} = \frac{4-5}{4-5} - \frac{3}{7} = 1 - \frac{3}{7} = \frac{4}{7}$$

K can be expressed as a rational number:

$$\frac{3-\pi}{4} + \frac{8\pi^2}{32\pi} = \frac{3-\pi}{4} + \frac{\pi}{4} = \frac{3}{4}$$

83. **(B)** In the school district, the total spent on teachers' salaries is $1{,}698 \times \$54{,}100 =$

$91,861,800 annually. If the district's budget is $500,000,000, then the education budget is

$$\frac{\$91,816,000}{\$500,000,000} = 0.1837236... \approx 18.37\%$$

---

84. **(H)** If 2(OP) = 3(NO), that means OP is 1.5(NO). Let NO = x cm; then OP = 1.5x cm and NP = 2.5x cm. The following statements are true:

1) MN + 2.5x = 33
2) 2.5x + PQ = 51

Since PQ = 2(MN), we can substitute 2(MN) in for PQ. We get the following re-written equations:

1) MN + 2.5x = 33
2) 2(MN) + 2.5x = 51

If we subtract the first equation from the second, we find that MN = 18 cm, which means 2.5x = 15 cm. Divide both sides by 2.5 to get x = 6 cm.

---

85. **(B)** When the number of customers served each day is rearranged from smallest to greatest, we get: 103, 119, 123, 176, 202, and 231.

The median is the average of the two middle numbers when there is an even number of numbers. In our case, it's the average of 123 and 176: 149.5.

The mean of our data set is (103 + 119 + 123 + 176 + 202 + 231) ÷ 6 = 954 ÷ 6 = 159.

The difference is thus 159 − 149.5 = 9.5.

---

86. **(J)** Let x be the number of marbles Albert originally had, and let y be the number of marbles Jeamine originally had. After giving Albert 16 marbles, Jeamine has twice as many marbles as Albert does now. In mathematical notation:

$$y - 16 = 2(x + 16) \rightarrow y = 2x + 48$$

From the first sentence of the problem, we can also write this equation:
$x = \frac{3}{13}(x + y)$, which can be arranged as $13x = 3x + 3y$, or $10x = 3y$.

We can rewrite the equation $y = 2x + 48$ as $3y = 6x + 144 = 10x$. We can solve for x:

$$4x = 144 \rightarrow x = 36$$

Substitute 36 for x in the first rewritten equation to get $y = 2(36) + 48 = 120$.

The total number of marbles they had together is thus 36 + 120 = 156.

---

87. **(C)** Each cup of coffee costs Jacie $0.75 + $0.15 = $0.90. Since Jacie makes $2.25 per cup, her profit per cup is $1.35. But since Jacie needs to pay $560.00 per week, she needs to sell $560.00 ÷ $1.35 = 414.814 cups every week to break even. But since she cannot sell partial cups, she must sell 415 cups every week to break even.

---

88. **(G)** If the water level in the cup rose 1 inch, the total volume of the 6 marbles equals the volume of a cylinder with a height of 1 inch and radius of 4 inches.

The volume of a cylinder is $\pi r^2 h$, so plugging in 4 and 1 for r and h, respectively, yields $\pi(4)^2(1) = 16\pi$ in.^{3} The volume of one marble is thus:

$$\frac{16\pi}{6} = \frac{8\pi}{3} \text{ in.}^3$$

121

89. (B) Fay kayaked three-fifths of a kilometer upstream in 4 minutes, or 240 seconds. Her net rate, in m/s, is therefore:

$$\frac{0.6 \text{ km}}{240 \text{ s}} = \frac{600 \text{ m}}{240 \text{ s}} = \frac{60 \text{ m}}{24 \text{ s}} = \frac{5}{2} \text{ m/s}$$

Because her net speed upstream was 2.5 m/s, Fay's speed in still water would have been 5.0 m/s, since she was rowing against a current that was flowing at 2.5 m/s. Thus, Fay's downstream speed would have been 7.5 m/s.

At 7.5 m/s, it would have taken Fay

$$\frac{600 \text{ m}}{7.5 \text{ m/s}} = 80 \text{ s} \text{ to kayak downstream.}$$

It would have taken Fay $240 - 80 = 160$ s less if she had kayaked downstream.

---

90. (J) The two smallest distinct prime numbers greater than 35 are 37 and 41, which add to 78, which is also the sum of three consecutive even integers:

$x + (x + 2) + (x + 4) = 78$, which can be simplified to: $3x + 6 = 78$. Solve for x:

$$3x = 72 \rightarrow x = 24 \rightarrow x + 4 = 28.$$

---

91. (A) The box has dimensions of 20 cm per side (the cubed root of 8,000 cm³), so the sphere fits the box, since the sphere has a radius of 10 cm, or diameter of 20 cm. To find the amount of water that needs to be added to fill the box up, find the difference of the volumes of the box and sphere:

$$8,000 \text{ cm}^3 - \frac{4}{3}\pi(10)^3 \text{ cm}^3 =$$

$$8,000 - \frac{4,000}{3}\pi \text{ cm}^3 = 4,000\left(2 - \frac{\pi}{3}\right)$$

mL

92. (F) If B is the midpoint of AC, $x = 9$, since the distance from A to B is 8, which means that the distance from B to C is 8, as well. Since F is the midpoint of AB, F's coordinate is -3. G's coordinate is 5.

If y represents the range of numbers on the number line, then the range of values from F to G must include the numbers from -3 to 5. Only F truly represents this:

The absolute value inequality $|y - 1| \leq 4$ can be solved when it is broken down into the following two inequalities:

$$y - 1 \leq 4 \text{ and } y - 1 \geq -4$$

Solving for the first, we get $y \leq 5$ as the upper bound. Solving for the second, we get $y \geq -3$ as the lower bound, which perfectly denotes the range from F to G.

Note: The second inequality uses the "greater than or equal to" sign and -4.

---

93. (C) Let x represent the pounds of nuts used in the trail mix, y the pounds of chocolate, and z the pounds of dried berries. The cost of trail mix can be expressed as: $\$0.95x + \$1.30y + \$0.40z$.

Because $x = 2z$ and $y = 3z$, based on the ratio of 2 : 3 : 1, we can substitute $2z$ and $3z$ in for x and y, respectively, to get:

$$\$0.95(2z) + \$1.30(3z) + \$0.40z = \$1.90z + \$3.90z + \$0.40z = \$6.20z$$

Thus, the cost of trail mix is $6.20 for every pound of dried berries used, or 6 pounds of trail mix. (Remember the nuts and chocolates, too. Every pound of dried berries is mixed with 2 pounds of nuts and 3 pounds of chocolates, for a total of 6 pounds.) As $1.55 is one-fourth of $6.20, the amount of trail mix that can be bought is one-fourth of 6 pounds, which is 1.5 pounds.

94. (G) Use the distance formula of $d = rt$, where d stands for distance, r for rate, and t for time.

Amos drove 450 miles at an average rate of 75 miles per hour. To find the time it took him to get there, apply the equation above to get $450 = 75t$ or $t = 6$ hours. On the way back, Amos also drove 450 miles, but at a rate of 60 miles per hour. The time he spent driving home was $450 = 60t$ or $t = 7.5$ hours.

Thus, the total time driving was 13.5 hours and the total distance was 900 miles. Amos's overall rate for the trip was $900 = 13.5r$ → $r = 66.67$ miles per hour.

95. (C) The inequality for the range of x values is $-4 \leq x \leq 6$, after dividing every term of the inequality by $\frac{3}{2}$. Similarly, the inequality for the range of y values is $-6 \leq y \leq 2$, after dividing every term by $\frac{2}{3}$.

This means that the range of values for z can be expressed by the inequality $-6 \leq z \leq 6$, since all of the unique values of x and y are part of the range of values for z.

96. (J) Let x be the number of pens and y the number of pencils. Write a system of equations and then manipulate the equations as below, to be able to eliminate a variable:

$3x + 8y = \$3.05 \xrightarrow{\times 4} 12x + 32y = \$12.20$

$4x + 3y = \$3.07 \xrightarrow{\times 3} 12x + 9y = \$9.21$

Subtract the bottom equation from the top to get $23y = \$2.99$ or $y = \$0.13$. Using substitution, we can find x:

$3x + 8(\$0.13) = \$3.05$ →
$3x + \$1.04 = \$3.05$ →
$3x = \$2.01$ → $x = \$0.67$ →
$x + y = \$0.13 + \$0.67 = \$0.80.$

97. (B) In order to find the proportion of the circle trapped between line m and the transversals s and t, we must find x.

The angles of the triangle have measures of $x°$, $(x - 5)°$, and $[180 - (x + 70)]°$. $x°$ is given in the figure. $(x - 5)°$ is true because of the vertical angle theorem. $[180 - (x + 70)]°$ is true because the third angle of the triangle is supplementary to $(x + 70)°$. Thus:

$x° + (x - 5)° + [180 - (x + 70)]° = 180°$ →

$x + (x - 5)° + (110 - x)° = 180°$ →

$(x + 105)° = 180°$ → $x = 75$

As such, the proportion of the circle trapped between lines m, s, and t is:

$$\frac{75°}{360°} = \frac{5}{24}$$

98. (K) The area of the smaller square is 48 yd^2, since its area is half that of the square with area 96 yd^2. The side length of this square is $\sqrt{48}$ yd, which can be rewritten as $\sqrt{16 \times 3}$ yd, or further as $4\sqrt{3}$ yd. The perimeter would therefore be $4 \times 4\sqrt{3}$ yd = $16\sqrt{3}$ yd.

99. (A) First, convert cubic yards to cubic feet:

1 yd = 3 ft → 1 yd^3 = 27 ft^3

Since the original price of the concrete is \$96.00 per cubic yard, that translates to \$96.00 per 27 cubic feet.

With a 15% discount, the price becomes:

\$96 − 0.15(\$96.00) = \$81.60 per 27 cubic feet, which is equal to \$3.02 per cubic foot (divide \$81.60 by 27), when rounded to the nearest cent.

AE

100. (H) Since we are looking at the distance traveled by the center of the circle with radius 1 inch, we can break the problem down into two distinct components: the distance the center travels parallel to the edges of the square and the distance the center travels when rounding the corners of the square.

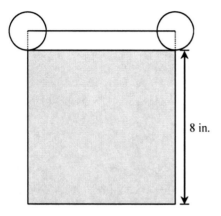

As you can see, the distance parallel to the side of the square is the same length as the side of the square itself. And since there are four sides, the distance that the center of the circle travels parallel to the sides of the square is 32 inches.

What's more tricky is figuring out the distance the center of the circle travels along the corners of the square.

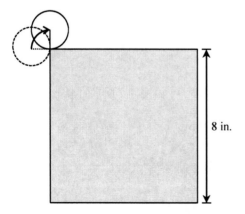

Notice in the diagram that the center of the circle must pivot. In doing so, it travels the distance of the circumference of a quarter circle with a radius of 1 inch, or $\frac{1}{4} \times 2\pi r$, where r is 1 inch, in this case. Thus, for each corner, the center of the circle travels $\frac{1}{2}\pi$ inches. Since there are 4 corners, the center travels a total of 2π inches.

All told, the center of the circle travels:

$32 + 2\pi$ inches around a square whose side length is 8 inches.

SHSAT
NYC EDITION
TEST KEY 2

AK

Answer Key – Test 2

VERBAL

SCRAMBLED PARAGRAPHS

Paragraph 1
USTQR

Paragraph 2
TQUSR

Paragraph 3
USQRT

Paragraph 4
RTSUQ

Paragraph 5
SRUQT

LOGICAL REASONING

11. C
12. H
13. B
14. K
15. D
16. G
17. B
18. J
19. A
20. H

READING

21. E
22. J
23. D
24. J
25. A
26. G
27. D
28. K
29. B
30. H
31. D
32. F
33. E
34. H
35. B
36. J
37. C
38. K
39. A
40. J
41. D
42. K
43. C
44. J
45. D
46. G
47. B
48. K
49. A
50. J

Answer Key – Test 2

MATHEMATICS

51. D		76. K
52. H		77. E
53. D		78. G
54. G		79. A
55. B		80. H
56. J		81. D
57. D		82. H
58. H		83. B
59. E		84. J
60. K		85. C
61. D		86. H
62. G		87. C
63. A		88. H
64. G		89. A
65. C		90. K
66. J		91. E
67. C		92. G
68. F		93. E
69. A		94. J
70. K		95. D
71. B		96. F
72. K		97. B
73. D		98. J
74. J		99. C
75. E		100. G

VERBAL EXPLANATIONS ▶

Answer Explanations – Verbal
Practice Test 2

SCRAMBLED PARAGRAPHS

Paragraph 1 (USTQR)

The lead sentence mentions New York City's Board of Health's December 5, 2006, decision to ban *trans* fats in city restaurants.

Sentence U follows the lead because it connects the lead to the next sentence, which is S, since S discusses the first milestone victory for healthy living. S discusses the FDA's requirement that all packaged foods list *trans* fats under their Nutrition Facts. S comes after U because the FDA's requirement was passed on January 1, 2006, 11 months earlier than New York City's Board of Health's decision, so chronologically, S happened first.

T comes after S because neither Q nor R makes sense after S. Thus, T acts as a transition. R must follow Q because Q introduces who Normann is. Thus, it only makes sense that Q follows T, which completes the paragraph.

Note: For this paragraph, we had to unscramble it backwards chronologically.

Paragraph 2 (TQUSR)

The lead sentence introduces the notion that the turkey tail mushroom may be able to provide some insight about how cancer may be combatted.

T follows the lead because it generally discusses how cancer works. Q follows T because Q provides the backdrop for how cancer cells exploit a "flaw" in the body's defense and repair mechanisms. Moreover, Q follows T because the key biological processes mentioned in U include defense and repair mentioned in T. U follows Q by explaining how exactly cancer cells get circumvent the body's defense and repair mechanisms. S comes after U because it shows how the turkey tail mushroom can fight against cancer cells. Finally, R comes last because it expands on what was said in S.

Easy Clusters: QU is an easy cluster to make because U follows Q, since U refers to the cytokines brought up by Q. SR is an easy cluster because S provides additional details about the turkey tail mushroom.

Note: Neither S nor R comes after the lead sentence because not enough context has been provided for either to come after the lead. T does not come after Q and before U because U does not follow naturally from T. Since we know R comes logically after S, and S can't come immediately after the lead, either Q or T comes immediately after the lead. But since it doesn't make sense for T to come after either U or R, T must come first, which makes sense, since T provides an introduction to how cancers develop.

Paragraph 3 (USQRT)

The opening sentence talks about the success of the movie *300*. U follows the opening sentence because it refers to the movie by telling the reader what historical event the movie was based on. S follows U because it expands on U by providing additional details.

Q follows S because Q expands on S's mention of the massive Persian onslaught by making an estimate about the size of the Persian army and concluding that, regardless of the actual numbers, the Greeks were vastly outnumbered. R comes after Q because T logically follows R, since T refers to a victory that had already been mentioned and R states that the Persians had prevailed.

Easy Clusters: SQ and RT are easy clusters to make. Once it becomes obvious that S follows U and U comes after the lead, the complete order is revealed.

Paragraph 4 (RTSUQ)

The lead sentence puts forth the question why Uncle Sam is the name for the personification of the United States.

R comes after the lead because it states that no one knows the answer to the question posed by the lead sentence. Furthermore, it speculates that it would make sense for "Uncle Sam" to have its origins traceable to someone famous or important. T follows R because T states that several theories have been posited and the one that's most commonly accepted attributes Uncle Sam to someone who was not famous or important in society. S follows T because it is the first time that the name Samuel Wilson is introduced, and both Q and U refer to Samuel Wilson by his last name.

U comes after S because U explains in more depth about Samuel Wilson's job as a meatpacker. Samuel Wilson had to stamp "U.S." on the barrels of beef he sent out. Q comes after U because Q discusses what happened after the soldiers received the barrels of beef. Moreover, Q makes the paragraph come full circle and we understand how the United States started to become personified as Uncle Sam.

Easy Clusters: RT and SUQ are the easiest clusters to make. After realizing that R must come after the lead, the order of the sentences becomes apparent.

Paragraph 5 (SRUQT)

The lead sentence states that James Marshall and John Sutter did not want to share the news of their discovery of gold at Sutter's Mill but that it was perhaps inevitable that word would eventually get out.

Sentence S comes after the lead sentence because it explains why Marshall and Sutter did not want to share the news of their discovery of gold and why they were unable to contain their excitement. R follows S because R is about the consequence of Sutter and Marshall's inability to keep their news completely contained; at least one newspaper reported that gold had turned up at Sutter's Mill. U

comes after R because U references the report made by the newspaper. Q comes after U because Q discusses just how frenzied the local people in San Francisco became once they had proof that gold actually existed at Sutter's Mill. Finally, T comes last because it is about how news of finding gold spread from California to the entire nation and consequently resulted in the gold rush of 1849.

AE

LOGICAL REASONING

11. **(C)** The only solid piece of information we are given is that Jerry made 100 people laugh during his stand-up routine on Thursday night. We are not given information about how Jerry usually does with his routines. As such, it is not logically valid to conclude that Jerry is the funniest comedian. Nor is it valid to conclude that Jerry is a professional comedian, since the problem does not state that an amateur comedian cannot make more than 80 people laugh during a stand-up routine. C is correct; if Jerry is not the funniest professional comedian, there are other times when Jerry does not make at least 80 people laugh.

A is incorrect. There is no information to support the notion that no other comedian could make more than 80 people laugh per routine. B is incorrect, as it assumes that making 100 people laugh on Thursday night put his average over 80, but there isn't enough information to support such an assumption. D is incorrect; making 100 people laugh once is not the same as making 80 or more people laugh, on average, during his stand-up routines. E is incorrect because it assumes that Thursday night's performance made him the funniest comedian.

12. **(H)** Convert the sentences in the problem into logic if-then statements:

    1) If Won is at home, then he either writes or relaxes.
    2) If Won writes, then he does research.
    3) If Won relaxes, then he hums.

    Since these statements are given to be true, the contrapositive statements—and only the contrapositive statements—are also true:

    1) If Won is not either writing or relaxing, then he is not at home.
    2) If Won is not doing research, then he is not writing.
    3) If Won is not humming, then he is not relaxing.

H is correct, since Won has two options at home: write or study. If Won is writing, then he is also doing research, and if Won is relaxing, then he is also humming.

F is incorrect because Won doesn't have to be home to relax. G is incorrect because Won could be home doing research without writing. It's just that if Won is writing, then he must also be doing research, but not necessarily the other way around. J is incorrect because he could be humming while not relaxing. K is incorrect for the same reason G is incorrect.

13. **(B)** The simplest way to approach this problem is to add the total number of years that Sunnie spent studying various art media. This equates to $3 + 5 + 5 + 6 = 19$ years. Divide 19 by 3, since she can study a maximum of 3 art media per year, and we're looking for the least number of years Sunnie could have studied the different art media. Since 3 goes into 19 six times with a remainder of 1, Sunnie had to have spent at least 7 years studying the various media.

14. **(K)** Draw a chart or diagram to solve this problem, as below, where N stands for name and O stands for lunch order:

	1	2	3	4	5	6	7
N	J	P	S	D	C	H	B
O			P				

We can reasonably deduce from the problem that three students ordered spaghetti, since there's no mention that at least one of the students didn't buy lunch.

The key to solving this problem, after drawing in the above diagram, are the first two conditions listed in the problem. The two kids who got hamburgers stood in line next to each other. There are four possible ways that could happen: 1) J and P, 2) D and C, 3) C and H, or 4) H and B. Try plugging those combinations in to see what happens. You should notice some logical contradictions.

If J and P both bought hamburgers, and three kids ordered spaghetti, then out of the last four spots, at least two kids who ordered spaghetti will have to stand next to each other, which goes against the conditions of the problem. The same is true if either both D and C or both H and B ordered hamburgers. Thus, it can only be the case that both C and H ordered hamburgers. This is the only choice that provides spacing between the kids who ordered spaghetti. Having figured this out, we can draw the following chart or diagram:

	1	2	3	4	5	6	7
N	J	P	S	D	C	H	B
O		P		H	H		

From this, we can deduce that both D and B bought spaghetti because if either one of them didn't, then both J and P had to have bought spaghetti, which is contrary to the conditions given by the problem. At this point, there are two charts or diagrams that could accurately express the possible outcomes because, between J and P, it is unclear as to which bought spaghetti and which bought pizza.

	1	2	3	4	5	6	7
N	J	P	S	D	C	H	B
O	S	P	P	S	H	H	S

OR

	1	2	3	4	5	6	7
N	J	P	S	D	C	H	B
O	P	S	P	S	H	H	S

Thus, the correct answer is K.

15. **(D)** The only valid conclusion we can arrive at from the logic of the problem is that some of Birch School's athletes play at least 3 sports: field hockey, lacrosse, and either basketball or soccer. Thus, D is correct.

Note: B is incorrect because it is possible that none of the Birch School athletes who play field hockey and lacrosse also play soccer—

they could all play basketball instead. C is incorrect because it is possible that no Birch School basketball player plays lacrosse.

16. **(G)** The best way to approach this problem is to draw a chart or diagram that matches the children with their favorite games.

	J	P	S	L	A
C		X			
Ch		X			
G	X	X		X	X
B		X		X	X
S	X	O	X	X	X

(Ch represents checkers, O marks a favorite, and X marks not a favorite.)

The above chart was filled out as much as possible from the given conditions. From here, we can see that Stephen's favorite must be go. Also, because LaToya and Antoinette only have chess and checkers available, we can deduce that Jackson's favorite is backgammon:

	J	P	S	L	A
C	X	X	X		
Ch	X	X	X		
G	X	X	O	X	X
B	O	X	X	X	X
S	X	O	X	X	X

Thus, in order to fully know everyone's favorite game, if we know either of LaToya's or Antoinette's favorite game, then we can complete the entire chart. Thus, G is the correct answer.

17. **(B)** Draw a diagram or chart to solve this problem. We start out with:

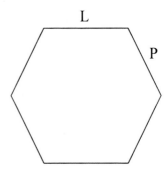

We realize that, since that magenta is directly across from turquois, the following configurations are possible:

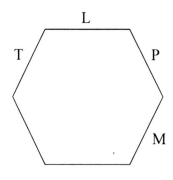

and

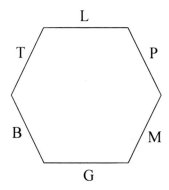

But since turquois is sitting immediately to the left of burgundy, the second choice does not work. Thus, the correct configuration is:

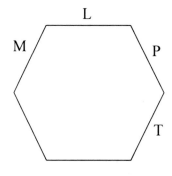

And we see that gold is between burgundy and magenta, which is represented by choice B.

18. **(J)**   Draw a diagram or chart to solve this problem, such as the following:

Entrée	Beverage	Dessert
S	J	~Y
C		B
M		~Y
F	I	

(The symbol ~ represents the word "not".)

Since the yogurt does not come with either the juice or the macaroni, the yogurt must come with the fish.

Entrée	Beverage	Dessert
S	J	
C		B
M		
F	I	Y

We now know that the root beer can come with either the chicken or the macaroni.

Case 1: Root Beer with Chicken

If the root beer comes with the chicken, the lemonade comes with the macaroni, and it is not known whether the fruit goes with the sandwiches or the macaroni.

Entrée	Beverage	Dessert
S	J	
C	R	B
M	L	
F	I	Y

Case 2: Root Beer with Macaroni

If the root beer comes with the macaroni, the fruit comes with the sandwich, since the fruit is not packaged with the root beer. This means the chicken comes with lemonade and macaroni comes with potato chips.

Entrée	Beverage	Dessert
S	J	F
C	L	B
M	R	P
F	I	Y

Note: It is tempting to look for an answer choice to go along with case 2, but do not fall for this trap. Instead, go through a careful analysis using the process of elimination, based on what we know from the two cases, particularly case 1, since that is open-ended.

Choice F is incorrect because even if we know that the sandwich comes with fruit, we are left with the question of which beverages the chicken and macaroni come with.

Choice G is incorrect because even if we know that the chicken comes with the root beer, we don't know what desserts the sandwich and macaroni come with.

Choice H is incorrect because knowing that the macaroni comes with the lemonade does not resolve which desserts come with the macaroni and the sandwich.

Choice K is incorrect because we already deduced that the fish comes with the yogurt, and that didn't reveal all of the exact pairings.

The correct answer choice is J. If the macaroni comes with the fruit, then the macaroni does not come with the root beer and comes with the lemonade instead. This in turn means that the root beer comes with the chicken. This then leaves the sandwich with the potato chips.

Entrée	Beverage	Dessert
S	J	P
C	R	B
M	L	F
F	I	Y

19. **(A)** Find the overlaps of the words to solve this problem and the next.

The following words have overlaps throughout the sentences: *we, going, today, later*.

We can see that *we* and *going* are present in both the first and second sentences, which means that they are represented by the letters Y and M. But note that the position of a letter is never the same as that of the word it represents. We see that in the second sentence that M is in the same position as *going* is in, which means M must represent *we*. Thus, choice A is correct.

Note: Having established that M represents *we*, we know that Y represents *going*.

20. **(H)** The letter J shows up in both the second and third sentences. The only word that shows up in both the second and third sentences is the word *later*. Thus, the correct answer is H.

READING ▶

READING

(Cell Phones)

21. **(E)** This passage is about the development of the first cell phone and why it was invented. Thus, choice E is the best answer.

A is incorrect because the passage does not discuss the complications that arose during the development and invention of the first cell phones. Although the first cell phones were not necessarily practical for daily use because of their heft, their size was not a complication that arose during their development. B is incorrect because it only discusses a small portion of what the passage is about. The statement made by B is not factually inaccurate, but it is not the main purpose of the passage. Much of the passage is about how the first cell phone was invented. C is incorrect because it is not the main idea of the passage, although the author does agree that cell phones are going to become more ubiquitous around the world. D is incorrect also because it only focuses on a small bit of the overall focus of the passage.

22. **(J)** The author assumes that the readers know who Alexander Graham Bell is. Even though you are not supposed to bring in outside knowledge while answering problems, this problem does not ask you to bring in outside knowledge. This question is simply asking you to realize that there was something significant about Alexander Graham Bell. We know this to be true because while Alexander Graham Bell is mentioned by name, his grandson's name is not. Thus, choice J is correct. Nothing else is mention of Alexander Graham Bell's grandson, thus choices F, G, and H are wrong. There is not enough information in the passage to suggest Alexander Graham Bell's grandson's age, his role (if any) in the development of the DynaTAC cell phone, or his role (if any) in Bell Labs. Similarly, K is incorrect because there is no mention of Alexander Graham Bell's father.

23. **(D)** In lines 26-29, the passage states that the first cell phone weighed as much as 30 ounces. Then in lines 41-43, the passage states that some modern cell phones weigh as little as 3 ounces. Thus, choice D is correct.

Choice A is incorrect because there's nothing in the passage to indicate that Bob Barnett worked for Motorola. Neither is there any indication that Motorola changed its name to Ameritech. Thus, B is wrong. C and E are also wrong because it's unsubstantiated by the passage. Note that these answer choices are trying to confuse you with the development of the first cell phone and the placement of the first call using the first commercial cell phone. In any case, the first commercial cell phone, which was released some 10 years after the first working prototype, was also manufactured by Motorola, not, as the answer choices want you to think, Ameritech. It happened to be that the first call was made by an Ameritech executive.

24. **(J)** The only answer choice supported by the passage is J. In lines 23-25, the passage states, "It weighed as much as or more than most contemporary ultrabook laptops do…"

F is incorrect because it assumes the audience knows what the world's population is. Furthermore, even if the total number of cell phone subscriptions totaled 84% of the world's population, this does not mean that each person that helps to constitute 84% of the world's population owns a cell phone; it is possible for a person to have more than one cell phone subscription. G is incorrect. Even though the passage does note that the cost of producing phones will go down, the passage does not indicate that cell phone prices will decrease in all available markets. The lower cost phones will presumably allow manufacturers to better reach lower end or emerging markets. H is incorrect because it assumes too much. Although the passage does state that there were 5.9 billion subscriptions by the end of 2011, there's nothing to indicate that the total number of subscriptions reached

6.2 billion by the end of 2012. K is incorrect because it is also unsubstantiated.

25. **(A)** Lines 6-11 indicate that people have already begun using their smartphones in place of many other, increasingly antiquated gadgets, such as the mp3 player. Thus, the author would disagree with the statement that mp3 players are as relevant as they used to be.

B is incorrect because, while the statement is not supported by the passage, it is not disproved, either. Thus, the author would disagree more with the statement made in A. C is incorrect because the author would agree with the statement, as made evident by lines 30-33. D is incorrect because lines 2-6 indicate that smartphones are capable of doing today what only computers could have done even in the late 1990s. Thus, the author would agree with the statement made in D. E is incorrect because the passage does not provide enough information to figure out whether the DynaTAC 8000X was more or less affordable than modern cellphones. Thus, it is not as clear whether the author would disagree or agree with E's statement.

26. **(G)** Lines 27-30 indicate that the first cell phone ever made weighed up to 30 ounces, or two ounces shy of two pounds. This means that 32 ounces equals 2 pounds, or 16 ounces equals 1 pound. Thus, the DynaTAC 8000X, which weighed 16 ounces, weighed 1 pound. Thus, G is correct. None of the other answer choices are substantiated by the passage.

(Neurogenesis)

27. **(D)** The passage is about neurogenesis, what it is, and what research was conducted recently to advance our understanding of it. Thus, D is the correct answer. Although D is phrased in broad terms, it is not incompatible with the passage.

A is incorrect because the passage does not support the notion that the question of how the human brain works is now answered. In

fact, in line 57, the passage states that many questions about the human brain remain. B is incorrect because, while the use of nuclear weapons did end up being the modality by which more about the dentate gyrus was understood, the passage does not argue that such an understanding would have been impossible without the nuclear weapons detonations. C is incorrect because it is too narrow in focus. It is true that radioactive isotopes of carbon helped scientists understand how the dentate gyrus works, but that is not the primary purpose of the passage. E is incorrect because the purpose of the passage is not to show much there is left to understand about the human brain.

28. **(K)** Lines 53-56 state that no new neurons are added to the brain, with the exception of the dentate gyrus, by age 2. This means that the brain is fully grown and mature by age 2.

F is incorrect because we do not know if the dentate gyrus is producing fewer than 500 neurons per day by age 92. The passage only states in lines 46-49 that an estimated 700 new neurons are created per day in adults, with that number decreasing modestly with age. The word modestly is not defined or qualified, so it is impossible to say that by 92, adult dentate gyruses produce fewer than 500 neurons per day. G is incorrect because there is no mention in the passage that the neurons produced in the dentate gyrus could replace neurons in the rest of the brain. H is incorrect because lines 61-64 indicate that the dentate gyrus possibly plays a significant role in the process of learning. J is incorrect because it is not stated that the dentate gyrus is formed after the brain has fully matured.

29. **(B)** Lines 61-64 state that it is possible that the dentate gyrus plays a significant role in the process of learning, which includes memory formation and the development of personalities. Thus, B is the correct answer.

A is incorrect because it assumes that 700 neurons out of 100 billion are all that a dentate gyrus ever creates. On top of that, the math is incorrect. 700 out of 100 billion is 0.0000007%, not 0.000007%. C is incorrect because the passage does not suggest or state that the safety concerns brought up in lines 8-12 are unverified. D is incorrect because lines 48-49 state that the rate of neurogenesis decreases modestly as people age. E is incorrect because the passage states that the researchers used carbon-14.

30. **(H)** Lines 4-17 indicate that in 1998 a team of scientists provided the first true evidence of neurogenesis in the adult hippocampus. But because of safety concerns with the scientists' methodology, the results could not be replicated. Moreover, the method could not shed light on the extent to which neurogenesis occurs. Thus, H is the correct answer.

F is incorrect because it is not supported anywhere in the passage. G is incorrect because there's no mention in the passage that the team was trying to continue its research. The research had been concluded; the experiment could not be replicated due to safety reasons, but that's different from being unable to continue its research. J is incorrect because it's not a limitation of the applicability of the research. K is not supported by the passage, either—we don't know if the team would have been able to continue its research or not.

31. **(D)** Lines 64-68 state that it is ironic that the greatest force of mass destruction served to provide the radioactive matter necessary to better understand the brain. Thus, D is the correct answer.

A is not ironic. B is not necessarily true. There is not enough information provided by the passage to conclude that the 700 neurons created by the dentate gyrus are just as important as the 100 billion neurons in the rest of the brain. Neither C nor E is ironic.

32. **(F)** F is the correct answer because the overall tone of the passage is objective. That is, its purpose is to convey information.

The author is not condescending, which means to be arrogant or to look down on, so G is incorrect. The author is not zealous, which means overly eager, and presumptuous, which means the author assumes too much, so H is not correct. The author is not aggravated, so J is incorrect. The author does not appear ill-informed, so K is incorrect.

(Fats)

33. **(E)** This passage is about unsaturated and saturated fats and explaining their differences. Furthermore, the passage explains how the differences in the characteristics of the fatty acids leads to different health effects. Thus, E best encapsulates the main idea of the passage.

A is incorrect because the focus of the passage is not the prevention of obesity. Nor is the passage mainly about the health risks that obesity poses. Thus, B is incorrect. C is incorrect. Molecular geometry is important, but it's not the main idea of the passage. D is an accurate statement, but it is incorrect because it is too narrow in scope to be the main idea of the passage.

34. **(H)** Lines 4-11 list some of the health risks of obesity: coronary heart disease, hypertension, type 2 diabetes, and certain types of cancer. Type 1 diabetes is not listed as a health risk in the passage. Thus, H is the correct answer.

35. **(B)** Use elimination to arrive at the correct answer. Lines 16-19 indicate that saturated fats are solid at room temperature, whereas unsaturated fats are not. Thus, A is incorrect. Lines 32-37 indicate that the stereoscopic structure of unsaturated fats is different from that of saturated fats because of the double bonds that unsaturated fats have. Thus, C is incorrect. D is incorrect because the hydrogen saturation level per aliphatic chain determines whether a fatty acid is saturated or not. E is incorrect because lines 28-31 state that the relative straightness of the aliphatic

chains permit saturated fatty acids to come closer together in proximity. After elimination, B is the only answer that remains.

36. **(J)** The correct answer here is J. In lines 41-50, the passage states that each aliphatic chain of monounsaturated fatty acids contains one double bond, whereas the aliphatic chains of polyunsaturated fatty acids each contains more than one double bond.

37. **(C)** Lines 51-73 talk about how the clustering ability of saturated fats is the culprit behind saturated fats' virulence. And then the passage discusses the health ramifications of what happens when arteries get clogged.

   A is incorrect. While it might be inferable that unsaturated fats are less dangerous than saturated fats, it is not supported by the passage that they're harmless. B is incorrect because the passage does not discuss *trans* fats. While the consumption of saturated fats may lead to health problems, the problem with D is that it uses the word "inevitably." E is incorrect because it doesn't account for the number of children in the United States. Because the percent of obese children is less than 35.7%, saying that the obesity rate is over 35.7% is mathematically unsound.

38. **(K)** Lines 51-73 discuss the potential consequences of consuming saturated fats. The only one not listed is K. While cholesterol and calcium are two of the other components of arterial plaque, there is no indication that the consumption of saturated fats leads to their increased production.

(Rhinoceros Poaching)

39. **(A)** This passage is about why rhinoceroses are being poached to the brink of extinction, and, in the case of the black rhinoceros, extinction, despite the illegality of poaching and a possible unconventional solution to poaching. Thus, A is the correct answer.

B is not correct because the passage does not exhort readers to take action of any sort, although it does bring the issue of rhinoceros issue greater awareness. C is incorrect. This passage does discuss the extinction of Western black rhinoceroses, but that is not the entirety of the passage's focus. D is not correct because, like C, it is overly narrow in focus. E is incorrect because the passage advocates rhino horn trade, just a very regulated form of it. Moreover, the passage mentions nothing about the consequences of breaking the law.

40. **(J)** Use the process of elimination to arrive at the correct answer. Lines 7-12 state that rhino horns were believed to be a panacea capable of treating all manners of ailments, from fevers and measles to epilepsy.

F is incorrect because the passage does not suggest that rhino horns were believed to promote eternal life. G, while tempting, is incorrect because it is too narrow in scope; the rhino horn was believed to treat all manners of ailments, with fevers, measles, and epilepsy listed as examples of what rhino horns were used to treat. H is incorrect because the passage does not state or imply that rhino horns were used as topically applied analgesics. K is incorrect because the passage does not state that rhino horns were used to boost immune system health. Thus, J is the correct answer.

41. **(D)** Lines 13-18 state that poaching has increased over the years because demand for rhino horn has remained high, which led to a drastic increase in the price of rhino horn. Then, in lines 26-35 state that because the prices of rhino horns have increased, poachers were willing to take the risks necessary to obtain rhinoceros horns. Thus, D is correct. A is incorrect because the technology used to hunt rhinoceroses is not discussed by the passage. B is incorrect because there is no mention of rhinoceros hunting becoming an extreme sport. C is incorrect because the passage does not give any other reason for poachers hunting rhinoceroses now than that they want to make money. In other words, C

does not properly reflect why poachers are doing the poaching. For all we know, from C, the poachers could be poaching for sport. E is incorrect because the passage does not state that no government is actively policing the poaching of rhinoceros horns.

42. **(K)** Lines 29-35 indicate that demand drives prices up and that the increased prices make poachers more willing to take risks.

F is incorrect because it cannot be inferred from the passage. In economics, a lower supply shifts the demand curve, so that the price does tend to increase, so F is not an incorrect statement in itself, but it cannot be inferred from the passage. The passage only mentions demand driving prices—supply constraints are not discussed. Furthermore, if a product is not in demand, then regardless of its available supply, the price won't go up. In economics, this is called a bad, rather than a good. Thus, while F is a very tempting choice, it is incorrect. G is incorrect because the passage does not establish how heavy a rhinoceros horn is; lines 14-15 state that rhino horns can fetch $65,000 per kilogram, but that is all. H is incorrect because a greater supply of a product may drive prices down, but it may not. J is incorrect because increased demand usually drives up the prices of a product.

43. **(C)** C is the correct answer. In lines 18-21 and 39-55, the passage discusses how legalizing and tightly regulating the trade of rhino horn may actually save rhinos from poachers.

A is incorrect because the passage does not mention using a wildlife preserve as a means to stop the illegal poaching of rhinoceroses. B is incorrect because the passage does not advocate drastically lowering the price of rhinoceros horns (probably because no government agency could control the price of rhino horns anyway, since rhino horns are being traded illegally). D is incorrect because it is not mentioned. It may be too difficult for government agencies to shut down black markets; otherwise, the black markets would

have been shut down already. E is not mentioned by the passage.

44. **(J)** J is the correct answer. Lines 39-43 state that rhino horns can be shaved or cut off without any physical repercussions to the animal, since rhino horns can grow back.

F is incorrect because rhinos do not need to be killed for their horns to be extracted. G is incorrect because the passage does not state that the species and subspecies of rhino alters the value of the horn, so G is unsubstantiated. H is incorrect. Rhino horns are believed to have curative properties, but the passage does not state that the horns have been scientifically proven to have curative properties. K is incorrect because it is also unsubstantiated.

(Cornelius Vanderbilt)

45. **(D)** The passage is about the success of Cornelius Vanderbilt and how he achieved that degree of success. The passage also mentions how he made his mark on U.S. history as a railroad tycoon and how he amassed the greatest amount of wealth for his time.

A is incorrect. The passage is not about the rise and fall of the steamship industry. In fact, there is no mention of the fall of the steamship industry at all. B is incorrect because it is not discussing how to succeed generally; it discusses how Vanderbilt succeeded. C is incorrect because the passage is not just about discussing Vanderbilt's wealth. E is incorrect because the passage is not about America.

46. **(G)** Use elimination to find the correct answer. F is incorrect because Vanderbilt did landscape as a teenager (lines 10-12). H is incorrect because Vanderbilt was at one point a sailboat passenger ferry operator (lines 12-14). J is incorrect because Vanderbilt was a railroad tycoon (lines 55-56). K is incorrect because Vanderbilt owned a steamboat fleet (lines 39-42).

Vanderbilt was never a military supplies procurement officer. He delivered military supplies during the War of 1812, but he wasn't an officer in the military. Nor did he procure supplies; he delivered them.

47. **(B)** In lines 21-42, the passage discusses how Vanderbilt saw that the future of the ferry business was in steamboats, not sailboats. Thus, he gave up his sailboat ferrying business in order to learn how to operate a steamboat. This decision ultimately led him to be able to make a fortune and own a fleet of steamboats. Thus, he made a series of very intelligent decisions based on the foresight that he had. In other words, he was perceptive, so B is the correct answer.

A is incorrect. While he may have been fortunate to some extent, the passage does not imply that it was luck that allowed him to succeed. C is incorrect because cunning implies using trickery or deceit and manipulation. He didn't do any of that. The same reasoning applies to D, which is why D is not correct, either. E is incorrect because clearly his brilliance was possible, since he made it happen.

48. **(K)** In lines 14-17, the passage states that Vanderbilt grew his sailboat ferry business by being a skilled sailor and pricing his fares aggressively to undercut his competition. Then, in lines 35-39, the passage states that Vanderbilt applied the same principles he used to grow his sailboat ferry business to growing his steamboat ferry business. Thus, we can infer that Vanderbilt used his skill and aggressive pricing to succeed.

F is incorrect because there's no mention of Vanderbilt charming his passengers with humor and conversations. G is incorrect because the passage does not state that Vanderbilt knew the waterways better than anyone else did. H is incorrect because there's no mention in the passage about by how much Vanderbilt undercut his competition. J is incorrect because the passage does not state or suggest that Vanderbilt spread rumors and offered extreme discounts.

49. **(A)** Lines 43-54 state that Cornelius Vanderbilt leveraged his success in his steamboat operations and invested in various ventures in Central America. This led to his entry into the transatlantic steamship industry. This further led to Vanderbilt's acquisition of railroads to allow him to connect passengers who needed passenger between waterway and railway. Thus, A is the correct answer.

B is incorrect because the passage does not state that Vanderbilt acquired more than half of the startup railroads in the United States. C is incorrect because there is no mention in the passage about the construction of the Panama Canal. D is incorrect because, while Vanderbilt's decision to learn how to be a steamboat operator did eventually lead to his entry into the railroad industry, Vanderbilt's entry into the transatlantic steamship industry more directly led to Vanderbilt's initial entry into the railroad industry. E is incorrect for a similar reason to D; Vanderbilt's ability to adapt to the times and capitalize on opportunities did eventually lead to his entry into the railroad industry, but his entry into the transatlantic steamship industry more directly led to Vanderbilt's entry into the railroad industry.

50. **(J)** Lines 26-29 state that the steamboat made the sailboat obsolete as a passenger ferry because the steamboat could transport passengers more quickly, reliably, and cost efficiently. Thus, J is the correct answer.

F is incorrect because the steamboat was more reliable than the sailboat was. G is incorrect because the passage does not state or imply how many times more people the steamboat could hold than a sailboat could. H is incorrect because it is not mentioned whether a steamboat could operate in smaller bodies of water. K is incorrect; it doesn't follow that a steamboat is more cost efficient because it is more expensive. Furthermore, the passage does not suggest the steamboat was much more expensive than the sailboat.

MATH EXPLANATIONS ▶

Answer Explanations – Mathematics
Practice Test 2

51. **(D)** The least common multiple of 84 and 189 can be found using prime factorization:

Prime factors of 84:

$84 = 2 \times 42 = 2 \times 6 \times 7 = 2 \times 2 \times 3 \times 7$

Prime factors of 189:

$189 = 9 \times 21 = 3 \times 3 \times 3 \times 7$

Because 84 and 189 share 3×7 as the greatest common factor, we can do the following to find the least common multiple:

$(3 \times 7) \times (2 \times 2) \times (3 \times 3) = 21 \times 4 \times 9 = 756$

But since we are looking for the quotient when 756 is divided by the greatest common factor, all we need to do is look above and take away 21 from $21 \times 4 \times 9$ to get 36 as the quotient. This is D, since $6 \times 6 = 36$.

52. **(J)** $(\sqrt{24})(\sqrt{6}) = \sqrt{144} = 12$

53. **(D)** Let B represent the amount Bella will invest, D the amount Damien will invest, and L the amount Lucius will invest. The following is true:

B + D + L = $42 million
B = 1.5D; D = 2L

Rewriting the first equation in terms of D, we get:

1.5D + D + 0.5D = $42 million →
3D = $42 million → D = $14 million

54. **(G)** 140 is the 20th multiple of 7. And 7 goes into 300 42 times. The 42nd multiple of 7 is 294. Thus, there are a total of 23 multiples of 7 that fall within the range of 140 to 300, inclusive.

140 is the 10th multiple of 14. 294 is the 21st multiple of 14. Thus, there are 12 multiples of 14 from 140 to 300, inclusive.

To find how many multiples there are of 7 in the range that are so not multiples of 14, we must subtract 12 from 23: $23 - 12 = 11$.

55. **(B)** $1/17 = 0.0588235\ldots$

Thus, the best approximation for the decimal number above is 0.0588, which, expressed in scientific notation is: 5.88×10^{-2}, since scientific notation is expressed in terms of one digit to the left of the decimal.

56. **(J)** First multiply both sides of the equation by 72:

$$\frac{25}{8} = \frac{(x+1)^2}{72} \rightarrow$$

$$(x+1)^2 = \frac{25 \times \cancel{72}^{9}}{\cancel{8}_{1}} = 25 \times 9 = 5^2 \times 3^2 = 225$$

Since the square root of 225 is 15, $x + 1 = 15$, and $x = 14$.

57. (D) Let R and C represent the number of candies Richard and Carlos ate today, respectively. Further, let C_y represent the number of candies Carlos ate yesterday. We can set up the following equations:

$R = 2C_y - 7$
$C = C_y + 5$

Because R = 13, we can make the following equation: $2C_y - 7 = 13$

Solving for C_y, we get $2C_y = 20$ and $C_y = 10$.

Substitute 10 for C_y to find C = 10 + 5 = 15.

---

58. (H) Because 4 different positive integers have a product of 42, the numbers are 1, 2, 3, and 7. The median of the smaller three integers is thus 2; the largest integer, 7, is 5 greater than 2.

---

59. (E) Because BC is common to both ratios, we can set a term for BC that works for both ratios:

CD : BC = 3 : 2 = 6 : 4
BC : AB = 4 : 1

Since these are ratios, for the values of the lengths, we can say CD = 6x units, BC = 4x units, and AB = x units. Thus, the total length of AD is 11x units. We are, however, looking for the length of BD, which is 10x units. Thus, E is the correct answer.

Note: Remember that x must be an integer.

---

60. (K) Rewrite the equation: $m^2 - 5m - 36 = 0$. Upon factoring, we get: $(m - 9)(m + 4) = 0$.

Thus, the solutions for the equation are: $m = 9$ and $m = -4$.

61. (D) Since $x = 7$ and $xy = 91$, $y = 13$.

Plugging in the values of x, y, and xy into the equation, we get: $91(7 + 2)(13 - 3)$. This, in turn, can be rewritten as $91 \times 9 \times 10$, which can further be simplified to $91 \times 90 = 8190$.

---

62. (G) First, find that the common denominator for the fractions in the parentheses is 45 and rewrite the problem accordingly:

$$\left(\frac{4}{9} - \frac{7}{15}\right) \div \frac{13}{10} = \left(\frac{20}{45} - \frac{21}{45}\right) \div \frac{13}{10} = -\frac{1}{45} \div \frac{13}{10}$$

Dividing by a fraction is the same as multiplying by that fraction's reciprocal:

$$-\frac{1}{45} \div \frac{13}{10} = -\frac{1}{{}_9\cancel{45}} \times \frac{\cancel{10}^{2}}{13} = -\frac{2}{117}$$

---

63. (A) First, draw point D into the diagram and start labeling, based on the information given:

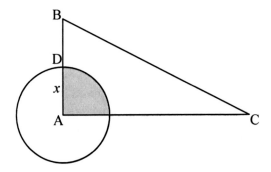

Let x represent the length of AD. Since the ratio of AD to AB is 1 to 2, AB is 2x. And since the ratio of AB to AC is 2 to 3, AC is 3x. Furthermore, we know that the area of the triangle is 12. Thus, ½(2x)(3x) = 12, or $3x^2 = 12$. This means $x^2 = 4$ and $x = 2$.

Since the area of the shaded region is a quarter circle, since angle BAC is a right angle, the area of the shaded region can be determined as follows:

Area of shaded region = ¼ × π × r^2 = ¼ × π × 2^2, where r, the radius, is 2 units, since r is x in this case. Thus, the area of the shaded region is ¼ × π × 4 = π square units.

.

---

64. **(G)** Let F be Fernando's age and A be Alexa's. We get the following equations:

F = A + 5
F + 9 = 3A

Using substitution, we get:

(A + 5) + 9 = 3A → A + 14 = 3A → 2A = 14 → A = 7

---

65. **(C)** This is an arithmetic word problem. To find the number of hours Tanner skied on the fifth day, first add the number of hours he skied on the first four days:

4 + 6 + 6 + 9.5 = 25.5

Subtract 25.5 from 32 to get 6.5 hours.

---

66. **(J)** Since P is an integer, and since M and N are distinct elements of Set A, M must be greater than N. Moreover, M is also a multiple of N. Thus, the possible combinations of M and N are as follows:

N = 3; M = 6, 9, 12, 15; P = 2, 3, 4, 5
N = 4; M = 8, 12, 16; P = 2, 3, 4
N = 5; M = 10, 15; P = 2, 3
N = 6; M = 12; P = 2
N = 7; M = 14; P = 2
N = 8; M = 16; P = 2

But since we are looking for unique values of P, we only count P = 2, 3, 4, 5, or 4 values of P.

---

67. **(C)** 9 jleps = 14 bwoks, so 27 jleps = 42 bwoks. Thus, 42 bwoks = 35 amooks. Dividing by 7, we get 6 bwoks = 5 amooks. Multiply both sides by 20, since we are looking for the value of 100 amooks. This results in 120 bwoks = 100 amooks.

---

68. **(F)** If 16 workers can build a house in 144 days, 1 worker can build a house in 144 × 16 = 2,304 days. To find how many workers are needed to build a house in 96 days, divide 2,304 by 96 = 24. Thus, 24 workers are needed to build a house in 96 days. Thus, 8 more workers are needed.

---

69. **(A)** Substitute 2 in for y:

$$3|x+2| = 5(2) + 7 = 17$$

Thus, $|x+2| = \dfrac{17}{3} \rightarrow x+2 = \dfrac{17}{3}, -\dfrac{17}{3}$.

Subtracting both sides by 2, we get:

$$\dfrac{17-6}{3}, \dfrac{-17-6}{3} = \dfrac{11}{3}, -\dfrac{23}{3}$$

---

70. **(K)** An equilateral triangle with side lengths of 10 has an area of: $25\sqrt{3}$ cm^2:

Since the area of a triangle is ½ × b × h, where b and h stand for base and height, respectively, we can find the height of an equilateral triangle by cutting the triangle in half to form two 30-60-90 right triangles. The resulting half triangle has a base of 5 cm. The hypotenuse is 10 cm, so the height is $5\sqrt{3}$ cm. Thus, for the whole equilateral triangle, b = 10 cm and h = $5\sqrt{3}$ cm. Thus, the area of the triangle is $25\sqrt{3}$ cm^2 and x = 5 and y = 3.

A circle's radius is xy, or 15, cm. The circle's area is then $15^2 × π$ cm^2 = $225π$ cm^2.

71. **(B)** Since every term is a multiple of 3, we know that there are 17 terms, since 17 × 3 = 51. Also, the sum of every two terms, starting from the beginning, is 3.

    Since there are 16 terms from 3 to 48, there are 8 sums of 3. Thus, the sum of the alternating sequence is 24 + -51 = -27.

72. **(K)** Set up a system of equations:

    $5p + 5e = \$5.75$
    $7p + 4e = \$6.69$

    Next, isolate the cost of the eraser. We know that the cost of 1 pencil and 1 eraser, from the top equation, is $1.15, by dividing every term in the equation by 5. Rewrite the system of equations:

    $1p + 1e = \$1.15$
    $7p + 4e = \$6.76$

    Multiply the terms in the first equation by 7 to get the equation $7p + 7e = \$8.05$.

    From this, subtract the bottom equation:

    $7p + 7e = \$8.05$
    $- 7p + 4e = \$6.76$
    $0p + 3e = \$1.29$ → $(3e = \$1.29) ÷ 3$ →
    $e = \$0.43$

73. **(D)** To find out how much time Marlon has to study, figure out how much time he has to sleep and how much time it takes to get to school:

    If he wants to sleep 8.25 hours, that's 8 hours and 15 minutes, since 0.25 hours is a quarter of an hour, and a quarter of 60 minutes is 15 minutes.

    It takes him 45 minutes to leave home, from the time he wakes up, and 30 minutes from the time he leaves his home to get to his classroom. That's 75 minutes.

Thus, the total time he needs to sleep and get to class is 8 hours and 90 minutes. Since 90 minutes = 1 hour and 30 minutes, 8 hours, 90 minutes is 9 hours, 30 minutes.

To find out how much study time Marlon will have, subtract 9 hours and 30 minutes from 10:30 am, which is his exam time. This means that Marlon will have to sleep by 1 am on the day of the exam.

If he starts studying at 11 am the day before the exam, he has 14 hours to study. (11 am to 11 pm is 12 hours, and 11 pm to 1 am is 2 hours, so 11 am to 1 am the next day is 14 hours.)

74. **(J)** Rewrite the expression, evaluating the terms in the parentheses first:

    $50(3.4)^2 – 100(0.3)^2 =$

    $50 × 11.56 – 100 × 0.09 = 578 – 9 = 569$

75. **(E)** The greatest possible sum of a and b: 26 + 43 = 69

    Least possible sum of a and b: 16 + 37 (37, since b has to be odd) = 53

    The mean of the sums: (69 + 53) ÷ 2 = 122 ÷ 2 = 61

76. **(K)** 40 laps, with each lap ¼-mile long, is 10 miles. 9 minutes per mile makes for 90 minutes. That is Phyllis's goal.

    If Phyllis met her goal exactly, she'd have finished an hour and half after she started, which was at 2:45 pm.

    2:45 + 1:30 = 4:15 pm.

    Since she beat her goal by 7 minutes, she finished at 4:08 pm.

77. (E) From the absolute value inequality, we can set up two inequalities that satisfy the absolute value inequality:

$x + 17 \leq 33$
$x + 17 \geq -33$

Solve for the first inequality to get: $x \leq 16$.

The second inequality yields: $x \geq -50$

Since the range of values that satisfies x is from -50 to 16, both inclusive, there are 67 possible integers. (Don't forget about 0!)

---

78. (G) The ratio of butter to flour is 4 to 5, and the ratio of eggs to flour is 8 to 3.

Since flour is common in the ratios, we need to find a common amount for flour, which would be $3 \times 5 = 15$.

Multiply the ratio of butter to flour by 3, so that the amount of flour becomes 15. Thus, for every 15 grams of flour, there will be 12 grams of butter.

Also multiply the ratio of eggs to flour by 5, so that the amount of flour becomes 15. Thus, for every 15 grams of flour, there will be 40 grams of eggs.

As we can see, for 15 grams of flour, there are 12 grams of butter and 40 grams of eggs, for a total of 67 grams. Thus, the individual components can be expressed as a fraction of 67.

Since there are 402 grams of cake batter total, we divide 402 grams by 67:

$402 \div 67 = 6$

Since the total mass of raw eggs and butter in 67 grams of cake batter is $40 + 12 = 52$ grams, the total mass of raw eggs and butter used in 402 grams of cake batter is therefore: $52 \times 6 = 312$ grams.

79. (A) Here, since order does not matter, we can solve this problem using combination theory.

There are 6 students to choose from, and the captain must select 5. The number of different groups of 5 that can be chosen from 6 is:

$$\binom{6}{5} = \frac{6!}{(6-5)!5!} = \frac{6 \times \cancel{5 \times 4 \times 3 \times 2 \times 1}}{(1!) \times \cancel{5 \times 4 \times 3 \times 2 \times 1}} = 6$$

It is also possible to manually count the number of groups that can be made, since our numbers are small:

Let the 6 students be A, B, C, D, E, and F. If groups of 5 are made, we can have the following unique groups, noting that A, B, C, D, E is the same as A, C, D, E, B, for instance, for the purposes of grouping, since order does not matter:

1: A, B, C, D, E
2: A, B, C, D, F
3: A, B, C, E, F
4: A, B, D, E, F
5: A, C, D, E, F
6: B, C, D, E, F

Notice how each student appears 5 times across the 6 unique groupings. We know we have counted them all.

---

80. (H) If point B is placed such that AB is one-fifth of BC, there are two places that B can go—either before A or between A and C. (B cannot come after C because then AB would be greater than BC.)

When B comes before A:

$A - B = \frac{1}{5}(C - B)$
$-6 - B = \frac{1}{5}(12 - B)$
$-30 - 5B = 12 - B$

$4B = -42 \rightarrow B = -10.5$

When B comes between A and C:

$B - A = \frac{1}{5}(C - B)$
$B - (-6) = B + 6 = \frac{1}{5}(12 - B)$
$5B + 30 = 12 - B$
$6B = -18 \rightarrow B = -3$

Thus, B can be -10.5 and -3.

---

81. **(D)** The total height of the first tree the students plant is $263 + 11 = 274$ centimeters. The second tree is 317 centimeters tall, and 246 centimeters of it are above ground. That means 71 centimeters of it are below ground.

Since the first tree is 11 centimeters below ground, the second tree is $71 - 11 = 60$ centimeters more below ground.

---

82. **(H)** Clara has 352 stamps. 154 are nature-themed and 110 are sports-themed, so she has $352 - (154 + 110) = 88$ architecture-themed ones. The ratio of nature to sports to architecture stamps is $154 : 110 : 88$, which equates to $77 : 55 : 44$, or $7 : 5 : 4$.

If she picks 64 stamps at random, the number of stamps will likely reflect the ratio we just found. Since $7 + 5 + 4 = 16$, which is a factor of 64, we can multiply each term by 4 to get $28 + 20 + 16 = 64$.

Thus, Clara is likely to pick 28 nature-themed stamps and 16 architecture-themed ones. The difference between these numbers, which is what the problem is asking for, is $28 - 16 = 12$.

---

83. **(B)** Since the height and base of each of the smaller, congruent right triangles are 4 cm and 3 cm, their hypotenuse is 5 cm, using the Pythagorean Theorem:

$3^2 + 4^2 = c^2 \rightarrow c^2 = 25 \rightarrow c = 5$

The large triangle is an isosceles triangle, with two of its sides each measuring 3 hypotenuse lengths of the smaller triangles. In other words, two of the sides of the large triangle each has a measure of 15 cm.

The third side of the large triangle measures 6 times the side length of a smaller triangle. The third side of the large triangle could either be $6 \times 4 = 24$ cm or $6 \times 3 = 18$.

Thus the perimeter of the large triangle can be either $15 + 15 + 24 = 54$ cm or $15 + 15 + 18 = 48$ cm. Since 54 cm is not one of the answer choices, 48 cm is correct.

---

84. **(J)** To find how much area the gray areas comprise, let's first see how much of the squares are covered by the circle.

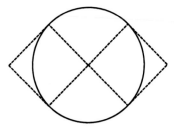

The overlapping areas of the circle and squares are quarter circles (a square has 4 right angles), with each quarter-circle having a radius of 10 feet (the side length of each square). Thus, to solve this problem, we need to know the area of each of the quarter-circles and the area of the squares.

The area of each square is $s^2 = (10 \text{ ft})^2 = 100 \text{ ft}^2$. The area of a quarter-circle $\frac{1}{4} \times \pi r^2 = \frac{1}{4} \times \pi (10 \text{ ft})^2 = 25\pi \text{ ft}^2$. Thus, the area of each shaded region is $100 \text{ ft}^2 - 25\pi \text{ ft}^2$.

Since there are two shaded regions, we multiply this result by 2 to get $200 \text{ ft}^2 - 50\pi \text{ ft}^2$.

85. **(C)** Draw a Venn diagram to solve this problem, accounting for the fact that 5 students do not play any instruments at all. Thus, the total number of students within the Venn diagram must be 42. Let x represent the number of students who play both cello and guitar, but not also violin; y the students who play both guitar and violin but not cello; and z those who play both violin and cello but not guitar.

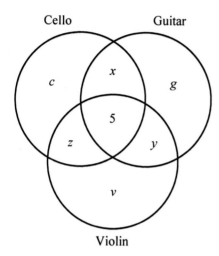

Cello   Guitar

Violin

The problem asks us to solve for $x + y + z$, the students who play exactly two instruments. To do so, find the number of students who play exactly one instrument, so let c represent the number of students who only play cello, g those who play only guitar, and v only violin.

Then we can write the equation $c + g + v + x + y + z + 5 = 47 - 5 = 42$.

Because 24 students in total play cello, 22 guitar, and 17 violin, we can write:

$c = 24 - (x + z + 5);$
$g = 22 - (x + y + 5);$
$v = 17 - (y + z + 5);$

After substituting these into the above equation, we get:

$[24 - (x + z + 5)] + [22 - (x + y + 5)] + [17 - (y + z + 5)] + x + y + z + 5 = 42$

This simplifies to:

$(24 + 22 + 17 - 5 - 5 - 5) - 2(x + y + z) + x + y + z + 5 = 42$

$(63 - 15) - 2(x + y + z) + x + y + z + 5 = 42$

$48 + 5 - (x + y + z) = 42$
$53 - (x + y + z) = 42$
$(x + y + z) = 53 - 42 = 11$

---

86. **(H)** The carnival sold, in terms of dollars, $12x + 9y$. Since it sold $5n$ times as many adult tickets as it did junior tickets, we know $x = (5n)y$. Rewrite the revenue expression as:

$12[(5n)y] + 9y = 60ny + 9y = 3y(20n + 3)$

Thus, the revenue generated is a product of a multiple of 3 and 23, 43, 63, 83, etc.

Use elimination to find the correct answer. 316 isn't divisible by 3, so F is not correct.

$930 \div 3 = 310$. 310 is not further divisible by 3 and does not have a units digit of 3, so G is not correct.

$1{,}563 \div 3 = 521$, which is not further divisible by 3, and does not have 3 as a units digit, so J is not correct.

$2{,}130 \div 3 = 710$, which is not further divisible by 3, and does not have 3 as a units digit, so K is not correct.

$1{,}161 \div 3 = 387$. $387 \div 3 = 129$. $129 \div 3 = 43$, which would mean $n = 2$.

---

87. **(E)** We need to find which fractions are the smallest:

$\frac{17}{3} = 5\frac{2}{3} = 5.\overline{66}$

$\frac{28}{5} = 5\frac{3}{5} = 5.6$

$\frac{45}{8} = 5\frac{5}{8} = 5.625$

As we can see, $\frac{28}{5}$ and $\frac{45}{8}$ are the two smallest. To find their average, first we find their sum:

$\frac{28}{5} + \frac{45}{8} = \frac{28 \times 8}{5 \times 8} + \frac{45 \times 5}{8 \times 5} = \frac{224}{40} + \frac{225}{40} = \frac{449}{40}$

To find the average, divide the sum by 2:

$\frac{449}{40} \div 2 = \frac{449}{80}$

---

88. **(J)** When both hoses are on, water pours in at a rate of 8 gallons per minute. Because of the cracks, the net rate of water being poured in is $(5 + 3) - 2.5 = 5.5$ gallons per minute. After an hour, 5.5 gal/min × 60 min = 330 gallons. 330 gallons represents 60% of the pool's capacity, so the pool's capacity is:

$330 = 0.6x \rightarrow 3{,}300 = 6x \rightarrow x = 550$ gal
After an hour, then, $550 - 330 = 220$ gallons remain to be filled. If the first hose is turned off, and the second one remains on, the net rate of water flow into the pool is:

3 gal/min − 2.5 gal/min = 0.5 gal/min

In order to fill 220 gallons at 0.5 gal/min, we divide 220 by 0.5 to get 440 minutes.

---

89. **(A)** To find the total value of the goods transported, multiply the value of the goods transported and number of vehicles that transported the listed value of goods for each row and then find their sum:

$1,000 × 55 = $55,000
$2,000 × 20 = $40,000
$3,000 × 15 = $45,000
$4,000 × 10 = $40,000

$1,000 × (55 + 40 + 45 + 40) =
$1,000 × (180) = $180,000

---

90. **(J)** Distribute the negative sign and combine like terms:

$(3x - 5y) - (7 + 8x - y) =$
$3x - 5y - 7 - 8x + y =$
$-5x - 4y - 7$

Since none of the answer choices look exactly like the solution above, we look to see which answer choice can be made to look like the solution.

F is incorrect. $-5x - (4y - 7) = -5x - 4y + 7$

G, H, and J are incorrect because $-6y$, $-2y$, and $11x - 6y$, respectively, are incorrect.

$-(5x + (4y + 7)) = -(5x + 4y + 7) = -5x - 4y - 7$, so K is correct.

---

91. **(E)** Find the middle height, if there is an odd number of data points, or the mean of the middle two heights, if there is an even number. Since there are 33 data points, the former rule applies. The median here is 41.

---

92. **(G)** Let x be the list price of the shirt. The price David would pay online with the coupon is 75% of x, or $0.75x$.

The price David would pay in-store before applying the extra member discount is $0.8x$. Apply the member discount:

$0.8x - 0.05(0.8x) = 0.8x - 0.04x = 0.76x$

Thus, the amount David would pay online is $0.01x$ less than what he would pay in-store. $0.01x = 1\%$ of x.

---

93. **(E)** The first square is shaded and then every fourth one after that is shaded. Thus, every $4^{th} + 1$ square is shaded.

To determine which squares are shaded, divide by 4 and see if the remainder is 1:

$123 \div 4 = 30$ R3, so A is incorrect.
$256 \div 4 = 64$ R0, so B is incorrect.
$312 \div 4 = 78$ R0, so C is incorrect.
$474 \div 4 = 118$ R2, so D is incorrect.
$569 \div 4 = 142$ R1, so E is correct.

---

94. **(J)** The trains travel towards each other at a combined $60 + 90 = 150$ miles per hour. As such, they will pass each other in 3 hours. At 3 hours, train A has traveled 180 miles (60 miles per hour × 3 hours), meaning train A has $450 - 180 = 270$ miles remaining to reach station B. At 60 miles per hour, train A will reach station B in $270 \div 60 = 4.5$ hours, from the time it passed train B.

---

95. **(D)** The first and last cards are lettered cards. Below are the possible numbers of cards that could occupy each spot, from first to last.

4	3	3	2	2	1	1

Since the cards have to alternate between lettered and numbered cards, it's irrelevant that the question points out that last card has to be a lettered card. Thus, there are 4 lettered cards that could be first, and 3 numbered cards that could be second (or the first numbered card).

After picking the first lettered card, there will be 3 lettered cards left, so the third card (or second lettered card) will have 3 choices. The same logic and rationale can be extended down to the last cards, as is represented above numerically.

Thus, the total number of ways the cards can be arranged is: $4 \times 3 \times 3 \times 2 \times 2 \times 1 \times 1 = 144$ ways.

96. **(F)** The cost of Ellie taking a cab for 1 day:

Distance = 40 miles for a one-way trip. Thus, the cost of a one-way trip is

$\$2.50 + \$0.05(40) = \$4.50$.

Over 3 days, she needs 6 one-way trips, so her cab fare amounts to: $\$4.50 \times 6 = \$27.00$.

Ellie's cost of driving to work over 3 days:

Distance = $80 \times 3 = 240$ miles. Her cost per gallon is $4.00. Thus,

240 miles ÷ 30 miles per gallon = 8 gallons.

8 gallons × $4.00 per gallon = $32.00.

Ellie would save $\$32.00 - \$27.00 = \$5.00$ by taking the cab for the three days.

---

97. **(B)** The two digit numbers that are evenly divisible by 8 are: 16, 24, 32, 40, 48, 56, 64, 72, 80, 88, and 96.

Notice also that $16 + 96$, $24 + 88$, $32 + 80$, $40 + 72$, and $48 + 64$ all equal 112. Thus, the sum of these 10 numbers is actually $5 \times 112 = 560$.

Since we didn't yet include 56, $560 + 56 = 616$.

The average of 616 across 11 numbers is 56, which was the middle number in the arithmetic sequence.

Also, another way to look at it is: $560 + 56 = 56(10 + 1) \div 11 = 56$.

98. (J) Franklin made a total of \$50.00 + \$283.80 + \$634.70 = \$968.50 with his returns on his various investments.

To find out how much money he would have made, if he had instead put all his money into a mutual fund, we first need to find out what percent his return on his mutual fund investment was, which can be found by dividing the return on investment by the amount invested or deposited. Thus, for the mutual fund, this is:

$634.70 \div 5{,}770.00 = 0.11$ or 11%

Franklin invested or deposited a total of \$2,500 + \$4,730 + \$5,770 = \$13,000.

An 11% return on \$13,000 is \$1,430.

Thus, if Franklin had invested all of his money into the mutual fund, he would have earned \$1,430 − 968.50 = \$461.50 more.

99. (C) Solving the equation for x, we get:

$$\sqrt{36 + x^2} = 6.5$$

$$36 + x^2 = (6.5)^2 = 42.25$$

$$x^2 = 42.25 - 36 = 6.25$$

$$x = \pm\sqrt{6.25} = \pm 2.5$$

Thus, the smallest possible value of x is -2.5.

100. (G) The truck traveled 7,700 miles in 20 days. On average, then, the truck traveled 385 miles, or $385 \times 5{,}280 = 2{,}032{,}800$ feet, per day.

Since the radius of each tire is 1 foot, the circumference of each tire is 2π feet. Substituting $\frac{22}{7}$ for π, we get a circumference of approximately $\frac{44}{7}$ feet.

To find the average number of revolutions made by each tire per day, we divide the distance by the circumference, as such:

$$\frac{385 \times 5{,}280}{\frac{44}{7}} = 385 \times 5{,}280 \times \frac{7}{44} =$$

$$385 \times \overset{120}{\cancel{1{,}320}} \times \frac{7}{\cancel{44}} = 385 \times 120 \times 7 = 323{,}400$$

Note: The reason this works is that the distance traveled can be expressed as:

$$\text{Distance} = \frac{\text{circumference}}{\text{revolution}} \times \text{revolutions}$$

So when you divide distance by circumference (which is actually circumference per revolution, since 1 revolution leads to a distance equal to the circumference), we are left with the number of revolutions.

SHSAT
NYC EDITION
TEST KEY 3

AK

Answer Key – Test 3

VERBAL

SCRAMBLED PARAGRAPHS

Paragraph 1
RUQST

Paragraph 2
QUSRT

Paragraph 3
USRTQ

Paragraph 4
STQRU

Paragraph 5
TURQS

LOGICAL REASONING

11. D
12. G
13. E
14. H
15. B
16. F
17. D
18. H
19. A
20. K

READING

21. D
22. B
23. A
24. H
25. A
26. K
27. B
28. H
29. D
30. H
31. C
32. K
33. B
34. F
35. E
36. J
37. B
38. F
39. B
40. F
41. E
42. J
43. E
44. G
45. E
46. J
47. C
48. G
49. C
50. J

Answer Key – Test 3

MATHEMATICS

51.	B	76.	F
52.	G	77.	D
53.	C	78.	K
54.	J	79.	D
55.	C	80.	H
56.	K	81.	C
57.	A	82.	J
58.	G	83.	B
59.	E	84.	G
60.	K	85.	D
61.	B	86.	G
62.	F	87.	B
63.	C	88.	F
64.	H	89.	B
65.	B	90.	H
66.	H	91.	D
67.	A	92.	J
68.	J	93.	A
69.	B	94.	F
70.	J	95.	B
71.	A	96.	H
72.	J	97.	C
73.	B	98.	J
74.	K	99.	E
75.	A	100.	G

VERBAL EXPLANATIONS ▶

Answer Explanations – Verbal
Practice Test 3

SCRAMBLED PARAGRAPHS

Paragraph 1 (RUQST)

The lead sentence states what we think of when we think of history.

Sentence R comes after the lead because it extends the statements made by the lead sentence. U comes after R. U follows R by also discussing natural history. U further states that sometimes proving the sequence of natural history is difficult for a lack of proper evidence. Q comes after U because Q states that as long as we have the means to determine our natural history's past, we can develop a more "honest" view of natural history than human history, in some cases. S comes after Q because S states that all we need are accurate ways of analyzing the past and that we need ingenuity, perceptiveness, and the ability to draw logical conclusions. T comes after S because T refers to the mental faculties discussed by S.

Easy Clusters: QST is an easy cluster. Q introduces the idea of needing an accurate means of determining the past of natural history, S discusses what mental faculties those accurate means require, and T discusses that humanity has shown itself capable of using those mental faculties.

Note: If you find yourself unsure as to whether Q or U comes after R, you can use logic to bail yourself out, once you understand that QST is a cluster. If you put QST immediately after R, then U has to come last, but that would not make sense. Thus, U precedes Q, and the order is RUQST.

Paragraph 2 (QUSRT)

The opening sentence starts the paragraph with a discussion of the Great Barrier Reef as the world's largest coral reef system and one of the seven natural wonders of the world.

Q comes after the lead because it makes specific reference to the Great Barrier Reef when it states, "This massive coral reef system". U follows Q because U states that coral reef systems will continue to face challenges in the future in the form of greenhouse gases. S follows Q because S mentions that carbon dioxide accounts for several billion tons of greenhouse gases and poses one of the greatest threats to coral reefs. R comes after S because R discusses the other threat to coral reef systems: the warming of oceans. T is the conclusion because it is about what we can do to protect our ecology.

Easy Clusters: USR is an easy cluster because S alludes to the greenhouse gases mentioned in U. R follows S as the other threat to coral reefs. Once it is obvious that Q comes first and T comes last, then the entire order becomes obvious, after the cluster has been made.

Paragraph 3 (USRTQ)

The opening sentence indicates that the paragraph will be about an elderly woman riding in a barrel over Niagara Falls.

U follows the lead because it follows the lead's statement that you would think your grandma was kidding if she said she would ride in a barrel over Niagara Falls. S follows U because S introduces a woman who actually decided to go over Niagara Falls. R comes after S because R follows through with the mention that Taylor survived the drop and became the first person to do so. T follows R because T says that though Taylor survived the fall, she did not achieve the fame she sought. Q follows T because Q extends the discussion about Taylor's legacy as a daredevil.

Tip: Q is the conclusion because it completely changes direction and no other sentences can follow Q logically.

Paragraph 4 (STQRU)

The lead sentence introduces information about the Concorde jet.

S comes after the lead. It discusses what the Concorde jet was capable of, in terms of speed, and how it served as a symbol of luxury. T comes after S because it refers to the New York City to London itinerary and how the Concorde could cut the travel time in half. T also mentions that the Concorde jet was not free from criticism. Q comes after T because it mentions the first criticism of the Concorde jet. R comes after Q because R discusses another criticism of the Concorde jet, which is that the jets were not cost effective. U comes last because it discusses how and why the Concorde jet finally became retired.

Easy Clusters: STQR is an easy cluster. ST is an easy cluster because S and T both discuss the route from New York City to London and the flight time involved. TQ is an easy cluster because Q naturally follows T, and R comes after T. Thus, all told, STQR is an easy cluster.

Paragraph 5 (TURQS)

The lead sentence discusses the Wright plane as the first heavier-than-air aircraft to take flight.

Sentence T comes after the introductory sentence because it references the lead sentence's first historic flight. It also discusses how inventors, engineers, and aviators have worked to make aircraft fly faster. U comes after T because it discusses how planes are now able to fly at tremendous speeds. R comes after U because R's mention of "remarkable milestone" is referring to U's mention of man flying faster than the speed of sound. Q follows R because Q says that it was theorized that supersonic flight was not possible because supersonic flight would eviscerate the aircraft. S follows Q because S states that Yeager proved the theorists wrong.

Note: TU and QS are easy clusters to make, with TU coming first. What might not be as apparent is why R comes after U and not after S. Thus, it might be tempting to place R after S. The problem with placing R after S is twofold. First, S is a better conclusion sentence, since its tone is one of more finality. The other, and more important, problem with placing R after S is that R introduces the *X-1* rocket plane in more detail. Thus, it makes more sense for R to come before S.

LOGICAL REASONING

11. **(D)** This question requires you to work with conditional statements and their contrapositives.

The first statement is: If my car is broken, I will ride the bus. The contrapositive of this statement is: If I do not ride the bus, my car is not broken.

The second statement is: If I am limping, I will ride the bus. The contrapositive of this statement is: If I do not ride the bus, I am not limping.

Thus, the hypothesis of the contrapositive statements "if I do not ride the bus" has two conclusions: "my car is not broken" and "I am not limping". D is the only answer choice that properly expresses this.

A is wrong because "my car is broken" does not logically follow from "if I am limping". B is wrong because it does not logically follow, from the conditional statements presented in the problem, that I cannot drive if I am limping. Although it is a reasonable conclusion to make, what's reasonable is irrelevant to a logic question. C is wrong because I can ride the bus for other reasons than my car being broken or my limping. E is wrong because it doesn't follow that I am limping from my car being broken.

12. **(G)** Create a chart or diagram to solve this problem. Since we need to find the least number of times Larry eats 3 meals per day during a week, we minimize the overlaps, as such:

	1	2	3	4	5	6	7
B	X	X	X	X	X		
F	X	X				X	X
S			X	X	X	X	X
P							

By the time we get to pasta, however, there must be at least one day during which Larry eats 3 meals. Thus, G is the correct answer.

13. **(E)** Use elimination to arrive at the correct answer.

A is incorrect because the facts state that no student at school X hears of game Z before entering the school. That does not mean no one else has heard of game Z. For instance, it is possible that students at other schools have heard of game Z or parents of students at school X have heard of game Z. B is incorrect because there is not enough information to support the idea that Joshua has friends at school X. C is incorrect for the reason stated above to show why A is incorrect. D is incorrect because there is nothing to support the idea that game Z has spread to other schools. Thus, E is the correct answer.

14. **(H)** Keep count of how many times the boat must cross the river.

If there are 4 boys, then 2 can enter the boat to cross the river the first time, leaving 2 boys at the starting side of the river. 1 boy is dropped off on the other side, and the boat goes across the river again to retrieve another boy. As of now, the boat has made 2 trips.

Another boy enters the boat, leaving 1 boy at the starting side of the river, and the boat goes across the river to drop this second boy off. The boat comes back for the last boy. As of now, the boat has made 4 trips.

The last boy enters the boat, and both boys go across the river. Since both boys in the boat can now get off the boat, the boat has made a total of 5 trips.

15. **(B)** The only logical conclusion that can be drawn from the facts is that some people in Huntsville are good at bowling. It does not follow that someone good at bowling can also hit a bull's-eye with every shot.

Just because Trey knows how to shoot rifles and is good at bowling does not mean he is capable of hitting a bull's-eye with every shot. Thus, A is incorrect. C is incorrect because there is not enough information to support that Trey lives in Huntsville. D does not logically follow from the information. Whether he lives in Huntsville or not has no bearing on whether he can hit a bull's-eye with every shot. E is incorrect because it cannot be concluded that the majority of people in Huntsville can score a bull's-eye with every shot.

16. **(F)** Draw a table or diagram to help you solve this problem. Nature was sold second and inventions last, and we know culture and space were sold before architecture, which Fannie made, so architecture was the fourth sold.

First Sold

1.	–
2.	– Nature
3.	–
4.	Fannie – Architecture
5.	– Inventions

Last Sold

Since we can't fill in any more information, see which answers we can eliminate.

F is correct because Fannie's sketch had to have been sold fourth, which means that Greta's sketch could not have been sold third, since Daisy's sketch was sold immediately after Greta's sketch was sold. G is incorrect because it is possible that the culture sketch was sold third. H is incorrect; the nature sketch could have been sold either before or after the culture sketch. J is incorrect because Greta could have created the space sketch. K is wrong because Edgar could have done the inventions sketch.

17. **(D)** Draw a diagram or chart for this problem. Since Kris was immediately before Omar in line, Kris could be either third or fourth.

First in Line

1.		
2.	J	J
3.	K	
4.	O	K
5.		O

Last in Line

We don't have enough information to draw any other conclusions, so we look to the answer choices to see which we can eliminate.

A is incorrect because May could be either first, third, or fifth. B is incorrect because either Nick or May was last if Omar was fourth. C is incorrect because Kris was either third or fourth, not first. E is incorrect because Nick could also be third in line.

D is correct because if May is third, then Kris is not third. That means Kris is fourth, which makes Omar last in line.

18. **(H)** Draw a diagram or table to solve this problem. Janice held her breath the third longest. Margo held her breath longer than Luke did, and Baxter lost his breath immediately before Sally did—in other words, Sally held her breath longer than Baxter did. This means that we can construct two possible diagrams.

Held Breath Most

1.	S	
2.	B	
3.	J	J
4.		S
5.		B

Held Breath Least

Since Margo held her breath longer than Luke did, we can fill in the chart above to completion, for both scenarios.

Held Breath Most

1.	S	M
2.	B	L
3.	J	J
4.	M	S
5.	L	B

Held Breath Least

We can see now that either Luke or Baxter held his breath the shortest. Thus, H is the correct answer.

19. **(A)** For "decoding sentence" question types, try to figure out what as many of the letters mean as possible.

Notice that all of the sentences contain the word "the" and the letter H. No other word or letter appears in all four sentences. Thus, H represents "the". Further notice that the first three sentences all contain "with" and T. Thus, "with" is represented by the letter T. The word "talked" is found in the first and third sentences, as is the letter L, so "talked" is represented by L.

20. **(K)** To find out which word Q represents, we look to the third sentence, which is the only sentence in which Q appears. But we see that F also appears in the third sentence. "Dirk" and "server" are the two words left in the third sentence, after deducing as much as possible while solving for question 19 above. But because "Dirk" and "server" do not appear in any of the other sentences and because Q and F do not appear in any of the other sentences, it's impossible to tell which letter represents which word.

READING

(Nitrogen)

21. **(D)** The passage is about nitrogen's importance and the dangers excess nitrogen poses ecologically, if abused or left unregulated. Thus, D is correct.

    A is incorrect. While nitrogen can be harmful, it is only harmful when used excessively. Also, nitrogen is probably more helpful than harmful, seeing as how we continue to use nitrogen excessively in many cases to sustain agriculture. B is incorrect. Even though the passage does mention that nitrogen is an incredibly important element, the passage also focuses on the problems nitrogen can pose. C is incorrect. Excess nitrogen can cause illnesses in infants, but that is only a portion of what the passage is about. E is incorrect because the passage draws no connection between the atmospheric compositions of nitrogen and oxygen and their impact on society.

22. **(B)** Nitrification is discussed in lines 17-26. They state that if we had not been able to discover a way to synthesize fertilizer by converting atmospheric nitrogen into ammonium nitrate through the process of nitrification, our planet would not be able to support its current population size. Thus, since ammonium nitrate is the end product of nitrification, and fertilizer is synthesized by incorporating nitrification, we can conclude that ammonium nitrate is essential to the synthesis of fertilizer. Thus, B is correct. But let's see why the other answer choices do not work.

    A is incorrect because there is no mention of using the positive and negative ions being used together as a magnet. C is incorrect because the passage does not discuss the relative strength of the ions. D is incorrect because there is no mention in the passage of the abundance of potassium and phosphorous in soil. All we know is that they are essential macronutrients for vegetative growth, from

lines 15-17. E is incorrect because the passage does not compare the importance of oxygen and nitrogen to our survival. Both are essential, so this is a moot point, anyway.

23. **(A)** Lines 30-33 state that soil microbes convert the ammonium found in the fertilizer to more nitrate. Thus, A is the correct answer since it properly reflects the function of soil microbes.

24. **(C)** Lines 56-66 discuss methemoglobinemia. The symptoms are listed specifically in lines 58-60: diarrhea, vomiting, and lethargy are first listed. Then, the passage discusses cyanosis, which is when the baby experiences a shortness of breath and his skin, lips, or nail beds may turn a grayish or bluish hue. Thus, high fever is the only symptom not mentioned in lines 56-66.

25. **(D)** Lines 47-52 indicate that the Safe Drinking Water Act was passed to control the maximum amount of contaminants that can be found in public water systems. Thus, A is correct. The Safe Drinking Water Act was passed to prevent public water systems from containing excessive levels of contaminants.

    B is wrong because the passage does not state that the act was passed to ensure that all water found in the United States was safe for drinking, just the water in public water systems. C is wrong because the 10 mg/L concentration was for the amount of nitrate that can be found in public water systems, not for every contaminant. D is wrong because the passage does not mention whether people would be experimented on, in order to find safe contamination levels. E is incorrect because the act was passed to protect all people in the United States, not just infants.

26. **(K)** Use elimination to arrive at the correct answer for this question.

    F is incorrect because infants *could* develop methemoglobinemia if they drink water with nitrate concentrations in excess of 10 mg/L;

the passage does not state that they necessarily will. G is incorrect because lines 34-41 state that excess nitrate can leach into groundwater, lakes, and streams and can cause the asphyxiation of the aquatic life in affected bodies of water. H is incorrect because lines 9-14 indicate that while nitrogen is the most abundant element in our atmosphere, the opposite is true of nitrogen's availability in soil. J is incorrect because it is not possible to tell from the passage whether we'd have zero nitrate run-off while being able to enjoy the same bounty of crops.

K is correct because the passage states that nitrogen is essential to plant life in lines 12-26. And without nitrification, our planet would not be able to support its current population. Thus, it can be inferred that plant life is essential to our survival. Even if you have no idea what *asphyxiation* means—it means deprivation of oxygen—we can deduce that it is bad from the context in lines 34-46. The passage states that nitrate provides nourishment for plants. Then note the word *however* in line 35. This indicates that there are cons to nitrate run-off.

(Caffeine)

27. **(B)** This passage is about caffeine and how it is used by humans and how it can affect insect species, too, in effect serving as a pesticide. Thus, B is the best answer choice.

A is incorrect; it focuses too narrowly on one portion of the passage. Caffeine is an extremely important global commodity, yes, but that is not the main idea of the passage. C is incorrect because the passage does not conclude that caffeine will eventually replace other pesticides and insecticides. D is incorrect. Caffeine's potency as an insecticide is an important piece of the passage, but the passage does not compare caffeine's potency to those of insecticides and pesticides. E is incorrect because human productivity is not the main idea of the passage.

28. **(H)** Use elimination. In lines 23-26, the passage states that caffeine in plants paralyzes and kills insects, so F and G are incorrect. Also, in lines 40-50, the passage describes how caffeine can kill insects and even humans in sufficiently high doses. In lines 32-36, the passage states that caffeine can depress food consumption and interfere with reproduction, so J and K are incorrect.

Seizures are the only effect not listed by the passage as a way caffeine can affect living organisms. Thus, H is correct.

29. **(D)** D is correct; lines 18-26 state that plants use caffeine to act as a natural pesticide.

A is not correct; it is not stated that caffeine prevents insects from coming near the plants. B is incorrect because it is not stated that caffeine is bitter or that caffeine's bitterness is used to repel insects. C is incorrect because there is no mention in the passage that caffeine causes plants to produce a more potent toxin that kills or paralyzes pests. (The passage does mention that when caffeine is combined with other toxins, the effect is amplified, but the passage does not state that plants do this.) E is incorrect; it is not stated that caffeine helps eaten leaves regenerate.

30. **(H)** Lines 40-48 discuss caffeine's lethality based on the bodyweight of the organism, specifically discussing how much caffeine would be needed to be lethal to humans. Thus, H can be inferred from lines 40-48.

F is incorrect; the passage infers that it is possible for humans to die of caffeine overdose. G is incorrect because the passage does not state or infer that it is safe for people over 60 kilograms to ingest 10 grams of caffeine. 60 kilograms of bodyweight × 170 milligrams per kilogram of bodyweight = 10.2 grams, suggesting that people over 60 kilograms may not die from ingesting 10 grams of caffeine, but it cannot be inferred that doing so would be safe. J is incorrect because the passage does not discuss age's role in the impact caffeine has on people. K is incorrect because caffeine as a global commodity is not discussed in lines 40-48. Furthermore, the statement made in K is not supported by the passage. While caffeine is an important global commodity, it cannot be inferred caffeine generates more revenue than any other.

31. **(C)** Lines 61-66 indicate caffeine may pose a threat to the ecosystem, including plants. By hurting the earthworms and other animals needed to keep the soil healthy, caffeine may impact plant-life. Also, caffeine may damage and harm marine life. Thus, C is correct.

   A is incorrect because concerns about the artificial pesticide industry are not discussed by the passage. B is incorrect because it is not logical. Farmers would be happy if caffeine were "too" efficient at killing unwanted pests. D is incorrect; caffeine leaked into our drinking water would probably not cause widespread caffeine addiction. E is not correct because the passage does express concerns about the use of caffeine as a pesticide.

32. **(K)** The passage states in lines 36-40 that mosquitos need to be able to swim to the surface for air. This implies mosquitos cannot hold their breaths indefinitely. K is correct.

   F is incorrect because the passage does not state or hint at whether mosquitos are born on the surface of water or not. G is incorrect; the passage does not state or hint at whether mosquito larvae alternate between living on land and in water. H is incorrect; the passage neither suggests nor states that mosquito larvae have gills. J is incorrect largely for the same reasoning as the reason G is incorrect.

(Akkadian Empire)

33. **(B)** This passage is about how the Akkadian Empire came to be, from providing background information of Akkad to showing how Sargon was able to help his empire flourish. Thus, B is correct, as lines 18-20 indicate that the Akkadian Empire was the oldest recorded empire.

A is incorrect because it is too narrow in scope. The passage does discuss how Sargon overthrew the king of Kish, but that is not the main purpose of the passage. C is incorrect because it is not supported by the passage. There is no indication that Sargon set precedent for all subsequent emperors in history. D is incorrect because it is too narrow in scope. E is incorrect because the author's purpose is not to speculate whether Akkad succeeded because Lugalzagesi did not receive aid.

34. **(F)** In lines 11-13, the passage states that empires showcased the hallmarks of human achievement throughout history. F is correct.

   G is not correct because the passage does not support the idea that empires served as a basis for modern systems and methods of governance. H is incorrect because it is too narrow in scope. Empires did serve as hubs for commerce and trade, but they also highlighted religious, philosophical, legal, and technological achievements. J is incorrect because it is not supported by the passage. It is unknown whether the citizens of empires enjoyed the luxury and power of their empires. K is incorrect because it is unsupported by the passage. The passage does state in lines 30-31 that the ziggurats in Sargon's time commanded great attention, but that is not the same as saying ziggurats unified multitudes of people under the same religion. Moreover, it is not known if all empires had ziggurats.

35. **(E)** Use elimination to arrive at the correct answer. E is correct because it is not mentioned or implied by the passage that the Akkadians planned to learn as much from the Sumerians as they could in order to overthrow the Sumerians at a later date.

   A is incorrect because the passage does mention in lines 30-31 that Sumer's monolithic mud-brick temples commanded great attention. B is incorrect because lines 31-33 indicate that irrigation techniques allowed formerly parched lands to be arable. C is incorrect because it can be inferred from lines 35-

36, which state, "There was much the Akkadians could learn from the Sumerians, so that's what they did", that Sumer possessed more knowledge about certain topics than Akkad did. Thus, in at least that regard, Sumer was more advanced than Akkad was. D is incorrect because lines 33-34 state that Sumerians used cuneiform, which was a writing system of wedge-shaped characters.

36. **(J)** Lines 44-50 state that it was unfortunate for Lugalzagesi did not receive the aid of the other Sumerian city-states because of the lingering animosity between the city-states of Sumer and Lugalzagesi from when he brought Sumer under his control. This suggests that the animosity came from a hostile takeover. Thus, J is correct.

K is incorrect because the passage does not compare Sumer and Akkad's system of laws, so it is not possible to infer from the passage that Sumer had a far more advanced system of laws than Akkad did. G is incorrect because it is an overstatement. Lines 13-15 state that many of the earliest empires began alongside or near rivers, but they do not suggest that all of the earliest empires began alongside rivers. H is incorrect. While Sargon's position of trust as the cupbearer for the king of Kush did give him better access to the king, it's not possible to say that he wouldn't have become emperor otherwise. It is possible that he could still have had have found another way to achieve his goal of becoming a ruler. K is incorrect because the passage does not support the idea that cuneiform was the most advanced writing system of its time. The passage only states that cuneiform was a writing system based on wedge-shaped symbols.

37. **(B)** Lines 56-73 state that razing the walls around the cities allowed Sargon to promote trade and commerce, which consequently brought in more tax revenue for Sargon. This allowed Sargon to increase his military might and support royal artists and scribes, who glorified Sargon in their works.

A is incorrect because the passage does not state that Sargon's governors were plotting to overthrow him. C is incorrect because the passage does not mention wall maintenance fees. D is incorrect because the passage does not mention the idea that people wanted to move more freely between cities but were not able to do so because of the city walls. E is incorrect because there is no mention in the passage of the increased facility of military deployment after the walls were torn down.

38. **(F)** Lines 59-62 discuss the commodities that were traded throughout Mesopotamia. These were pearls, ivory, olive oil, wood. Precious metals such as copper and silver are mentioned in lines 62-66, but there is no mention of gold. Thus, F is correct.

(WWII Theft)

39. **(B)** This passage opens with a discussion of theft crimes and briefly highlights one of the most daring theft crimes committed by an individual before transitioning to the theft crimes committed by Nazi Germany during World War II. Thus, B is the correct answer.

A is incorrect because the passage is more than about the magnitude of theft crimes. C is incorrect because the main idea of the passage encompasses more than just the fact that many pieces of art, jewelry, and china stolen by Nazi Germany remain at large. D is incorrect because it is only something discussed by the passage, not the passage's main idea. E is incorrect; Germany's dismal economic conditions did serve as a trigger for World War II, but this passage is not about Germany's role in World War II.

40. **(F)** Lines 19-30 discuss the Treaty of Versailles, which was the treaty that ended World War I. As part of the treaty, Germany was forced to pay reparations, which did not help Germany's economy. F is correct.

G is incorrect because, according to the passage, other foreign nations imposed export tariffs on German goods, not the Treaty of Versailles itself. H is incorrect because the passage does not state or suggest that the Treaty of Versailles caused Germany to go bankrupt. J is incorrect. Though it can be inferred from the passage that the Treaty of Versailles forced Germany to pay Britain and France greater reparations than to any other country, this comparison point was not why Germany's economy became even worse. That is, even if Germany did not have to pay reparations to any other country, the Treaty of Versailles still triggered the worsening of Germany's economy. K is incorrect because it overstates what the passage states. The passage states that the Treaty of Versailles led to Germany's plummet into a seemingly inescapable abyss; it does not state that Germany actually fell into an inescapable abyss; that would mean Germany is still in that abyss.

41. **(E)** Use elimination. A is incorrect. Lines 7-14 describe Jack Roland Murphy's theft of the Star of India and Midnight Star Sapphire. However, there is nothing in the passage to indicate that these were the largest gems ever crafted. B is incorrect. While Germany's dire economic situation did help to catapult Hitler to power, we don't know if Hitler would not have come to power regardless. C is incorrect because it uses the same faulty reasoning used by B. While it is true that the tariffs other countries imposed on German exports probably did make it harder for Germany to make reparation payments, it's impossible to tell from the passage whether Germany would have been able to make reparation payments without much difficulties, if the other nations had not imposed export tariffs. D is incorrect because it is not known whether all the stolen valuables will be recovered, much less returned to their rightful owners. Thus, by elimination, E is correct.

E is correct. Because of Nazi Germany's looting of valuables, a valuable part of human history, in the form of art, has been lost. Lines 63-65 say that as much as 20% of Western fine artworks had been stolen. And

even still, over 100,000 paintings and other pieces remain at large (lines 69-71).

42. **(J)** The irony with the other nations' imposition of export tariffs on German goods was that they imposed the tariffs to try to punish Germany for World War I. Little did they realize, though, that they were providing Germany with the fuel to eventually conquer and dominate them in World War II. The answer was provided in lines 27-33.

43. **(E)** Lines 60-63 say that Germany looted more than $400 million in gold from the countries they occupied and then another $140 million from individuals. Thus, E is the best answer. In total, Germany plundered over $540 million in gold during the war.

44. **(G)** Lines 42-51 state that Hitler marginalized the significance of a sound economic policy but that even he realized he needed money to build up his military. D is correct.

F is incorrect because the 20% of Western fine artworks that the Nazis stole amounted to over 100,000 pieces of paintings. H is incorrect because the passage states that General Patton recovered some of the gold; *some* does not equate to *most*. J is incorrect because it is not supported by the passage; we do not know if the gems that Jack Murphy stole were the largest or not. He might have stolen them because of their convenience. K is incorrect because it is not known whether Germany's looting was not sufficient to allow Germany to win the war. There may have been other reasons aside from monetary ones that Germany lost the war—the passage states in lines 58-60 that "their piratical modus operandi was, by many metrics, extremely successful".

(Black Armbands)

45. **(E)** This passage is about the incidents that occurred to several children, how that turned

into a lawsuit, what the outcome of the lawsuit ultimately was. The passage serves to report on events that took place, so E is correct.

A is incorrect because it does not illustrate the primary purpose of the passage. While it can be inferred from the passage that the Supreme Court wields much authority, it is not the primary purpose of the passage. B is incorrect because the passage's primary purpose is not to show how easily rights and freedoms can be obfuscated, which means "to confuse, bewilder, or stupefy; to make obscure or unclear." It is true that the passage does discuss the obfuscation of children's rights, but that is only a part of the passage's primary purpose. C is incorrect because the passage is more objective than it is argumentative or insistent. D is incorrect for a similar reasoning as to why C is incorrect.

46. **(J)** Lines 19-23 indicate that John and Mary Beth Tinker and Christopher Eckhardt wore black armbands to school in order to protest the government's involvement in Vietnam. Thus, J is correct. The children wore black armbands to express anti-war sentiments.

47. **(C)** Use elimination to arrive at the correct answer. A is incorrect because the question it poses is answered in lines 45-51, which state that the children's fathers were approached by the Iowa Civil Liberties Union and that suit was filed after securing the support of the American Civil Liberties Union. B is incorrect because lines 3-6 state that the first amendment of the Bill of Rights protects the freedom of speech. D is incorrect because line 64 states that there are 9 Supreme Court justices. E is incorrect because lines 1-2 state that the Bill of Rights was adopted on December 15, 1791.

D is the only one unanswered. It is not mentioned how long it took for the children's fathers' suit to reach the Supreme Court.

48. **(G)** Lines 51-52 state that the children and their fathers lost in District Court. After losing, they appealed their case to the United States Circuit Court and lost there, too, which left them with no choice but the United States Supreme Court. The question asks what happened immediately after the District Court's decision and that is that they appealed to the U.S. Circuit Court. G is correct.

49. **(C)** According to the passage, in lines 51-56, the District Court dismissed the complaint and held that the regulation of the armbands was within the school board's power on the ground that the regulation was reasonable in order to prevent disturbance of school discipline. This means that the District Court ruled in favor of the principals, thus C is correct.

50. **(J)** In lines 61-71, the passage discusses how the Supreme Court of the United States overturned the lower courts' decisions. The Supreme Court held that 1) the children were not being disruptive in their wearing of armbands and 2) First Amendment rights cannot be denied in schools without evidence to show that the rights were denied in order to maintain order. J accurately reflects this.

F is incorrect because clothes can probably disrupt discipline, particularly if the clothing is antagonistic or hostile to a certain class of people or if the clothing is too revealing. G draws an improper logical conclusion. Just because a school can deny freedom of speech rights in order to maintain order and discipline does not necessarily mean schools can limit any Amendment rights as long as the limitations are justified. The word *any*, in particular, is what makes this choice incorrect. H is incorrect because the author would probably not agree with the statement that students have no privacy rights in school. K is incorrect because the phrase "however they want" is incorrect. The author would not agree that students should be able to say whatever they want in school.

MATH EXPLANATIONS ▶

Answer Explanations – Mathematics
Practice Test 3

---

51. (B) GCF(10, 15) = 5; LCM(10, 15) = 30

LCM(10, 15) – GCF(10, 15) = 25

(GCF stands for greatest common factor, and LCM stands for least common multiple.)

---

52. (G) First, find x in terms of y:

$6y - 3 = 2x + 5$

$2x = 6y - 3 - 5 \xrightarrow{\text{yields}} 2x = 6y - 8$

$x = 3y - 4$

Then find $3x + 4$:

$3x = 3(3y - 4) = 9y - 12$

$3x + 4 = 9y - 12 + 4 = 9y - 8$

---

53. (C) Distribute $8y$ across the terms in the parentheses:

$8y(3z - 7zu) = (8 \times 3)(yz) - (8 \times 7)(yzu) = 24yz - 56yzu$

---

54. (J) $T = 150\% \times 800 = 1.5 \times 800 = 1{,}200$

$S = 15\% \times 1{,}200 = 0.15 \times 1{,}200 = 180$

---

55. (C) To qualify for the race, each runner must run 5 laps in $68 \times 5 = 340$ seconds.

Kyle ran a total time from 4 laps of $64 + 72 + 74 + 66 = 276$ seconds. In order to qualify, Kyle needs to run the final lap in no more than $340 - 276 = 64$ seconds, which is 1 minute and 4 seconds.

---

56. (K) Convert the division of a fraction to a multiplication of the reciprocal of the fraction and then simplify the expression:

$$\frac{7}{35} \times \frac{5}{24} \div \frac{3}{7} =$$

$$\frac{\cancel{7}^{1}}{\cancel{35}_{5}} \times \frac{5}{24} \times \frac{7}{3} =$$

$$\frac{1}{\cancel{5}} \times \frac{\cancel{5}}{24} \times \frac{7}{3} = \frac{7}{72}$$

---

57. (A) Hernando is 13 years old. 8 years ago, he was 5 years old, which was half as old as his cousin was then. Thus, 8 years ago, Hernando's cousin was 10 years old. Hernando's cousin is currently 18 years old. In 7 years, Hernando's cousin will be 25 years old.

---

58. (G) Use elimination to see which expressions are false.

$(x + y)^2 = x^2 + 2xy + y^2$, so I is not always true. It is only true when x or y is 0.

II is always true. $(x - y)^2 = x^2 - 2xy + y^2$ and $(y - x)^2 = y^2 - 2xy + x^2$, so $(x - y)^2 = (y - x)^2$.

III is not true because x and y have to be positive integers, so $2xy \neq 0$.

Thus, only II must be true.

59. **(E)** Simplify the expression.

$$\frac{m\,\cancel{n}}{\cancel{n^2+m}}\left[\left(\frac{\cancel{m+n^2}}{n-m}\right)\left(\frac{m-n}{\cancel{n}}\right)\right]=\frac{m(m-n)}{n-m}$$

Since $m - n = -(n - m)$, we can use substitution and then cancel to get a final, simplified answer of -m.

---

60. **(K)** The length of LM is $0 - (-7) = 7$. The length of MN is $4 - 0 = 4$.

The sum of the lengths of LM and MN is 11. The product of the lengths is 28. The difference of the sum and product of the lengths of LM and MN is therefore $28 - 11 = 17$.

---

61. **(B)** The easiest way to solve this problem is to draw a rectangle around points A, B, and C such that A, B, and C lie on the perimeter of the rectangle. If A is on the left side of the rectangle, C on the top side, and B on the corner of the bottom and right sides, then we get a diagram that looks like the following:

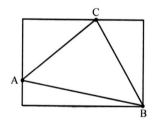

Since A has coordinates of (-7, -2) and B has coordinates of (3, -4), we can determine that the width of the rectangle is $3 - (-7) = 10$. And since C has coordinates of (-1, 3), we can determine the height of the rectangle to be $3 - (-4) = 7$.

Thus, the area of the rectangle is $10 \times 7 = 70$. From this, we can find the areas of the three resulting right triangles and subtract their sum from the area of the rectangle to find the area of triangle ABC.

Using the coordinates of the points, we can labeling the side lengths as follows:

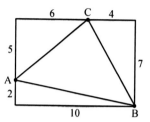

<u>Areas of the right triangles:</u>

To find the areas of the three right triangles, we can look at the labeled sides above:

Upper Left: $½ \times 6 \times 5 = 15$
Upper Right: $½ \times 4 \times 7 = 14$
Bottom: $½ \times 2 \times 10 = 10$

The sum of the areas of the right triangles: $15 + 14 + 10 = 39$.

The area of triangle ABC: $70 - 39 = 31$

---

62. **(F)** Rearrange the equation to get y by itself on one side of the equation:

$$3x - 5y + 4 = 16 + y \;\rightarrow\; 6y + 16 = 3x - 4$$

$$6y = 3x + 4 - 16 = 3x - 12$$

Divide both sides by 6 to get $y = 0.5x - 2$

---

63. **(C)** First, recognize that $x = 5$, since 5.49 rounded down to the nearest whole number is 5, and $y = 6$, sine 5.51 rounded up to the nearest whole number is 6.

$60 \div 5 = 12$, and $60 \div 6 = 10$, so the difference of the quotients is 2.

64. **(H)** $t^2 - u^2 = 115$, which can be rewritten as:

$(t - u)(t + u) = 115$, by using the principles of polynomial factoring.

To solve this problem, we will need to know the factors of 115: 1, 5, 23, and 115. Thus, there are 2 viable scenarios for t + u:

First, $t + u = 115$, then $t - u = 1$.
Second, $t + u = 23$ and $t - u = 5$.

Since the first $t + u = 115$ is not an answer choice, $t + u = 23$ must be true.

65. **(B)** Angles x and y are supplementary, which means $x + y = 180$. Since $x = 3y$, we substitute $3y$ for x:

$3y + y = 180$

$4y = 180 \xrightarrow{\text{yields}} y = 45$

$5y = 5 \times 45 = 225$

66. **(H)** From the graph, we see that the population of Urbantown doubles every 10 years. Since we are looking for 400% of Urbantown's population in 1990, which was 400, we are looking for when Urbantown's population will be 1,600. In 2000, Urbantown's population was 800, so in 2010, the population will be 1,600, according to the graph.

67. **(A)** The box has dimensions of 6 in. (0.5 ft.), 7 in., and 3 in. Thus, there are 2 faces that are 6 in. by 7 in., 2 faces that are 6 in. by 3 in., and 2 faces that are 7 in. by 3 in. Thus, the surface area of the box is:

$2 \times (6 \times 7) + 2 \times (6 \times 3) + 2 \times (3 \times 7) =$

$2 \times [(6 \times 7) + (6 \times 3) + (3 \times 7)] =$

$2 \times (42 + 18 + 21) = 2 \times 81 = 162 \text{ ft}^2$

68. **(J)** In order for the rational expression to be an integer, the numerator must be a multiple of 4.

Since $j = 14$, $3(j + k) = 42 + 3k$. The closest multiple of 4 that $42 + 3k$ can be is 44. Thus, $3k = 2$, which means that $k = \frac{2}{3}$.

69. **(B)** When $m = 7$ and $n = 8$,

$m \Phi n = \dfrac{7 + 8}{3} = 5$

We are then looking for $5 \Phi 7$.

$5 \Phi 7 = \dfrac{5 + 7}{3} = 4$

70. **(J)** Cheryl and her friend ate a total of:

$d + (d + 4) = 14$ pieces of candy

$2d + 4 = 14$

$2d = 10$

$d = 5$, so $d + 4 = 9$

71. **(A)** When x is divided by 7, the remainder is 4. This means that $x = 7n + 4$, where n is an integer. Thus, $2x = 2(7n + 4) = 14n + 8$. In other words:

$2x = 14n + 7 + 1 = 7(2n + 1) + 1$

This means that when $2x$ is divided by 7, then, the remainder is 1 because $7(2n + 1)$ is perfectly divisible by 7, whereas 1 is not.

72. **(J)** The mass of the brick of gold is found by multiplying the density of gold by the volume of gold. Since we know the density of gold to be 19.3 grams per cubic centimeter, we need to know the volume, which is:

9 cm × 10 cm × 0.003 m

To convert from m to cm, we multiply by 100, so 0.003 m is the same as 0.3 cm. Thus, the volume of the gold brick in cubic centimeters is: 9 × 10 × 0.3 = 27 cm^3.

The mass of the gold brick is therefore:

19.3 $\frac{g}{cm^3}$ × 27 cm3 = 521.1 g, so J is correct.

---

73. **(B)** If M,NOP,QRS,TU7.14 is divided by 10,000, we move the decimal space to the left by 4 spaces to get MNO,PQR.STU714. Thus, N is in the ten thousands place.

---

74. **(K)** From 1 to 20, there are 6 multiples of 3: 3, 6, 9, 12, 15, 18. Of these, 12 is also a multiple of 4. So we are looking for the probability that Magnus will roll 3, 6, 9, 15, or 18 on his next turn. There are 20 numbers total, and 5 numbers we are looking for. Thus, the probability of rolling a multiple of 3 but not 4 is 5 out of 20 or ¼.

---

75. **(A)** To find the perimeter of the figure, find the sum of the lengths of the following: the longer side of arc AD, AB, BC, and CD.

In the figure, OA and and OD are radii of length 6. Since B and C are midpoints, OB and OC have lengths of 3, and AB and CD have lengths of 3, as well.

The length of BC can be determined using the Pythagorean Theorem:

$3^2 + 3^2 = 18 = (BC)^2$

BC = $\sqrt{18} = 3\sqrt{2}$

Since a quarter circle was removed from circle O, the length of arc AD is ¾ × the circumference of circle O. The radius of circle O is 6, so the circumference of circle O is 2π(6) or 12π. Thus, the arc length of AD is ¾ × 12π = 9π.

The perimeter is therefore:

$9\pi + 3 + 3 + 3\sqrt{2} = 9\pi + 6 + 3\sqrt{2}$

This form is not apparent from the answer choices, but by partially factoring, we get:

$9\pi + 3(2 + \sqrt{2})$

---

76. **(F)** 50% of 7 is 0.5 × 7 = 3.5. 7% of 50 is 0.07 × 50 = 3.5. 3.5 + 3.5 = 7, so F is the correct answer. 100% of 7 is 1.0 × 7 = 7.

---

77. **(D)** Let the distance Jarvis jumped be represented by x. Jesse jumped $\frac{7}{6}x = 21$ feet.

Multiply both sides by $\frac{6}{7}$ to find $x = 18$. Thus, the combined distance Jesse and Jarvis jumped was 18 + 21 = 39 feet.

---

78. **(K)** To find the number of saplings Roger planted, divide 300 by 15 to get 20. But because he planted a sapling at the very beginning of the stretch, add 1 to 20 to get 21. Thus, he planted a total of 21 saplings.

Let x represent the number of saplings Roger started out with. The number of saplings Roger has left over is one more than half the saplings he started out with. The number of saplings he has left over is $x - 21$, so we can write:

$x - 21 = 1 + ½x$

Solving for x, we get: $½x = 22$ → $x = 44$

79. **(D)** The key to solving this problem is recognizing that $m^2 - n^2 = (m + n)(m - n)$. Thus, if $m^2 - n^2 > 0$ and $m + n < 0$, then it must be true that $m - n < 0$ because it is impossible for a positive number to have one negative factor and one positive factor. Thus, D is correct.

80. **(H)** To find s from the perimeter, write the following equation: $2s + 2(2s - 1) + 3(s + 4) + 11 + 13 = 196$. Combine like terms to get:

$$2s + (4s - 2) + (3s + 12) + 24 =$$
$$9s + 34 = 196$$
$$9s = 162$$
$$s = 18$$

81. **(C)** Let r represent the radius of the smaller circles. The area of each of the smaller circles is πr^2. The combined area of the shaded region is $\pi r^2 + \pi r^2 = 2\pi r^2$.

The area of the larger circle is $\pi(2r)^2 = 4\pi r^2$, since the radius of the larger circle is twice that of the smaller circles.

The area of the unshaded region is the area of the larger circle minus the area of the shaded region:

$$4\pi r^2 - 2\pi r^2 = 2\pi r^2$$

The ratio of the areas of the shaded region to unshaded region is $2\pi r^2 : 2\pi r^2 = 1 : 1$.

82. **(J)** Marsha's average score on 4 tests was 94, so her point total was $4 \times 94 = 376$.

The sum of her first three test scores was $93 + 89 + 92 = 274$. Thus, her fourth test score was 102.

Marsha's highest score was 102 and her lowest score was 89. $102 - 89 = 13$.

83. **(B)** To find the median number of ice cream sales, organize the numbers in order and then find the middle number:

166, 177, 178, 185, 191, 199, 206

Thus, 185 is the median.

The mean is determined by:

$$\frac{166+177+178+185+191+199+206}{7} = \frac{1,302}{7} = 186$$

The difference between the median and mean is $186 - 185 = 1$.

84. **(G)** Betty is k years old, and Lacey is 16 years older, so Lacey is $16 + k$ years old. In 12 years, Lacey will be twice as old as Betty is then. In mathematical terms, this is:

$$12 + (16 + k) = 2(k + 12)$$

Simplify and combine like terms:

$$28 + k = 2k + 24$$

$$k = 28 - 24 = 4$$

Thus, Lacey is $4 + 16 = 20$ years old now.

85. **(D)** The rectangle portion measures almost 8 grid squares high by 11 squares wide. Since 1 cm translates to 5 ft, the dimensions of the rectangle measure approximately 40 feet by 55 feet or 2,200 ft^2.

The triangle portion has a base of 11 cm and a height of 3 cm. This translates to 55 ft by 15 ft. The area of a triangle is $\frac{1}{2} \times 55 \times 15 = 412. 5$ ft^2.

The total area would be approximately 2,612.5 sq ft. The closest answer is therefore D.

86. (G) Divide 613 by 52 to find out how many people can ride the roller coaster at a time.

$613 \div 52 = 11 \text{ R } 41$

This means that the roller coaster will have to operate 12 times for the 613 people to ride. Since each ride is 140 seconds long, it'll take 1,680 seconds for everyone to finish the ride at least once.

1,680 seconds $\div$ 60 seconds/minute = 28 minutes exactly

87. (B) To find the sums of A and B, recognize that A and B are arithmetic sequences.

The sum of an arithmetic sequence is given by the formula:

$S_n = \frac{n(a_1 + a_n)}{2}$, where S_n is the sum of n terms, and a_1 is the first term of the sequence and a_n is the nth term of the sequence.

In set A, there are 25 terms. The sum of the terms of set A is: $\frac{25(2+50)}{2} = 650$.

In set B, there are also 25 terms. The sum of the terms of set B is: $\frac{25(1+49)}{2} = 625$.

Thus, $x - y = 650 - 625 = 25$.

88. (F) Carlos has a total of $6 + 5 + 4 + 3 + 2 = 20$ flashcards.

The probability that he'll pick a yellow flashcard first is $\frac{5}{20} = \frac{1}{4}$. Since he is not returning the flashcard, there are 19 flashcards left, and 4 are yellow, so the probability he'll pick a yellow flashcard for his second is $\frac{4}{19}$.

The probability he'll pick both yellow is the product of the probabilities:

$$\frac{1}{\cancel{4}} \times \frac{\cancel{4}}{19} = \frac{1}{19}$$

89. (B) 270 moths are gray. $450 - 270 = 180$ are white. There are $270 - 180 = 90$ more gray than white moths. Set up a proportion to find the difference in the number of gray and white moths in the forest:

$$\frac{90}{450} = \frac{x}{20,000}$$

$$\frac{1}{5} = \frac{x}{20,000}$$

$x = 20,000 \div 5 = 4,000$

Thus, there are about 4,000 more gray moths than white ones in the forest.

90. (H) The circle has a radius of 5, so if the circle passes through the point (5, 0) and the center of the circle has integer coordinates, the center of the circle can have any of the following possible coordinates:

(0, 0), (10, 0), (5, 5), and (5, -5).

F is incorrect because if the circle has center (5, 5), then (5, 10) would lie on the circle's boundary. G is incorrect because if the circle has center (0, 0), then the circle would pass through the point (0, 5). J is incorrect because if the circle has center (10, 0), then the circle would pass through the point (10, 5). K is incorrect because if the circle has center (0, 0), then the circle would pass through the point (-5, 0).

H is correct because (0, 0) can be a center, but not a point on the circle's boundary,

since the circle must have a center with integer coordinates.
Note: If the center did not have to have integer coordinates, (0, 0) could lie on the circle's boundary. Below is the proof.

Let the point (a, b) be the center of the circle, such that both (0, 0) and (5, 0) lie on the boundary of the circle. Since the radius of the circle is 5, we can apply the distance formula twice to solve for a and b.

From (0, 0), we get:

$$5 = \sqrt{(a-0)^2 + (b-0)^2}$$
$$a^2 + b^2 = 25$$

From (5, 0), we get:

$$5 = \sqrt{(a-5)^2 + (b-0)^2}$$
$$(a-5)^2 + b^2 = 25$$

Subtract the resulting equations to get:

$(a-5)^2 - a^2 = 0$
$-10a + 25 = 0 \rightarrow 10a = 25 \rightarrow a = 2.5$

Substitute 2.5 for a to find b:

$(2.5)^2 + b^2 = 25 \rightarrow 6.25 + b^2 = 25$
$b^2 = 25 - 6.25 = 18.75 \rightarrow b = \pm\sqrt{18.75}$

Thus, there are two possible circles that pass through the points (0, 0) and (5, 0), but both circles have centers that do not have integer values.

---

91. **(D)** If the ratio of girls to boys is 7:5, let $7x$ represent the number of girls and $5x$ represent the number of boys. The total number of students is therefore $7x + 5x = 12x = 48$.

$x = 4$, which means $7x = 28$ and $5x = 20$. There are then $28 - 20 = 8$ more girls than boys in the class.

92. **(J)** $11^2 + 12^2 = 121 + 144 = 265$

$15^2 = 225$, $16^2 = 256$, and $17^2 = 289$

265 is between 16^2 and 17^2, so J is the best answer.

---

93. **(A)** Kaylee started with x pens. Lou started with $x - 2$. After Kaylee gave Lou half her pens, Lou has $(x - 2) + \frac{1}{2}x$ pens = $1.5x - 2$ pens, and Kaylee has $\frac{1}{2}x$ pens. Lou gives Ilene half of his new total, so he now has $\frac{1}{2} \times (1.5x - 2) = 0.75x - 1$ pens.

Ilene started out with 3 fewer pens than Lou started out with, so Ilene started out $x - 5$. After receiving half of Lou's, Ilene has $x - 5 + (0.75x - 1) = 1.75x - 6$ pens.

Ilene then gives a third of her new pen total to Kay. One-third of $1.75x - 6$ is

$$\frac{1}{3} \times (1.75x - 6) = \frac{1}{3} \times \left(\frac{7}{4}x - 6\right) = \frac{7}{12}x - 2$$

Since Kaylee had $\frac{1}{2}x$ pens before receiving pens from Ilene, Kaylee now has:

$$\frac{1}{2}x + \left(\frac{7}{12}x - 2\right) = 37 \text{ pens}$$

$$\frac{6}{12}x + \left(\frac{7}{12}x - 2\right) = \frac{13}{12}x - 2 = 37$$

$$\frac{\cancel{13}}{12}x = \cancel{39}^{3} \rightarrow \frac{1}{12}x = 3 \rightarrow x = 36$$

---

94. **(F)** Since ¼-inch represents 2 meters, 1 inch represents 8 meters. 1 square inch then represents 64 square meters:

¼ in = 2 m $\rightarrow$ 1 in = 8 m

$(1 \text{ in})^2 = (8 \text{ m})^2 \rightarrow 1 \text{ in}^2 = 64 \text{ m}^2$

Now we can set up a ratio:

$$\frac{x \text{ in}^2}{96 \text{ m}^2} = \frac{1 \text{ in}^2}{64 \text{ m}^2}$$

Solving for x, we get:

$$x \text{ in}^2 = \frac{1 \text{ in}^2}{2\,\cancel{64} \text{ m}^2} \times \cancel{96}^{\,3} \text{ m}^2 = 1.5 \text{ in}^2$$

---

95. (B) The area of the shaded region is the sum of the areas of the two right triangles:

The first right triangle has an area of $\frac{1}{2} \times 3x \times 4x = \frac{1}{2} \times 12x^2 = 6x^2$

The second right triangle has an area of $\frac{1}{2} \times 5x \times 5x = \frac{1}{2} \times 25x^2 = 12.5x^2$

The total shaded area is then $6x^2 + 12.5x^2 = 18.5x^2$. Thus the area is a multiple of 18.5.

Since we are trying to find out which answer choice cannot be the area of the shaded regions, we look to see which answer choice is not a multiple of 18.5, when x is an integer.

A is incorrect because if $x = 1$, the shaded area will be 18.5. C is incorrect because it would mean $x^2 = 4$, so $x = 2$, which can work. D is incorrect $166.5 \div 18.5 = x^2 = 9$, which means $x = 3$, which can work. E is incorrect because $1850 \div 18.5 = x^2 = 100$, which means $x = 10$, which can work.

B is correct because the area cannot be 37, as that would mean $x^2 = 2$, and x would not be an integer.

---

96. (H) To solve this problem, find the remainder when 187 is divided by 13: $187 \div 13 = 14 \text{ R}5$

Thus, since 5 people are left over, they will sit together at the last table.

---

97. (C) The greatest multiple of 3 in set L is 87. It is the 29th multiple of 3.

The greatest multiple of 9 in L is 81. There are 9 multiples of 9 in L.

Thus, the number of multiples of 3 but not of 9 in L is $29 - 9 = 20$.

---

98. (J) The ratio of ducks to cows is 3 to 2. Let $3x$ represent the actual number of ducks and $2x$ the actual number of cows, for a total of $5x$ animals on Young McDonald's farm.

The number of legs can be expressed by $2(3x) + 4(2x) = 6x + 8x = 14x$. There are $14x$ legs on the farm. For the number of legs to be a perfect square, x must be at least 14.

Thus, the least number of animals on the farm is $5 \times 14 = 70$.

---

99. (E) 16.5 feet = 1 rod → 66 feet = 4 rods
4 rods = 1 chain → 66 feet = 1 chain

5,280 ft/mi ÷ 66 ft/chain = 80 chains/mi
Thus, there are 80 chains per mile.

---

100. (G) The volume of a cylinder is given by the formula $V = \pi r^2 h$, where r is the radius of the circular base of the cylinder and h is the height of the cylinder.

If the radius is tripled, and the height is halved, then the volume of the new cylinder can be given by

$$V = \pi(3r)^2(\tfrac{1}{2}h) = \pi(9r^2)(\tfrac{1}{2}h) = \frac{9}{2}\pi r^2 h$$

Thus, the volume of the new cylinder is 4.5 times or 450% of the volume of the original cylinder. Thus, G is correct.

CPSIA information can be obtained at www.ICGtesting.com
Printed in the USA
LVOW09s1957300915

456356LV00030B/796/P